REINVENTING ANGLICANISM

BRUCE KAYE

A vision of confidence, community and engagement in Anglican Christianity

FOREWORD BY IAN T. DOUGLAS

CHURCH PUBLISHING
New York

First published 2003 by
Openbook Publishers,
205 Halifax Street
Adelaide, South Australia 5000

USA edition published 2004 by
Church Publishing Incorporated
445 Fifth Avenue
New York, NY 10016

A catalog record for this book is available from the Library of Congress.
ISBN 0-89869-455-8

Cover design: Karyn Edwards
Layout: Mark Thomas
Typeset in Garamond Classico 10pt
Printed by Openbook Publishers, Australia

For Toby and Molly and their generation,
in the hope that they might experience a reinvented Anglican faith.

CONTENTS

FOREWORD

BY IAN T. DOUGLAS

Every now and then a book comes along whose message is not only profoundly important and forward-looking but also critically needed for the times. This book is one of them.

In many ways the Anglican Communion—the family of thirty-eight churches with seventy-five million members in one hundred and sixty-four countries that trace their histories somehow to the Church of England—is experiencing both the worst of times and the best of times. Divisions and disagreements over human sexuality threaten to tear at the fabric of the Anglican Communion as church leaders in one continent declare 'impaired communion' with churches in another continent. At the same time, in parishes and dioceses across Anglicanism, as well as in wider secular society, more and more people are wondering about what it means to be an Anglican and what the Anglican Communion is all about.

The election and consecration of the Rt. Rev V. Gene Robinson as Bishop of New Hampshire in late 2003, a homosexual man living in a lifelong committed relationship with another man, has occasioned a firestorm of scrutiny and media attention about the beliefs and practices of the Episcopal Church in the United States and the wider Anglican Communion. At the beginning of 2003 most individuals outside of the church (to say nothing of those within the fold) would have known little about the odd collection of Christians called Anglicans. Today, however, that is no longer the case, as articles in the *New York Times* or stories on CNN discuss the possibilities of schism in the Anglican Communion or debate the authority of the Archbishop of Canterbury and the other Anglican primates.

What is missing in most of these discussions, both in the secular media as well as in many church circles, is a nuanced, reasoned, and sensitive reflection on the history, challenges, and calling of Anglicanism today. Those of us looking for an informed and constructive discussion of what it means to be an Anglican in these times, however, are richly resourced in *Reinventing Anglicanism*.

Bruce Kaye's presentation of the priorities and possibilities of Anglicanism is not a rehashed tracing of the spread of the Church of England from the sixteenth-century Reformation to this day. No, Kaye is about a much more important and fundamental task. Beginning with Bede, the historian of early English Christianity in 731, and continuing through current post-colonial global realities, Kaye wants to recast, 'reinvent,' Anglicanism for the twenty-first century and beyond. His project is to free Anglicanism from the legacies of Tudor imperialism and British colonialism. He offers instead a view of Anglicanism as a Christian tradition that is confident in a plurality of cultural contexts, grounded in a community of interdependent diversity, and engaged with the world in a visionary and respectful manner. Kaye's task is thus fundamentally missiological: he wants to outline a vision for how Anglicanism can best serve and advance God's mission of reconciliation in today's hurting and broken world.

Kaye's recasting of Anglican history and resulting vision is not some disembodied discussion of ecclesial essentials. Using good incarnational theological method, Kaye grounds his vision for Anglicanism within the experience and story of his own church in Australia. The Australian case study is particularly useful because it highlights all of the dynamics of contemporary Anglicanism without being encumbered with the highly charged debates and political positions over human sexuality found in the Episcopal Church in the United States.

Kaye knows intimately of what he writes. He has traversed the Anglican Communion in his position as General Secretary of the Anglican Church in Australia and as a member of major Anglican councils such as the Inter-Anglican Theological and Doctrinal Commission, and the Anglican Communion Trust. In the halls of Anglican power from London to Sydney and from New York to Cape Town, Kaye is considered a clear-thinking, honest, and fundamentally fair churchman who puts the needs of the Anglican Communion above any personal interest or agenda. He is a widely respected theologian, scholar, and teacher, having held posts at the University of New South Wales, Australia, and the University of Durham, England. He continues his teaching ministry as the inspiration behind and founding editor of the new international *Journal of Anglican Studies*. Above all, Bruce Kaye is a man of deep faith in Jesus Christ who believes in the possibilities of the Anglican Communion. *Reinventing Anglicanism* is his gift to the Anglican Communion. There is much to be received in this gift. And there is much to be learned from this most important book for these tumultuous times of change and possibility in Anglicanism.

Ian T. Douglas is Professor of Mission and World Christianity at the Episcopal Divinity School in Cambridge, Massachusetts.

INTRODUCTION

There is no doubt that conflict and hostility make for good television, at least as perceived by those who produce television programs. Such conflict feeds our voyeuristic interest in power. Malcolm Muggeridge, who in his day had a vivid sense of the power of the press and television, records an occasion when a friend suddenly confessed to him that he did not know if he was licking the right boots. It introduced a discussion of what Muggeridge described as that 'inexhaustibly fascinating' subject of power. This interest of the media in power may account for the steady stream of stories about power politics and conflict in Anglican churches. The 1998 Lambeth Conference was a media bonanza, because it combined all the elements for dramatic media stories: conflict which involved bishops, sex and race. Within days of the announcement in January 2002 of the retirement of George Carey as Archbishop of Canterbury the British papers were littered with stories of intrigue and power plays for the appointment of his successor. In Australia the press love to portray conflict among the Anglicans, especially among the bishops.

Even taking into account the fascination of the media with conflict, it nonetheless seems to me that there has been increasing conflict among Anglicans in the last forty years. There have been serious conflicts before, I am sure, but we have been witnessing sustained conflict over a period of time. It is no accident that this has coincided with a period of quite remarkable change in the institutions of Anglicanism world wide as Anglicans have had to respond to changes in marriage patterns, the role of women and same sex relations, the advent of effective birth control and changing perceptions of authority.

But what actually is going on here? Two streams of influence have come together in this period to create a confluence of change and challenge to Anglicans' sense of their identity and the shape of their institutions. An endogenous stream flowing from the inner history of this tradition of Christianity has come to a point of significant crisis. The tradition of the Church of England and its style of Christianity has now moved outside the confines of the English culture and social institutions which formed it. It is now scattered in many countries and cultures which have little consonance with the English seed from which this straggling rose has sprung. The journey of this faith tradition has spread out into a delta of multiple streams and locations and it is not clear where the river runs. Secondly, there is an exogenous stream of external influences brought by the impact of global changes and by the variety of the local contexts in which Anglicans live and practise their faith.

This environment of change means that institutional authority is less strong and thus is open to more challenge. That inevitably means that there is more exercise of power in these communities, and that means life in the community is more political as people test the power of groupings. Because the church is essentially a voluntarist community and professedly religious, the conflict is verbal rather than physical. A great deal of rhetoric is to be heard in connection with people carving out elements of influence and territory. That rhetoric often focuses on three areas in this tradition: the English Reformation of the sixteenth century, the Bible (especially the New Testament) and the broader theological tradition of Christianity of which Anglicans are a part. People do not want to be called fundamentalists, though others think of them in those terms. Others do not want to be called liberals, though they are thought of in those terms. The naming game is really part of the rhetoric of claiming publicly defensible parts of the tradition for oneself and ascribing other less defensible parts to others.

If we are interested in the future of Anglicanism, how might we respond to this crisis? Obviously there are a number of different ways into the question, and a number are clearly represented in the literature. We might deal with the identity challenge by seeking to demonstrate that some particular marker or characteristic is the key identifier of Anglicanism. In the third quarter of the twentieth century there was a habit of saying that what marked Anglicanism out was that it sustained a liturgical pattern of worship. So dress and style of choreography were the bearers of Anglican identity. It hardly made sense if you lived in a predominantly Roman Catholic or Orthodox country. Episcopacy was claimed by some to be the distinctive mark, but that only made sense if your horizon was Geneva and its children. Yet others said synodical decision making, but other churches have that too. Some approached the problem by trying to find a distinctive Anglican doctrine or practice that marked out Anglican identity. It has been all very confusing and a little like the search for the lost chord. It is not surprising that the quest for the distinguishing marker seeped away into the sand.

A variation of this approach suggested that Anglicanism was identified by a certain characteristic ethos or style. Stephen Neill made this a popular approach, but it proved very difficult to be specific about the style, except that maybe it looked a little like the common room of an Oxbridge college.

Yet another approach to the identity issue has been to see Anglicanism as essentially a transitional form of Christianity whose great role is to be a bridge in bringing the churches back together again. So it used to be claimed that Anglicans were talking to more ecumenical partners than any other church. Such an approach looked to the Church of North India, and perhaps a little less enthusiastically to the Church of South India, as examples of the way for the future of the unity of the body of Christ. So the dialogue with Roman Catholics (ARCIC) took on great programmatic significance. This approach has now been given an extra impulse by the formation of a joint Anglican–Roman Catholic bishops group to work out the practical steps that might follow the agreements said to have been reached in the ARCIC declarations. Conceiving themselves as bridge builder in the process of ecclesial and ecclesiastical incorporatism has been and is still a way that Anglicans are using to deal with their identity problems.

Organisational development and acceptance is another way. Thus we notice the emergence in the Anglican Communion of new organisational arrangements which are increasingly episcopal. The growth in size and presentational significance of the Lambeth Conference of Bishops in the second half of the twentieth century has been a remarkable feature of worldwide Anglicanism. The establishment of the Anglican Consultative Council reverted to a more conciliar model, with representatives from the provinces, including bishops, clergy and lay people. But now we have seen the emergence of a meeting of the primates, at first once, then occasionally, and now each year, initially for consultation and private encouragement and support, but now with a public agenda and a program of activities which compete for funds in the budget. The development of economical and fast international air travel and of efficient and sophisticated communications has meant that it is possible for the role of the Archbishop of Canterbury to be extended and enhanced, though that process has placed great strains on the incumbent, not least in relation to his responsibilities in the Church of England.

All of these approaches are very understandable and are undoubtedly ways of handling the identity challenge facing Anglicans at the beginning of the twenty-first century. Another way of looking at the present issue is to look at the rhetoric used in the debates between Anglicans. Getting behind the rhetoric to find out what people really believe is always difficult. But an examination of the rhetoric would provide a basis not so much for identifying what people using the rhetoric actually believe in the quiet of their own rooms, but rather would reveal what they think are the elements in Anglicanism to which they can publicly appeal with advantage. One fascinating aspect of such an approach would be what it revealed about the nature of the power which was consciously or unconsciously being used and adopted by the deployment of this rhetoric.

The issue of power, politics and authority has been opened up in a most helpful way by Jeffrey Pfeffer. While he is primarily concerned with the business corporation, his analysis is germane to the present situation of Anglicanism. He makes a distinction between power, which is the effective changing of another's behaviour, and authority, which is power exercised within an agreed institutionalised framework. This is not dissimilar to the contrast between binary and ternary relationships developed by Alistair Mant. A binary relationship is, for example, one between a master and a servant—a one-to-one power relationship. A ternary relationship is one which exists within the framework of agreed values and structures to which both parties are committed.[1] In an open and social

---

1   Mant, A, *Intelligent Leadership*, pp 4–7.

context, power in Pfeffer's sense becomes political power. In order to highlight the qualities of political power Pfeffer has in mind, I list some of the contrasts he makes between dimensions in a bureaucratic model and a political power model.[2]

DIMENSION	BUREAUCRATIC MODEL	POLITICAL POWER MODEL
Goals preferences	Reasonably consistent	Consistent within social actors; inconsistent, pluralistic within the organisation
Power and control	Less centralised with greater reliance on rules	Shifting coalitions and interest groups
Decision process	Procedural rationality embodied in programs and standard operating procedures	Disorderly, characterised by push and pull of interests
Information and computational requirements	Reduced by the use of rules and procedures	Information used and withheld strategically
Decisions	Follow from programs and routines	Result of bargaining and interplay among interests
Ideology	Stability, fairness, predictability	Struggle, conflict, winners and losers

Clearly there is much in these comparisons which shows that a good deal of the activity in Anglicanism falls within what Pfeffer calls the 'political power model'. Given the present circumstances of Anglicanism, that should not be too surprising, though it is hardly a pattern to be content with in the long run.

2   See Pfeffer, J, *Power in Organizations*, p 31.

5

People often appeal to history in this rhetoric. That reflects the accepted traditional character of Anglicanism. This appeal to history is very often an appeal to the history of the sixteenth-century Reformation. It is of course not always clear whether this appeal to the Reformation is made because it is a publicly suitable appeal which can be fitted into the ambitions of activists or because of an unambiguous desire to retain the qualities of the Reformation. After all, the will to power is an all too human quality and can be presented in a myriad of ways, just as church politics can be very subtle and relentless.

But this appeal to history is not simply a matter of demonstrating what 'actually happened' in some Rankean sense. Rather, it is a matter of interpreting the past in the light of the present, or of seeking to give sense to the present in the light of the past. I believe that this process, properly conducted in the public arena of open conversation, is not only inevitable but essentially correct for Anglicans to be engaged in. It follows from this that such an interpretation of the Anglican past must be part of any continuing public conversation and, furthermore, that this conversation must be sufficiently informed to stand up to critical and scholarly examination. For this to happen, there needs to be some acceptance of the importance of this kind of conversation. That was the claim of Richard Hooker, as it was of Irenaeus and many others.

What is true in regard to history and the particular example of the sixteenth-century Reformation is equally true in regard to the other principal foci of appeal in Anglican rhetoric, namely Scripture and the ongoing theological tradition. These appeals are susceptible to the same kinds of conscious or unconscious corruptions, as they are also open to the kind of public conversation which can enhance both the understanding of the Anglican tradition and the quality of the contemporary conversation among Anglicans.

Rhetoric is a form of influence and an instrument of power in a loose-knit community such as the Anglican Communion, or indeed the various national Anglican churches. The management and manipulation of information is another form of power, and that would also provide an interesting point of entry into understanding the present identity issues in Anglicanism.

Similarly, patronage is a discrete exercise of power. It used to have a great deal of influence in the Church of England in clergy appointments in a formal sense. What I have in mind here, however, is the more informal exercise of patronage whereby the right people are enabled to find their way into the right places at the right time for them to be able to enlarge their own and their patron's influence. Tracking the lines of personal and institutional patronage would be a fascinating way into the issues of contemporary Anglican identity.

However, the position of this book is different from these approaches to the question. I have approached this matter by regarding Anglicanism as a tradition, indeed a discrete tradition within the broader tradition of Christianity. The present crisis in Anglicanism is created by the confluence of the two streams: the external historical developments of the second half of the twentieth century and the point of development from national church to international Communion of churches which is the story of the last three hundred years of Anglicanism. Each of these influences has an ambiguous impact on contemporary Anglicanism and is capable of moving the tradition in different, even mutually contradictory, directions. The future of Anglicanism will depend to a great degree on how the tradition responds to these two forces. It will need to find the resources within its own journey to enable it not only to respond but also to reinvent itself in a way that is both creative and faithful. In that sense my position on Anglicanism at the dawn of the twenty-first century is that it is a discrete tradition of Christianity in need of reinvention.

In order to give the discussion some focus, I shall take Australia as an example of the problems. It serves that purpose well because it has some of the problems in sharp form and it also happens to be the form of Anglicanism I know best.[3] I recognise that this example will not meet every particular form of the Anglican issues, but the conversation in global Anglicanism must inevitably be to some extent a conversation from different particulars. Writing from within a particular part of the tradition enables others to listen in on the conversation. This example may also contribute in another way, in that Australian Anglicanism is under-represented in the literature, largely because Australians in the past have tended not to record their story or to have written about its meaning. A small contribution on that front might be useful.

Conscious of these limitations and fully recognising that Australia is different

---

3   In 1995 I set out my own thoughts on this subject in *A Church without Walls.*

from other places, even though it highlights the central issues before Anglicanism at the present time, I believe that the form of Christianity embodied in Anglicanism is a modest but important part of the general spectrum of Christianity and that its reinvention is a pressing question for Anglicans and others. From this position this book seeks to present an argument which tries to take the tradition seriously and pays attention to the current dynamics in Anglicanism by looking at those elements most used in the contemporary rhetoric, namely the New Testament, the English Reformation of the sixteenth century and the ongoing theological tradition. These sources will be looked at selectively: the New Testament in order to raise some issues sharply, the Reformation to test its relevance and to engage with its place in the journey of Anglicanism, and the theological tradition in order to illustrate a few ways forward. Those elements will be referred to in relation to three crucial issues for modern Anglicans: what kind of confidence can they have in the present uncertain times, what kind of community can or should they be, and how can they appropriately engage with their contemporaries?

This approach to Anglicanism leads me to view Anglicanism as a tradition with certain qualities.

1. Anglicanism has survived, as one of the discrete traditions within western Christianity, because it contained within it crucial elements of a theological kind which have made it resilient. Those marks are:

   a. a conception of God who is participating in the human condition—an incarnational God

   b. connectedness in its ecclesial conceptions—a real sense that God is present

   c. an instinct about authority which derives from this and which is marked by qualities of open-endeddness, porous borders, tentativeness, contingency awareness, and an authority experienced and exercised by the whole people of God

   d. enmeshment in the social and cultural context and thus being guided by an awareness of both contingency and providence in regard to both ecclesial and social institutionality

   e. a particular way of dealing with origins in relation to Scripture which sets it in a context of continuity with the early church.

2. The current 'moment' which faces Anglicanism is one of a series in its history. Some of the earlier moments include
    a. the Saxon–Celtic interface, marking out a tradition of influence and a monastic presence
    b. the Roman invasion, or mission, of Augustine, marking out a conception of territory and organisation
    c. the Norman conquest, marking out a pattern of control and, for the church, legal separation and some institutional independence
    d. the Tudor triumph, marking out a tradition of nationalism and statutory control which went along with a religious revival
    e. and the imperial colonial phase, marking a tradition taken to foreign parts in the clothes of empire, redolent of the domestic imperial conceptions of Tudor nationalism.

All of these moments have carried with them cultural influences which have shaped the particular presentations of the tradition and provided the opening point for subsequent generations. They have contributed to the accumulation of memory, of the furniture our predecessors lived with and which now occupies various rooms in the house of Anglican community memory. The earlier moments are mentioned here by way of illustration. The last two will be more fully dealt with in the course of this discussion.

3. The current situation is marked by two predecessor paradigms:
    a. Domestic national imperialism. The Reformation monuments are cast in the language and institutional assumptions of Tudor imperialism, and these distort the religious perception.
    b. Colonial imperialism. Here institutionalities in the church such as law, property and the means and power to decide are influenced by the assumptions of overseas imperialism.

4. To imagine what Anglicanism might be like in the future requires not just re-conceptualising but also gaining some critical distance from these predecessor paradigms. This is in fact a classic example of contextualised theology. The reinvention has to struggle with mental and institutional paradigms inherited from variations of English imperial notions going back to the sixteenth century. That struggle is complicated by the widespread attachment in Anglicanism to the sixteenth-century Reformation legislative monuments, which are clothed in Tudor political conceptions.

5. The underlying key issues in such a reinvention of Anglicanism are confidence to act in environments which are not always sympathetic, the nature of ecclesial community life in a voluntarist situation, and the pattern of engagement with the host society. These three issues constitute the key challenges in the reinventing of Anglicanism.

This book therefore begins with a brief account of the journey of Anglicanism and an interpretation of the Australian situation. The three central chapters are concerned with confidence, community and engagements with others. I argue that Anglicans should seek a confidence appropriate to an attempt at persuasive resonance with what God is doing in the creation, that Anglicans should be nurturing a community of interdependent diversity and that their engagement with their fellows should be that of respectful visionaries. The final chapter takes up some suggestions about imagination and change in the reinvention of Anglicanism.

The substance of the manuscript was completed in 2002, but events since then have only confirmed in my mind the relevance of the thesis argued here. September 11 and its associated uncovering of conflict and instability in our world, and the challenge to international institutions like the United Nations by the actions of so-called coalitions of the willing, are mirrored in the international politics of the Anglican Communion. We truly continue to live in interesting times, and in such times we do well to go back to our roots and discover how we might reinvent ourselves in ways which are at once creative and faithful.

Some authors are able to write in relative isolation. I am not one of those. This book represents a vast array of information and insights which I have learned from others over the years. Indeed, the exploration of the deeper roots of the Anglican tradition has been and continues to be a fascinating journey of learning and appreciation of the vast richness of the work of specialist scholars, especially in such areas as medieval and early modern history and social and political theory. In writing this book I have had numerous discussions with a number of people from which I have learned an enormous amount. My friends, particularly Keith Mason and Hugh Mackay, have heard the ideas in this book in a variety of forms over recent years. I have benefited greatly from their conversation. Stanley Hauerwas has also been a friend and conversationalist over many years, and I constantly find myself in his debt in that conversation. Phillip Browning has maintained a continuous stream of stimulation and encouragement, which I acknowledge. I hope that he will take that acknowledgment as encouragement for his own pilgrimage in the church. This book has gone through a number of gestations, and parts of the text at various stages have been read by a number of friends and colleagues. I am grateful to them all for their comments and only wish that I had the wisdom and courage to accept all their advice. I am grateful to Chris Pfeiffer of Openbook Publishers for wise strategic advice and encouragement and to John Pfitzner and the staff at Openbook. Being a publisher of theology in Australia is a daunting task, and I salute the courage and determination of Openbook in sustaining that role. The community of St Michael's, Vaucluse, has heard a number of the themes in this book in the form of sermons. They are an infinitely patient community, which is just as well probably. My best thanks go to my wife Louise for her support. She has listened to her husband's ramblings, put up with his late nights and early mornings in the study with patience and interest, and experienced the occasional burst of excitement when she thought he had got something right.

Especially with a book such as this I want to express my thanks to that extraordinarily resilient community of people across the length and breadth of Australia who call themselves Anglicans. It has been my privilege to serve this community for the past nine years. Beyond them is that galaxy of God's people who for a millennium and a half have constituted the living members of the Anglican tradition and without whose faith and testimony we could not even begin to think about such a thing as reinventing Anglicanism.

CHAPTER ONE

THE JOURNEY OF ANGLICANISM

It was in going out to a place that he did not know that Abraham acted by faith, according to the writer to the Hebrews. 'By faith Abraham obeyed when he was called to set out for a place that he was to receive as an inheritance; and he set out, not knowing where he was going' (Hebrews 11:8). That journey motif has been used throughout Christian history to describe not only the lives of individuals but also the life of the people of God as the pilgrim church, the people of God following the call of God. That journey motif implies that this people know the God whom they serve and to whose call they respond, but it also implies that they are learning and discovering in the course of that journey. That truth is relevant not only to individuals and the whole Christian community but also to the groups and traditions which go to make up the whole. It is a model which applies to Anglicans and their tradition of faith.

Where that journey becomes distinctive and how its distinctiveness is to the be characterised are matters which we will explore during the course of this book. For the present, however, we need to clarify a little the nature of this journey and how it has been understood. It is not just an interesting story to be told while enjoying a cool drink under a gum tree; it is a life-changing question for Anglican communities and their friends, because in the present generation Anglicanism faces one of the most important interpretative questions in its history. As a tradition of Christianity formed and nurtured in the particularities of England's social and cultural experiences, Anglicanism now finds the centre of its numerical growth in the southern hemisphere. At the start of the third millennium more than half of all the people who go to Anglican churches in any given week do so on the continent of Africa. This numerical change and the different circumstances faced by Anglicans, together with new liaisons between different parts of the Anglican Communion, lay behind the notorious conflict at the 1998 Lambeth Conference over issues of sexuality.[4]

How are we to account for this tradition of Christianity? How can we characterise types of Christian faith as they develop over centuries of time? In this book I want to argue that Anglicanism is a discrete and particular tradition within Christianity and that it is best understood by looking first at its history and location. Such an approach enables us to mark out some of the leading characteristics of this tradition, and that will enable Anglicans to deal creatively and faithfully with the transition in which they are currently involved and in that process more faithfully reinvent themselves, their practices and understandings.

The first task, then, is to identify the journey of Anglicanism, and the first and contested interpretative question is when that journey should be reckoned to have started.

The beginnings of the journey

Anglican churches around the world claim to take their heritage back to the apostles and to Jesus himself. The constitution of the Anglican Church of Australia makes it an unchangeable part of its identity. The claim is that this church is the recipient and custodian of genuine apostolic Christianity. Those same churches also claim that they look to the Church of England as the particular line of heritage to which they belong within the broader compass of Christianity. Many again take the further step of identifying the monuments of the sixteenth-

---

4   See, for example, the account in Douglas, I T, 'Lambeth 1998 and the "new colonialism"', *The Witness*, May 2000, 8–12.

century Reformation as the particular expression of English Christianity to which they look. These monuments are the 1662 Book of Common Prayer, the Ordinal and the Thirty-nine Articles. In appealing to these Reformation monuments as 'classic texts', it is easy to forget that they were created in a very specific context and are particular kinds of documents. These monuments of the English Reformation were legal documents enacted by the king's parliament. That legal garb was itself not neutral on the political question of the relation between the Christian 'empire' of England and the 'imperium' of the bishop of Rome.

The English reformers of the sixteenth century appealed to the early church, and in particular to the first four centuries, against what they described as the innovations of the bishop of Rome. In doing so, they located the origins of their own ecclesial tradition in the earliest phase of Christianity. That claim is another side of their appeal to Scripture, which took the appeal back from the early church to the apostles and to Jesus himself as the historic incarnate Son of God. In making these claims, they knew clearly what was at stake: it was the identity of their own form of Christianity.

In their disputes with the Romans, the English reformers quite understandably sought to appeal to this longer and broader tradition stretching back to the apostles in order to secure their theological point against the bishop of Rome. Cranmer's essay on the doctrine of the Lord's supper is presented as the 'Catholic Doctrine'. He appeals to the New Testament and then, on a continuous line, to the early fathers of Christianity. He wished to show that his doctrine has a better and more apostolic pedigree than the innovations of his opponents.[5]

When the journey of Anglicanism began is thus a contentious issue. To claim, let alone simply to assume, that it dates from the sixteenth century calls for as much justification as any other proposed point of commencement. Space does not allow in this book for a comprehensive treatment of this matter, and therefore I can only point to the lines of an argument for my claim that the story must be construed as originating from the very early centuries of British Christianity. Given the privileged place in much contemporary Anglicanism of the sixteenth-century

---

5   See Kaye, B N, '"Classical Anglicanism": A necessary and valuable point of reference', *Reformed Theological Review* 56, no. 1 (1997).

monuments, that argument would begin with the understanding of the English reformers themselves that they were not innovators but reformers.

In their appeal to the past, priority was given to the apostolic past as contained in Scripture. Indeed Scripture is made the touchstone for knowing those things which it is necessary to believe in order to be saved. The appeal to Scripture is the core of the appeal to the apostolic past, and its authority for the Reformers reflects their instinct to be faithful in their tradition to the apostolic faith. It is in that faithfulness that they will be connected to the historic Christ and the incarnation of the Son of God. That framework of appeal to the past meant that these reformers saw Scripture as not alone but as pre-eminent and, in that pre-eminence therefore, always necessary and unique. The instinct to defend a practice by appeal to the ancient past and the pattern of development between that past and the present can be seen in the preface to the Ordinal. It makes the historically dubious claim that there had always been a threefold order of bishops, priests and deacons since the time of the apostles. That the accuracy of this appeal is not now accepted by historians does not remove the point that these reformers wanted to be able to locate their practice in a tradition which could claim a lineage back to the apostles.[6]

The English reformers were not uncritical of the recent past in England. The Preface to the 1662 Book of Common Prayer speaks of the 'late unhappy confusions'. The introduction 'Of ceremonies' deplores the diversity of the liturgical use of Salisbury, York, Bangor or Lincoln and decrees that henceforth in the nation there will be but one use. The political agenda and its assumptions which lay behind the various Acts of Uniformity and their significance in the journey of Anglicans will occupy us later, but it is clear that the appeal to the past by the English reformers served a rhetorical purpose and also at the same time revealed something of the traditional nature of the their faith.

The claim of the principle English reformers that they were the representatives of historic Christianity and that the pope was an innovator has been largely sidelined in recent centuries. In particular it has failed to hold ground in the public

---

6   See, for example, Luoma, J K, 'The Primitive Church as a Normative Principle in the Theology of the Sixteenth Century: The Anglican-Puritan debate over church polity as represented by Richard Hooker and Thomas Cartwright', PhD, The Hartford Theological Seminary, 1974; Luoma, J K, 'Who Owns the Fathers? Hooker and Cartwright on the Authority of the Primitive Church', *Sixteenth Century Journal* 8 (1977): 45–59.

argument about the identity of Anglicanism. On the contrary, the Roman rhetoric that this was a church brought forth late in time and occasioned by the marital difficulties of Henry has won wide acceptance. This reading of Anglicanism has been part of and has served some interests in various Anglican ecumenical dialogues. Even Anglican theologians have come to accept central elements of this claim. It is, of course, much simpler to construe Anglicanism as existing within a horizon which reaches only to the sixteenth century. There can be no doubt that at the Reformation a fundamental break with Rome occurred and that the English church claimed to be able to sustain itself from within its own resources. The point is also underlined by the defining presence given to the formularies of the English Reformation in many Anglican constitutions around the world. The Roman Catholic author Aidan Nichols has recently taken this as the basis for a sustained critique of the Church of England.[7] Even recent Anglican reports have given voice to this interpretation of Anglicanism, looking only as far as the sixteenth-century horizon.[8]

It is therefore apparent that the claim that Anglicanism can only properly be understood in the light of its long history back to the early centuries of British Christianity is actually highly contentious. For many it sounds like a claim designed to overthrow the reformed character of Anglicanism and thus to advance an agenda in the present which is subversive to that character. In part it evokes memories of earlier debates between Anglo Catholics and Evangelicals. Such suspicions are entirely understandable and indeed, in a certain sense, well founded. Whoever owns the past has first mortgage on the present and the future. More than that, any argument about the identity of Anglicanism will inevitably have to be about the past and where that past has led and is leading. Furthermore, any argument about the identity of Anglicanism will also be about priorities and direction in the present. This book is no exception to that.

However, if we pose the question of the historical horizon of the Anglican tradition in broader terms about western Christianity generally, we can get a little better leverage on the problem. What actually was the character of western

---

7   Nichols, Aidan, *The Panther and the Hind: A theological history of Anglicanism*. Edinburgh: T & T Clark, 1993.

8   Kaye, B N, 'Unity in the Anglican Communion: A critique of the "Virginia Report"', *St Mark's Review* 184 (2001): 24–31.

Christianity in late antiquity and the medieval and early modern period? Was it marked by such a level of uniformity which would make the inquiry about a discrete sub-group automatically improbable? It is easy to think that the highly centralised conception of the papacy today was the way it has always been. Clearly it has not been so. The pre-eminence of the pope was hard won, and the actual character of that pre-eminence emerged and changed over many centuries.

During the seventh century, moves by the pope for more power in Europe took place in a context of growing political regionalism and earlier ecclesiastical regionalism. Peter Brown goes so far as to describe this regionalism of the seventh century as a 'patchwork of adjacent, but separate, "micro-Christendoms." No longer bathed, unconsciously, in an "ecumenical" atmosphere based upon regular inter-regional contacts, each Christian region fell back upon itself. Each needed to feel that it possessed, if in diminished form, the essence of an entire Christian culture.'[9]

This period coincided in Britain with the consolidation of the new Saxon kingdoms and the determination to extend the range and reach of royal power. These rulers thought of themselves as Christian rulers of Christian kingdoms and, as a consequence, such rulers could think of themselves as caring for the souls of their people as well as their bodies. Such conceptions not only made for a complete coincidence of body and soul, sacred and secular, but also consolidated the politico-religious regionalism of the 'micro-Christendoms' of western Europe. It was in this context that the extraordinary library was established at Monkwearmouth in the north of England, with books and manuscripts collected from all over Europe in order to secure for England the resources to sustain its own faith and religious practices. This was the library in which Bede worked.

Patterns of regional autonomy can also be seen later in the eleventh century. In a letter to Gregory VII in 1075 William the Conqueror makes a nice distinction in his relationship to the pope. Gregory had sent a legate to collect back amounts of 'Peter's Pence' and also to order William to do fealty to the pope and his successors. 'I refused to do fealty, and I will not do it: for I did not promise it, nor

---

9 Brown, P, *The Rise of Western Christendom: Triumph and Diversity AD 200–1000*, Oxford: Blackwell, 1996, p 218.

do I find that my predecessors did fealty to yours.'[10] As to the money, it will be sent when it has been collected. William also would not allow anyone to 'to acknowledge as apostolic the pontiff of the city of Rome, except by his own order', and all communication from the bishop of Rome had to come through the king. Statute 13 of Richard II marked out the same independence from the bishop of Rome when it forbad the pope providing appointments in the English church. It is noteworthy that this statute goes to some trouble to recall the precedent for this in the action of Richard's grandfather King Edward. A further act under Richard forbad appeals to Rome.

This dimension overlays another movement in relation to diversity and centralising tendencies in the first five centuries of the second millennium. Through political force in the fourteenth century, English clergy obtained relief from papal obedience. The freedom of the church pointed to in Magna Carta was a freedom under the prince from the intrusion into the kingdom by the pope. Across the channel in France the synod of 1406/07 marks the origins of what was to be called 'Gallicanism'. The Gallican church relied on conciliar canon law in order to argue for relief from papal demands similar to the 'English liberties' of the fourteenth century. The 'English liberties' and 'Gallicanism' illustrate the way in which the religious regionalism was made possible by the growing political regionalism and was in close interaction with the emerging regional cultures.[11]

A different pattern of decentralising can be seen in the councils of Constance (1414–18) and Basel (1431–49). This reform movement looks more like the operation of the principle of subsidiarity within the church hierarchy rather than geographical regionalism. The revolutionary document from Constance, *Haec Sancta*, clearly sets out a claim to precede the pope in authority. 'First that this synod, legitimately assembled in the Holy Spirit, constituting a general council, representing the catholic church militant, has power immediately from Christ, and that everyone of whatever state or dignity, even papal, is bound to obey it in those matters which pertain to the faith and the eradication of the said schism.'[12] It is the claim to represent the whole church that is so striking here. It is the whole

---

10 Letter to Gregory VII [c 1075]. The text is readily available in Bettenson, H (ed), *Documents of the Christian Church*, London: Oxford University Press, 1956, p 217.

11 Stump, P H, *The Reforms of the Council of Constance (1414–1418)*, Leiden: E J Brill, 1994, especially pp 11–14, and Izbicki, T, *History*, 557–20. Generally on Gallicanism see Holt M P, *The French Wars of Religion, 1562–1629*, Cambridge, Cambridge University Press.

church which has authority, and because the council claims to represent that 'catholicity', it has supreme authority which can properly be said to come 'immediately from Christ'.

Recent scholarship on late antiquity and the early modern period points to a very differentiated picture of western Christianity. Furthermore, recent scholarship on the conciliar movement has shown that a number of forces were at work modifying and challenging the centralist and absolutist claims of the pope.[13] In this context it is not only possible that a distinct tradition of Christianity formed in Britain but also that this tradition actually proved to be just one particular example of a number of such local traditions, of which Gallicanism is another notable example.

The formation of such a tradition of English Christianity is really the work of centuries. However, the different nations within the island of Britain were first brought together conceptually by Bede in 731. A pious monk from Monkwearmouth, Bede was known throughout Europe for his learning. Part of the effect of Bede's *History of the English Church and People* was to show that now in the eighth century Saxon Britain could be portrayed as a Christian land. He opens his account with a survey of the peoples occupying the British Isles in their interrelationships. In the Preface he had reviewed the sources he had used to describe this people. His dedication of the work to King Ceolwulf refers to the king's desire to know something of the past and 'of famous men of our own nation in particular'.[14] 'Bede was the first author to treat the disparate groups of settlers as a single *gens Anglorum*, a 'nation of the English' ... a single people, newly established in their own Promised Land, the island of Britain.'[15]

12   Session 4, 30 March 1415. The text is quoted from Tanner, N P (ed), *Decrees of the Ecumenical Councils*, 2 vols, Washington: Georgetown University Press, 1990, vol 1, p 408. See also 'First it declares that, legitimately assembled in the Holy Spirit, constituting a general council and representing the catholic church militant, it has power immediately from Christ' (Session 5, 6 April 1415), Tanner vol 1, p 409.
13   See the work of Stump referred to above, and also Black, A, *Council and Commune: The Conciliar movement and the fifteenth-century heritage*, London: Burns & Oates, 1979, and *Guilds and Civil Society in European Political Thought* and Tierney, B, *Church Law and Constitutional Thought in the Middle Ages*, London, 1979, and, from an earlier generation of scholarship, Figgis, J N, *Studies of Political Thought from Gerson to Grotius, 1414–1625*, Cambridge: Cambridge University Press, 1907.
14   Bede, *A History of the English Church and People*, translated by Leo Shirley-Price and R E Lathan, London: Penguin Books, 1968, p 33.
15   Brown, *Rise of Western Christendom*, p 213. The same point is made by A Hastings in Hastings, A, *The Construction of Nationhood: Ethnicity, Religion and Nationalism*.

It is to Bede, more than any other, that we should look for the consolidation of earlier disparate traditions to create the basis for the particular and discrete Christian tradition that we can call Anglicanism. That tradition, of course, retained elements of the earlier period described by Bede which stretches from the Roman invasions by Caesar (60 BCE) and Claudius (46 CE) to the death of Archbishop Bertwold in 731 CE. During that period the Celtic and tribal monastic pattern gave way to the diocesan and centralised pattern of the Romans, but Bede's story shows clearly that the tribal and monastic traditions persisted for centuries.[16]

It should not be imagined that the discrete regional traditions in Western Europe did not see themselves as belonging to the Catholic Church. That point is clear in the conciliar formulations and is manifest in the interpretative commitments of Bede. Rather, what is being emphasised here is that within the compass of catholic Christianity there were discrete local versions, and Anglicanism was one of them. Furthermore, as this tradition wended its way through the centuries it developed its own memory and pedigree and thus also its own historical framework. That memory provided a framework for understanding particular parts along the way, even if some of those parts, like the sixteenth-century Reformation, constituted a radical change.

Anglicanism in its modern form is thus the result of a multiplicity of transitions from its seedbed in early Celtic and Saxon Christianity. These transitions have each had their own particular characteristics. The Romanising mission of Augustine had its impact on the Celtic traditions of British Christianity. The Norman invasion and the negotiated legal independence for the church courts secured by Lanfranc re-ordered the institutional shape of the church. Theodore's use of synods to renew the life and structures of the church left its mark, as have a multitude of other transitions, not least, of course, the sixteenth-century Reformation. The modern period has seen the tradition move overseas, first to America and then later to the growing parts of the British empire. While there were some common elements in the colonial experience, each was different. In Nigeria missionaries preceded direct colonial rule, and Anglicanism expanded in

---

16 See the summary of this period by Bonner, G, 'Religion in Anglo-Saxon England' in *A History of Religion in Britain*, edited by S Gilley and W J Sheils, 24–44, Oxford: Blackwell, 1994.

close tandem with English commercial activity. A colony was established in Lagos in 1861, but a protectorate of Northern and Southern Nigeria was not declared until 1900. Crowther, the first black bishop, worked on the assumption in this early period that 'commerce encouraged conversions'.[17] In India the missionary movement worked in the early nineteenth century mainly through education, though that changed with the more direct British rule after the Sepoy mutiny in 1857, when Anglicanism was more clearly associated with the direct British imperial rule. Australia began in New South Wales as a convict colony, and the church came in the person of a chaplain working under the disciplines of war in a military environment. Other Australian colonies began differently and developed different characteristics.[18]

The experience of the last two centuries shows that a similar process of transition has been at work, even though the precise details differ.[19] That transition involves the core religious tradition which was being exported and the specific cultural, institutional clothing of this tradition. Such a transition is not in principle new in Christianity generally, or in the longer history of Anglicanism, but it has been a transition in which elements of the exported form have proved to be extraordinarily resilient and resistant to analysis and change.

These matters have not gone unnoticed or unremarked upon. In the last decades of the twentieth century the obvious challenges to coherence, adaptation and faithfulness that have faced Anglicans around the world have produced a number of important interpretations of the present situation of worldwide Anglicanism to which we should now turn.

The recent search for an interpretation

In recent decades a number of writers have contributed significantly to the interpretation of the transition of the Anglican tradition from England to the international gathering of churches which now constitute the Anglican Communion. One of the earliest writers in this recent period was Stephen Sykes,

---

17 Sachs, W L, *The Transformation of Anglicanism: From State Church to Global Communion*, Cambridge: Cambridge University Press, 1993, p 168.
18 Kaye, B N, *The 1850 Bishops Conference and the Strange Emergence of Australian Synods*. Melbourne: Trinity College, 2000, pp 5–8.
19 See the historiography of the mission aspects of imperialism in Etherington, N, 'Missions and Empire' and Porter, A, 'Religion, Missionary Enthusiasm, and Empire'.

who in 1987 published *The Integrity of Anglicanism.*[20] He was prompted to write this book because of what he perceived to be a lack of integrity in conversations that Anglicans, mainly Anglicans in the Church of England, were conducting with other church traditions. He perceived a lack of serious theological work, he observed what he regarded as a somewhat facile interpretation of the idea of comprehensiveness, and he set out a notion of liberalism as being in itself not a substantial theological position but at most a qualification of other substantive positions.

The argument which Sykes put forward in this book was both innovative and rigorous. One of the most substantial parts of the book was his discussion of ecclesiology. The issue undergirded much of what he said in the various chapters of the book and came to sharp expression when he sought to define the limits of Anglican belief. He argued that the Church of England had definite convictions and plainly insisted on a high degree of conformity to them. The distinct convictions were those which informed its liturgical texts, and its insistence on conformity was embodied in canonical declarations made by every ordained person that he or she would use only the forms of service which were authorised by canon.[21]

Stephen Sykes has addressed the question of authority in Anglicanism on a number of occasions, and in a reflection published in 1992 he underlined two points.[22] The first is that Anglicans cannot claim exemption from the sociological rule that determines that authoritative texts require authoritative interpreters. He does not offer documentation or argument for this assertion, but clearly the force of the claim lies in its susceptibility to some kind of empirical proof. Sykes regards this principle as a sociological rule based upon the claim that classical texts exist as classical texts within a community. That seems to me to be relatively uncontroversial. However, the second part of the claim, that they gain their authority as they are interpreted by those who have responsibility within the

---

20 Sykes, S W, *The Integrity of Anglicanism*, London: Mowbray, 1978, Sykes, S, 'Foundations of an Anglican Ecclesiology' in *Living the Mystery*, edited by J John, 28–48, London: Darton Longman & Todd, 1994.

21 He returned to this point in Sykes, S, *Unashamed Anglicanism*, London: Darton Longman & Todd, 1995, p 217.

22 Sykes, S W, 'The Genius of Anglicanism' in *The English Religious Tradition and the Genius of Anglicanism*, edited by Geoffrey Rowell, 227–241, Wantage: Ikon, 1992, reprinted in *Unashamed Anglicanism*, pp 211–226.

community, is more problematic. It is not clear in this claim who those are who are responsible for this task in the church. Even so, this particular way of construing the question is only one particular way of reading the matter. Another is that the classical texts in a tradition community are always the subject of interpretative argument and that the authority of the texts depends upon the process of argument itself. In the field of science Steven Shapin[23] has recently shown that positional reliability was a key feature in the acceptance of new truth claims but that the trust engendered by the position of such people did not necessarily relate to the subject matter of the claim. In the particular case of the seventeenth century, which Shapin was investigating, social status played a significant role in establishing trust in relation to scientific assertions. If Stephen Sykes is claiming that Scripture is part of the package of authority that operates in the church and that it does so within the framework of that wider setting and because of that gains authority in the community, then it is a very controversial claim.

By putting it in this sociological way, Sykes is setting the issue in the wider context of human socialty and institutions.[24] I agree with that move in that it helps to open up the issues which were inevitably at work in bringing to consciousness in the early church the idea of having a list of authoritative books ('classic texts') and then by gradual consensus agreeing on the contents of that list. It also helps to understand the theological debates in history about the status and authority of the Bible in a more refracted way. But that point only draws attention to the opacity of what the move means in terms of notions of responsibility, power and interpretation. These points are not elaborated by Sykes in his short essay.

His second point is more important to him and more significant in terms of what I wish to argue in this book, namely that the problem of authority for Anglicans is not so much in the external organs of authority, whether synods or bishops meetings, but it lies 'in the hearts and minds of members of the church'. Sykes bases this interpretation of authority on what he describes as the plainly biblical theology that 'God's gifts are given to the whole people of God, and that the gift of leadership is only bestowed within that context'.[25]

---

23 Shapin, S, *A Social History of Truth: Civility and Science in Seventeenth-Century England,* Chicago, 1994, University Chicago Press.
24 See the more general discussion of these issues in Condren, Conal, *The Status and Appraisal of Classic Texts: An essay on political theory, its inheritance, and on the history of ideas,* Princeton, N.J.: Princeton University Press, 1985.
25 *Unashamed Anglicanism,* p 223.

This is a striking analysis of the authority issue. It sets it clearly in relation to ecclesiology and in symbiotic relationship to an understanding of the sociality that necessarily must characterise any conception of the church. His conception of Anglicanism, though strongly influenced in his earlier work by the English experience, provides a more general basis for understanding Anglicanism in its global and diverse social and political circumstances. That he relates his conception to a theology of the presence of God in the creation, and to a particular epistemological approach, takes the matter to a fundamental level of analysis. That emphasis enables him to underline that the action of God in his world 'involves an affirmation *both* of created sociality *and* of that which is new, surprising and unique'.[26] That he has come to shape his idea of Anglicanism in terms which focus on the members of the Anglican churches rather than the particularities of institutional arrangements makes his argument more suitable for understanding the variety of circumstances in which Anglicans live and practice their faith. This formulation draws attention immediately to the fact that Anglicanism exists as a voluntary association in most parts of the world. It reflects the new and distinctive position of Anglicanism in England pointed to in the English Act of Toleration (1689), which granted freedom of worship to dissenters, and in the more substantial moves to toleration in the nineteenth century. This plural environment became manifest in every part of the globe during the nineteenth and twentieth centuries.

Two other recent significant attempts to interpret the present position of Anglicanism serve not only to highlight the argument of this book but also to illuminate the issues involved in this discussion. Paul Avis has written on Anglicanism with a view to the ecumenical dimensions of the transition confronting Anglicanism.[27] William Sachs has approached the question more from the point of view of the way in which Anglicanism has been transformed into a worldwide Communion, but in the process he argues that it has not been able to resolve the question of an authority basis for its institutional life. Both review the historical tradition of Anglicanism since the sixteenth century, and

---

26 *Unashamed Anglicanism*, p 224.

27 Avis, P, *Anglicanism and the Christian Church*, Edinburgh: T & T Clark, 1989. He has revisited the Anglican idea of the church in *The Anglican Understanding of the Church: An Introduction*, London: SPCK, 2000.

each develops from that review a particular focus for dealing with the issues facing Anglicanism.

Paul Avis uses the notion of 'paradigm' to develop his argument. His review of Anglicanism uses three paradigms to interpret that history: the Erastian paradigm (the church is subject to the divinely ordered rulers) of the sixteenth century, exemplified in Archbishop Thomas Cranmer, the Apostolic paradigm (the church has its own integrity based on its apostolic origins and character), as recovered in the Tractarian revival of the nineteenth century, and the baptismal paradigm, which he sees as underlying the continuing history and experience of Anglicanism. He claims that Anglicanism has always thought of itself as a 'branch of the Christian church' in the sense that it has been grown from the common stock of apostolic Christianity. In that sense catholicity for him has to do with the qualitative issues of baptismal acceptance. In other words, baptism marks out the Christian as belonging to Christ and underlies the Anglican and catholic Christian experience.

That baptismal experience is different from the issues of particular ecclesial identity which is dependent on cultural norms and circumstances. On this view the church naturally fits into the cultural shape of the time and place in which it is located. Thus it is moulded by the medieval social structures, the nationalist patters of the sixteenth century, the imperial categories of the nineteenth century. The more Christians have become aware of their common heritage in catholic Christianity, the more they have become conscious of their different particular identities. Given this variegated model of ecclesiastical forms, how should Anglicans approach their self-understanding? The Erastian paradigm is dead, and the apostolic paradigm of the nineteenth century, exemplified in the Oxford Movement, is divisive and 'takes an aspect of catholicity for the whole. It makes the life of the whole body dependent on one particular instrument in that life— the ministry'.[28] An alternative paradigm is the baptismal model. 'Baptism is the fundamental sacrament of Christianity.'[29] This baptismal paradigm has never been absent from Anglicanism, and Avis tracks it through from the sixteenth-century reformers to the modern period. He then argues that the flourishing of a central type of Anglicanism which is focused on this baptismal paradigm would enable

---

28 Avis, *Anglicanism*, p 303.
29 Avis, *Anglicanism*, p 304.

the diversities of interpretation and disposition in the church both to be vital and to contribute to the whole. He is not arguing for a 'dominant liberal consensus, with its purely pragmatic attitude to truth, but genuine tripartite interaction' between the elements of catholic, liberal and evangelical within Anglicanism which would require the church to learn to contain conflict and to widen the bounds of diversity. The way ahead for Avis is to 'take the baptismal paradigm as a guide, to liberate the inner dynamic of Christian reality in the church ... and to ask What makes us Christians? What constitutes the church? What is essential to Christianity? How do historical determinants and canonical structures stand in relation to that?'[30]

There is much here with which I would like to agree, but it leaves unclarified the nature of the diachronic character of the Anglican tradition. True, the church fits into the cultural framework of its location in time and space. True, the fundamental Christian issue is Christological and in that sense is related to the role of baptism in Christianity. But it is also true that the past impacts on the way in which a tradition-shaped community can and does think and act in the particularities of its location. The baptismal paradigm may be a useful test for Christians in their Christian living and decision making, but inevitably the tradition in which they have been formed will shape that question differently. Moreover, the church institutionality and the tacit assumptions of its life will be similarly shaped by the inherited tradition. That tradition is also itself a conversation from within the present and with the particularities of the past.

The baptismal paradigm, therefore, does not seem to me to go far enough in configuring the nature of Christianity as necessarily a set of discrete traditions that depends on those traditions for its vitality. It does not address the issue of the particularity of those traditions and therefore is left with the question, as yet unguided and unshaped, as to what constitutes the church. The difficulty it seems to me is that the notion of 'paradigm' is not quite adequate or flexible enough to deal with the issue of traditionality in Christianity in general and in its several subsets, of which Anglicanism is one.

---

30 Avis, *Anglicanism*, p 311.

In one sense Paul Avis's argument could have been strengthened if he had taken his horizon for Anglicanism back beyond the sixteenth century, in that he could have shown even more clearly the limited value of the Erastian and the nineteenth-century 'apostolic' paradigms for the interpretation of Anglicanism. By default that would have strengthened his case for the baptismal paradigm. However, such an extension of the horizon would also have drawn attention to the wider diversity within western Christianity and the character of Anglicanism as a discrete tradition within that diversity which was at once more specific and more malleable than the model suggested by the baptismal paradigm.

Writing just four years after Avis, William Sachs approached the question in quite a different way. Also starting with the sixteenth-century Reformation, he traced the model of Anglicanism in terms of the establishment position of the Church of England. This picks up the theme highlighted by Avis under the heading of the Erastian paradigm. However, Sachs tracks this through the English experience in more detail. These different conceptions of the establishment are central to his understanding of what Anglicanism is all about. He draws out the problems faced by the church in changing political circumstances and the growth of empire.

It is in the twentieth century that the real issues of the transformation of Anglicanism arise. 'By 1945, what had once been the Church of England had evolved into the Anglican Communion.'[31] It was in this period that the glory of Anglicanism was to be seen, and it was manifest in liberal Catholicism, a tradition which had emerged in Anglicanism shaped by the culture of modernity. 'The Church of England was a product of the rise of the modern world, an arm of a modern nation integral to political arrangements, pivotal to the functioning of society.'[32] In this framework of modernity, society was ordered according to a cosmic order, which could be construed as a divine plan. This model of human society was rational and discounted affect. It was in effect a state model, whether that be the establishment pattern of the Church of England or the elite pressure group of the Episcopal Church of the United States of America.[33]

---

31 Sachs, *Transformation*, p 303.
32 Sachs, *Transformation*, p 304.
33 For an account of the changing models of national church in the United States see Douglas, I T, 'Whither the National Church? Reconsidering the Mission Structures of the Episcopal Church' in *A New Conversation: Essays on the Future of Theology and the Episcopal Church*, edited by R B Slocum, 60–78, New York: Church Publishing, 1999.

However, in the second half of the twentieth century changed social and political circumstances meant that there was a sustained assault on the establishment model, a loss of coherence in terms of theology and belief, and a revival of affect in the charismatic movement.

The result of these changes in the second half of the twentieth century was that Anglicanism became a 'global grass roots liturgical communion'.[34] This transformation appeared at first to have succeeded. However, the claim to a catholic character, the acknowledgement of an English heritage and openness to contemporary society did not satisfy the problem of having a way to resolve conflicts within the church. 'There seemed to be no definitive Anglicanism as the twentieth century waned.'[35] Modernity, which had been the basis of the flourishing of the liberal catholic ascendancy in the middle of the twentieth century, proved at the end of the century to be baggage which did not enable Anglicans to incorporate diversity while at the same time having some sense of their own identity.

As with the Avis analysis, this presentation draws attention to important elements in the experience of Anglicans especially in the last fifty years. Once again the analysis of Anglicanism commences from the sixteenth century, and that settlement is taken as a model. Furthermore, the establishment elements in the sixteenth-century settlement are taken as the model which goes forward. The analysis of the development in England of the church–state relations and its effect on the understanding of the church and the theological implications of those changes is detailed and illuminating. However, the conspectus of the analysis is kept to the issue of establishment. While I don't want to understate the importance and influence on the self-understanding of this church–state relationship in England, it is too narrow a point of reference for a full understanding of global Anglicanism. Furthermore, restricting the horizon to the sixteenth century limits the imaginable possibilities for understanding this tradition of Christianity.

Given the use of establishment as the key heuristic category, it is not surprising that the relevant notion from modernity for this analysis is the nation state.

---

34 Sachs, *Transformation*, p 336.
35 Sachs, *Transformation*, p 336.

Clearly the idea of the nation has had a significant influence on the experience of Anglicanism; that, after all, is true of Christianity in other parts of Europe and elsewhere. Sachs draws out the characteristic elements in the English experience in his historical survey but leaves it untouched and unincorporated into the analysis and the conception of Anglicanism which he presents. In terms of the development of the Anglican Communion, it is clear that there is a distinct relation with the state-supported and state-promoted colonialism of the modern period. That is true of the de-colonisation process as well. What Macmillan did for the British Empire, Fisher did for Anglicanism. Archbishop Geoffrey Fisher spent a good deal of effort encouraging Anglican churches in newly independent former British colonies to develop their own constitutions.[36] A similar process of ecclesiastical colonising and de-colonising can be seen in the relationship between ECUSA and South America and the Philippines, and also between Australia and Papua New Guinea. In this sense it is reasonable to say that aspects of modernity influenced, even shaped, the transformation of Anglicanism. But it is not the whole story, and the conspectus of the analysis is too narrow adequately to account for this religious tradition. Similarly, what Sachs calls 'affect', which he identifies with the charismatic renewal of the second half of the twentieth century, is in my view better understood as the residual critical impulse of romanticism. That same impulse was also at work in the evangelical revivals and the directing motivations of the Tractarians.[37]

However, in one sense Sachs is correct to focus on the state issue, in that it brings to the surface the issue of what kind of authority can operate and has operated in Anglicanism. Sachs laments that there appears to be no definitive Anglicanism at the end of the twentieth century, and the issue he focuses on is the absence of a centre of authority capable of settling conflict and dealing with the diversity which the twentieth century has witnessed among Anglicans. Given the controlling use of the category of the state for understanding Anglicanism, it is not surprising that this is how the problem is formulated. The problem is stated in terms of the categories used in the historical analysis. Why should it not be so? That shows laudable consistency in the argument. However, the categories are not critically examined in relation to any notion of the elements of Anglican theology.

---

36 See Piggin, S, 'Australian Anglicanism in a World-wide Context' in Kaye, B (ed), *Anglicanism in Australia: A History*, Melbourne, MUP, 2002, pp 200–222.
37 See Berlin, I, *The Roots of Romanticism* and Harris, R, *Romanticism and the Social Order 1780–1830*.

Furthermore, the analysis is too narrow both in terms of the issues and in terms of the chronological horizon adopted. An extension of both of these would have presented a different picture, and the problem would be similarly differently construed.

Another interpretation of the present circumstances of Anglicanism which makes use of notions of modernity and post-modernity is that offered by Ian Douglas.[38] Here, however, the focus is on colonialism as the determining predecessor model of Anglicanism. He uses the recent difficulties at the 1998 Lambeth Conference to argue that the old Anglo–American hegemony is now dead and that the roots of Anglican identity will not be found in any re-use of the colonial model. Indeed, the book he has jointly edited is entitled *Beyond Colonial Anglicanism.* The essays in this book specifically address the situation of Anglicanism in a post-colonial environment. More than that, they do so on the basis that the spread of Anglicanism and the emergence of the Anglican Communion have been effected in intimate connection with colonial expansion. That fact has created a particular kind of colonial Anglicanism beyond which these authors wish to go. The way to do this, according to the analysis of Ian Douglas, is to go back to the contextualising principle of the English Reformation. 'Anglicanism thus can be understood *as the embrace and celebration of apostolic catholicity within vernacular moments.*'[39]

Douglas uses the work of Lamin Sanneh to develop his idea of vernacular moment. Sanneh argued that the gospel only finds its truth when it is translated into the local vernacular. The point was developed in relation to his study of the impact of Christianity in Africa, and it constitutes a strong claim for the centrality of the principle of contextualisation as arising out of the very nature of the gospel. It is hard to argue with this point, since it lies within the flow of Christian history from the time of the apostles. Jesus' own actions and ways of speaking, Paul's use of Greek and Roman ideas and terms to express the gospel, his so called Hellenisation of Christianity, all point in this direction. However, it is not at all

38 Douglas, I T, 'Anglican Identity and the *Missio Dei*: Implications for the American Convocation of Churches in Europe', *Anglican Theological Review* 82, no. 3 (2000): 459–474 and Douglas, I T, 'The Exigency of Times and Occasions: Power and Identity in the Anglican Communion Today' in *Beyond Colonial Anglicanism*, edited by I T Douglas and Kwok Pui-Lan, 25–46, New York: Church Publishing, 2001. See also Harris, M, *The Challenge of Change: The Anglican Communion in the Post-Modern Era*, New York: Church Publishing, 1998.
39 Douglas, *Exigency*, p 35.

clear to me that the English Reformation could be regarded as especially distinctive in terms of this principle. That process had been going on for a long time in British Christianity. Certainly what happened at the Reformation was a certain re-patriation of church authority, though this was more in the nature of an assertion of English imperial autonomy at the political level than any distinctive theological principle. To define Anglicanism in terms of contextualisation is an important insight in the present global situation where a variety of old-style colonial forces are at work. It also has a strategic significance in regard to thinking about ecumenical relations. But I think something a little more specific can be said.

The analysis presented by these authors advances the level of discussion considerably. They clearly represent significant analytical endeavours, and they clarify some key issues. The use of the notion of paradigms by Avis and the use by Sachs of modernity as seen in the state with which Anglicanism was established both provide clear insights, though they are too narrow in the conception of Anglicanism both in terms of the categories used and the historical framework within which their analysis is set. If Sachs had adopted a more general conception of the relationship between Anglicanism and English society rather than notions of establishment, his analysis could have opened up wider horizons for interpreting the institutional circumstances of worldwide Anglicanism. As it is, his own categories of analysis in large measure create the impasse into which his argument leads.

All these interpretations are significant attempts to analyse the character of the religious tradition of Anglicanism. They all draw attention to the transitions that have taken place historically in the transformation which is implied in the spread of Anglicanism beyond the shores of England. They all draw attention to the centrality of the question of ecclesiology and of the relationship of the Christian community to the host society in which the church is located. They all draw attention to issues of institutionality, and they all draw attention to the critical question of the way in which authority could be construed in Anglicanism in a way that makes sense of the history of the present circumstances of the churches of the Anglican Communion. They all raise, however, to the forefront of our consideration the question of how exactly we might best approach the characterisation of Anglicanism and an analysis of its present circumstances.

Characterising Anglicanism as a traditon

The analysis in this book has been developed in terms of what I call a 'tradition critical' approach. This approach has led me to illustrate the argument by reference to the sixteenth-century Reformation, the New Testament and some recent theological discussion. These were by no means the only elements of the past which could have been mined for assistance in interpreting the present circumstances of Anglicanism. They were chosen because they suited the particular issues which seem to me to be important in terms of any reinventing of Anglicanism. The Australian situation has been taken as a helpfully typical expression of the wider issues facing Anglicanism. That approach already implies that what we are dealing with in Anglicanism is a tradition, and, more than that, a particular or discrete tradition within Christianity.

The notion of a tradition is in general terms well enough understood. It is a way of characterising a particular pattern of ideas, relationships, habits and actions which persist though time. Some traditions of this kind are short lived, others persist for millennia. Christianity and the other major religions are in this latter category. When we come to Anglicanism then, the scope of the tradition must include some sense of the way in which Anglicans believe, how they think, feel, pray, hope and live. Anglican faith, like the broader category of Christian faith, is a dispositional matter which is exemplified in a continuing historical community of people.

This connection in time between a community of people and understandings and experiences of meaning draw the notion of tradition into close connection with that of narrative. A narrative can be conceived of as the story of a theme or element located within a tradition. That narrative then becomes itself an interpretation of what is leading or important in the tradition. Narrative also embraces the overarching account of the meaning which holds the tradition together. Such a narrative does not contain all that could be said about a tradition, but it may tell us something which is critically important to understand other elements in the tradition.

In recent times Alasdair MacIntyre has made effective use of this combination to develop a notion of virtue and moral action. He argues that humans are a story-telling species and that they have become such through their history. As a consequence, '"an" action is always an episode in a possible history'.[40] This does not mean that our identity is founded on this continuity. Rather, it means that, while we may change over time, we are never not what we are and also what we have been. In other words, our identity, who we are, has a story attaching to it which may show that there is not a strict sameness over time in this observable character. That does not mean that I am not who I am, rather it means that 'the self inhabits a character whose unity is given as the unity of a character'.[41] Such individuals are by the nature of the case individuals in connection with others, and that community of experience is at the same time the social exemplification of the continuity that is reflected in the stories, the shared stories, of the individuals who make up the group.

In a later book MacIntyre developed the thought that such communities through time, as they were exemplifications of a tradition, had in that tradition a way of thinking which made sense of the stories and the experiences of the individuals and the community. They had a rationality, and they also had a sense of justice and of the virtues, which made sense within the framework of this rationality.[42]

A slightly different emphasis is given by Robert Bellah and his associates in their evocation of de Tocquville's account of the 'habits of the heart' of the citizens of the United States of America.[43] He thought that these habits of the heart made the operation of their democracy and their social institutions possible. Reaching beyond cognition to intuition and sentiment, de Tocqueville sought for an evocation of those habits which effectively made the social system work and which Bellah and his colleagues later tried to examine. It is a point for MacIntyre that their attempt to describe these things forced them to do so in large measure by a series of stories.

However, this emphasis on tradition is not universally popular, nor in many respects is it the consciously accepted way in which modern people think about their situation. MacIntyre is well aware of this and sets up his exposition in contrast to the impact of the Enlightenment on western culture. In the same year that MacIntyre published *After Virtue*, Edward Shils published his T S Eliot

---

40 MacIntyre, A, *After Virtue: A Study in Moral Theory*, London: Duckworth, 1981, p 16.
41 MacIntyre, *After Virtue*, p 217.
42 MacIntyre, A, *Whose Justice? Which Rationality?*, Notre Dame: Notre Dame University Press, 1988.
43 Bellah, R N, R Madsen, W M Sullivan, A Swidler, and S M Tipton, *Habits of the Heart*, Berkely: University of California Press, 1985.

lectures on 'Tradition'. Shils clearly sets out the fundamental attack on tradition posed in the Enlightenment and the scientific culture. The Enlightenment began with an attack on tradition, but, as Shils points out, in turn it became a tradition. Because of its objectivist conceptuality, it was a transportable tradition. Science was a universal human language and mathematics the rationality of the universe. The reality of the human condition is that we cannot live without some kind of order, some kind of chart of the world we inhabit. Furthermore, we cannot invent that whole chart ourselves, and for that reason traditionality itself is a virtue. 'Human beings need the help of the ancestors; they need the help which is provided by their own biological ancestors and they need the help of the ancestors of their communities and institutions, of the ancestors of their societies and their institutions.'[44]

Shils takes religious tradition as the archetypal tradition which reason has opposed. 'Traditions of religious belief are different from other intellectual beliefs but they also have a great deal in common with them.'[45] What makes the difference for Shils is the notion of the divine and the desire in a religious tradition to apprehend and experience that divine. For Christians and especially for Anglicans this point is turned around and in the process makes the issue much more demanding, for the Christian and the Anglican believes that the issue is not the apprehension of the divine by humans but rather the apprehension of human individuals and communities by the divine. The church is constituted not by its members finding God but by the action of God in finding the members of the church. Thus this religious tradition is a narrative of the divine initiative.

Because the knowledge which is part of this religious tradition is a knowledge of God which is personal and concerns the whole experience of individuals and the community, it is overthrown or undermined not simply, and often not at all, by cognitive or rational argument. Such things may contribute to the overthrow of this knowledge, but the alternative to belief is unbelief, and unbelief comes from an unsettling. Confrontation with alien religious traditions is thus always to some degree threatening, as is the transportation of religious traditions. The classic example offered by Shils is the settlement of the Israelites in the promised land, a settlement which involved a transition from a nomadic shepherding life to a

---

44 Shils, E, *Tradition*, London: Faber and Faber, 1989, p 326.
45 Shils, *Tradition*, p 94.

settled agricultural life. The transportation of Anglicanism from England would be another example, and the stripping of the English baggage in the period of de-colonisation would be another.

Characterising Anglicanism involves a demand to include the whole of the human condition. It must embrace the whole humanity, sentience, sociality, feeling and affect, persecution and behaviour. It must also take account of the content of the belief of these Anglicans about God, that there is a strong sense of divine initiative and that in theological terms the community being described is a community being brought into existence and sustained by such a God.

The great advantage of seeking to characterise Anglicanism as a tradition is that it enables these conditions to be met more successfully, and it draws attention to the historicality of the ecclesial experience and thus to the incarnational character of the divine action and providence. It also has the advantage of directly drawing attention to the untidiness of any characterisation. The experience of this community is always cast in the contingency of their particular circumstances. The perceptions and stories which they sustain are always partial and clouded by their sin, their moral and intellectual inadequacies.

Yet the very persistence of such a community constituted and sustained by a tradition which, despite its vagaries, can be characterised in some general ways indicates something of the power of that tradition. That tradition has to do with the way in which Anglicans understand and sense themselves to have experienced the action of the living God.

The marks of such a tradition will emerge in the course of the argument of this book. They draw attention to a sense of God as involved and participating, a God who is vitally at work in the created order. It is not surprising that the tradition has a continuing recourse to the incarnation. It was a prominent theme in the nineteenth century, but it lies at the heart of Richard Hooker's theology in the sixteenth century and is apparent in the devotional patterns of earlier centuries. It is in this context that the church is thought of as being created by God. Further, the church is for the same reason a community of inter-dependent diversity. The essential element in church is the connectivity and belonging, more than the particularities of institutional emphasis which occur from time to time in the story. Thus also the Christian life is essentially a pilgrimage set in the contingencies of life. Its story is not that of the oak tree that inevitably and necessarily in all its detailed form develops out of the acorn. The authority of this community arises from the totality of the experience of the community.

The commitment to the historicality of the experience of the church community means that the process of the pilgrimage has a certain assumed authority, a privileged position. However, it is not an absolute one, since life and the activity of God may change that. Institutions are thus part of the providence of God and the contingency of the human condition. For that reason they have a respected validity but not an absolute significance. Given this historicality and contingency, the appeal to the origins of the faith and the apostolic witness constitutes the ultimate but not the only authoritative reference point.[46] These are elements which will be illustrated in the theological interpretation of the Reformation, the apostolic experience in Corinth and recent theological work.

The global context

Given that Anglicanism can be effectively characterised in tradition terms, it is clear that historically this tradition has been through a number of significant transitions as a result of changes in the social, cultural and political context. It should not therefore be remarkable to note that the global context in which Anglicanism is now set will affect the nature of the current transition and any reinventing that might be attempted. But how to characterise the present global context in a way which is likely to be relevant to the dynamics of Anglicanism is not all that straightforward. There may be large-scale movements at work in the present time which affect Anglicans all around the globe in some way, but it will inevitably still be the case that local and regional forces will be at work and will undoubtedly affect the changes that are either likely or possible in Anglicanism.

We can see this in the inner ecclesiastical arena in terms of church constitutions. The problems facing Anglicans in England, the United States of America and Australia are quite different simply because of the structure of their different constitutions and the resources and power different parts of the church possess. Australia has a loose federation of dioceses with little resource power nationally. The USA has a stronger national constitution with higher levels of national canonical power but with relatively modest resource power compared to some

---

46   See Kaye, B N, *Web of Meaning: The Role of Origins in Christian Faith*, Sydney: Aquila Press, 2000.

dioceses and parishes. England has very strong national power canonically and a tradition of almost complete central resource power, which is only recently being diminished because of the poor performance of the Church Commissioners. Australia's strategic challenge is to hold together the scattered communities in the dioceses in some kind of national community in the face of institutional privileging of local initiative and independence. The USA faces the strategic challenge of accommodating local initiative and difference in the face of the central canonical power in the General Convention but relatively limited resource power in the national organisation. England is something of a mixture of these two, but with the effect that differences of opinion and emphasis tend not to be located in the dioceses but in extra-diocesan subsets of the national community.

However, there are also external political forces at work here. The relation between the Anglican church in Sri Lanka and the united churches in India are clearly affected by the political relations between the two countries. The political forces at work in Nigeria in relation to Islam and Christianity inevitably shape the possibilities for Anglicans in that country. At each of the meetings of the Provincial Secretaries which I have attended, members have shared their experiences of church life, and in almost all cases political conditions directly impact on the response of the Anglican church to their local context. How, indeed, could it be otherwise?

While we recognise the importance of this differentiating point, it is still the case that global dynamics will impact upon the transition of Anglicanism in the twenty-first century. In turning now to such global dynamics in brief form, I would like to underline that this is a characterisation of those elements which appear to me to be of some relevance to the position of Anglicanism. Inevitably, such a brief account can only point to some things and will be very selective and impressionistic.

Especially in western culture, which itself has a phenomenal influence on the whole world, the present is marked by an impression that modernity is in some sense coming to an end or is changing significantly. Attempts to interpret this often refer to post-modernity.[47] This language draws attention to an important shift in the social, political and cultural landscape. This shift is relevant to Anglicanism, because it already affects changes and the possibilities of change. It constitutes a major context in relation to which Anglicanism is itself changing, and it contributes to setting the frameworks for any reinventing.

There are, in my judgment, four elements relevant to Anglicanism in this movement: the nation state, colonialism, capitalism and globalisation. These all interact on each other and influence and interpret each other.

Robert Nisbet described the state as a form of revolution when it emerged out of medieval feudalism.[48] It seems to me that nationalism came to have a cohering effect on the identity of states alongside the emergence of the institutional forms of the state. In this I am inclined to the arguments of Adrian Hastings rather than those of Gellner, Hobsbawn and Anderson.[49] So the sixteenth century marked the high point of nationalism in Europe, even though the mechanisms of the modern state did not emerge until much later. During the nineteenth century the modern state gathered to itself sovereignty over a wide range of the elements of human life. In Australia this expressed itself in the separate colonies in terms of 'statism' as the state came increasingly to be seen as the vehicle to get things done and took over responsibility for social services such as education. The declining power of institutional religion in the modern state and the emergence of a pluralist concept of the state also meant that those religious traditions which were institutionally wedded to the state found themselves re-positioned in society. This was the common experience of Anglicanism in various parts of the world.

The latter part of the twentieth century has seen a re-configuration of the formerly complete sovereignty of the state.[50] Multinational enterprises have grown significantly in power, so that they are able to influence and modify the power of the states in which they operate.[51] Indeed, the selection of which state they will locate their activities in is itself a significant lever in their relations with

47 The literature on this theme is vast. Some key texts are Lyotard, J-F, *The Postmodern Condition: A Report on Knowledge*; E T of La Condition postmoderne: rapport sur le savoir, 1979, ed Manchester: Manchester University Press, 1984; Gellner, E, *Postmodernism, Reason and Religion*, London: Routledge, 1992; Jameson, F, *Postmodernism, or, The Cultural Logic of Late Capitalism*, London: Verso, 1991; and useful guides are Seidman, S, *Contested Knowledge: Social Theory in the Postmodern Era*, Oxford: Blackwell, 1994 and Ward, G (ed), *The Postmodern God. A Theological Reader*, Oxford: Blackwell, 1997.

48 Nisbet, R, *The Quest for Community: A Study in the Ethics of Order and Freedom*, first published 1953, ed San Francisco: Institute for Contemproary Studies, 1990, pp 89ff.

49 Hastings, A, *The Construction of Nationhood: Ethnicity, Religion and Nationalism*, Cambridge: CUP, 1997; Gellner, E, *Nations and Nationalism*, Oxford: Blackwell, 1983; Hobsbawm, E J, *Nations and Nationalism since 1780*, Cambridge: CUP, 1990; and Anderson, B, *Imagined Communities*, London: Verso, 1991.

50 See the perceptive discussions in Camilleri, J, and J Falk, *The End of Sovereignty: The Politics of a Shrinking and Fragmenting World*, Aldershot: Edward Elgar, 1992.

51 Corten, D C, *When Corporations Rule the World*, London: Earthscan, 1995.

states. Information technology has diminished the communication barriers of the borders of nation states and, as a result, international movements can have much easier sway in the influences on governments and community attitudes. The capacity of governments to control international financial movements has been similarly diminished in recent decades. All of these things have changed the character and extent of the sovereignty of the nation state.

Anglicanism is a tradition which has been shaped in a nation in which the public institutions have been influenced by a sense of consensus and the value of experience. The moderating influence of a 'common law' mentality in England distinguishes the entry of England into modernity from continental countries such as France or the United States of America. That does not mean at all that the high point of imperial political thinking in the sixteenth century was not marked in England—it certainly was. It is the clothing of this Tudor imperial mentality that makes the statutory monuments of the English Reformation (the 1662 Book of Common Prayer, The Thirty-nine Articles, The Act of Uniformity and the Ordinal) such a problem in the modern transition of Anglicanism.

A religious tradition like Anglicanism, with its English establishment mentality and an attachment to the sixteenth-century Reformation monuments, and one which is in any case committed at a profound theological level to social enmeshment, will be deeply affected by the late-twentieth-century changes in the nature and role of the nation state.

Colonialism is the second major development in the current world scene which impinges on the transition of Anglicanism. For millennia powerful countries and groups have established colonies. One only has to think of the Greeks and the Romans to consider the various reasons why such colonies are established. The colonial relationship is relevant to modern Anglicanism because of the colonial activity of England from the seventeenth to the twentieth centuries, not to mention the colonial activity of the USA and Australia. There have been various forms of colonising. On the one hand, there was direct state colonisation such as in New South Wales and Tasmania for the purpose of establishing a jail. More common are the examples of Virginia, India, Canada or South Australia, where the colonisation was conducted by state-supported private enterprise for commercial reasons.[52] The issue behind these various types of colonisation is hegemonic imperialism. Colonialism represents a relationship of power and influence.

During the nineteenth century the so-called old Commonwealth won levels of independence from Britain, and during the latter half of the twentieth century the remainder of the British empire gained independence. This is a well-known story of the establishment of independent nations, mostly within the British Commonwealth of Nations. This is the state colonialism that is most directly connected with Anglicanism, but it is by no means the only expression of colonialism in the twentieth century. During the twentieth century the two great power blocks of the capitalist West and the communist East struggled so vehemently in part because they were different manifestations of the same parent: modernity and its scientific technological mentality. One represented the corporatist implication of imperial modernity and the other the pluralist version. It is the imperial element here that adds weight to John Luckaks's interpretation of the twentieth century as a century of tyrants and Hitler as the archetype of the political dynamics of the century.[53] Certainly the twentieth century saw significant changes in the pattern of international relations. World War II and the Cold War which followed mark out this transition from the dominance of the state by military power to the dominance of commercial forces. World War II was won by superior technology and the capacity to deploy superior military resources. The Cold War was won by superior commercial capacity and the ability to deploy superior economic power and resources. The public device in this war was the arms race, which had the power to enthral and thus retain centre stage while serving the purpose of cultural and political conflict and commercial erosion.

Interpretations of the twentieth century differ, of course. Frances Fukuyama sees it as the triumph of liberal democratic society,[54] whereas Lukacks sees it as simply the introduction to a twenty-first century of continuing imperialisms, that is to say tyrants. One consequence of the conflicts of the twentieth century has been the rise to prominence of commerce as a world language of power. That power resides not just with nation states but also with multinational enterprises, and it creates new forms of colonisations.

52 Hobsbawm, E. J, *Industry and Empire: The making of modern English society, 1750 to the present day*, [1st American] ed New York: Pantheon Books, 1968.
53 Lukacs, J, *The End of the Twentieth Century and the End of the Modern Age*, New York: Ticknor and Fields, 1993.
54 Fukuyama, F, *The End of History and the Last Man*, London: Penguin Books, 1992.

At the social-political level there is a second wave of decolonisation to be seen in the old colonial territories. Former colonies are shedding the constitutions left by the former colonial powers, and indigenous peoples are seeking to roll back the key elements of colonial experience. One can see the latter at work at different stages in Canada, New Zealand and Australia, where the instrument used is the claim to human rights, that other side of modernity having its roots in romanticism. Isaiah Berlin has argued that Romanticism set out to protest against the Enlightenment in the name of individuality and ended up providing the basis of a number of social values, including the power of a claim to individual rights of various kinds.[55]

In Anglicanism these forces of colonialism have been and continue to be present. The Fisher project in encouraging independent church constitutions mirrored the Macmillan decolonisation phase, but resource power relations mean that older colonial attitudes within the Communion have persisted. At the 1998 Lambeth Conference another language of power emerged in relationships within the Communion, namely the language of vitality and active membership. The wealthy found themselves confronted with a different rhetoric, and they and the conference stumbled in public view. It is not surprising that coalitions between these two resources are combining to promote their agenda within the Communion, a project reaching out from both the United States of America and England.[56]

The economic residual from the Cold War has been capitalism, but it has emerged in that situation from a developing history of its own. Alfred Chandler has identified various stages of capitalism, referring to the source or control of the capitalist enterprise:[57] family capitalism, where families have provided and nurtured the capital for corporate enterprises, financial capitalism, where the capital was located in financial institutions, managerial capitalism, where the power of the senior management in corporations colonised the benefits of capital exploitation in corporations. This makes a lot of sense to me as a description of the inner development of the corporation as a vehicle for the capitalist enterprise.

---

55 Berlin, I, *The Roots of Romanticism*, London: Chatto & Windus, 1999.
56 On the English evangelical mission in worldwide Anglicanism see Dudley-Smith, T, *John Stott, the Making of a Leader: A biography: the early years*, and on the more recent North American mission see Douglas, I T, *Lambeth 1998 and the 'new colonialism'*.
57 See Chandler, A D, *The Visible Hand: The managerial revolution in American business*.

A more disturbing analysis of capitalism, which brings it into specific relationship with post-modernism, is that offered by Frederick Jameson in a famous article published in the *New Left Review* in 1984 and again later in an expanded form in 1991. He followed an analysis of the development of capitalism in terms of the development of power technology: steam (since 1848), electric and combustion engines (since the late nineteenth century) and electronic and nuclear power (since mid-twentieth century). In each phase the capitalism associated with these stages takes over the previous stage. Thus market capitalism is taken over by monopoly capitalism, which is taken over by what Jameson calls multi-national capitalism. It is this last stage in which we are located at the beginning of the twenty-first century. This analysis provides the outline of Jameson's analysis of post–modernism, which he sees as a form of 'American military and economic domination throughout the world'.[58] Thus the radical individualism noted by others in relation to post-modernism is actually, on this analysis, the other side of a radical form of divide and rule or of the observation that radical individualism invites tyrannies because of the absence of intervening constraints.

This element in the present global context affects Anglicanism, because it shapes the intellectual and conceptual framework within which Anglicans live and think. It is particularly relevant in that it is concerned with similar underlying questions about the nature of authority and power, the character of human social connections. In that Anglicanism is challenged with plural tendencies, it faces similar challenges and temptations about the configuration of power in its relationships. It ought not to surprise us if Anglicans are drawn to patterns of power which are at least singular if not tyrannical in one way or another. It would be hard in the present environment not to be drawn in that direction. These forces can be seen in the contemporary eddies and currents in the perennial tussle in Anglicanism between ministerial hierarchy and the voice of the people, in modern times expressed in the conciliar synodical instruments.

Already this discussion of present trends has drawn in concepts which are gathered under the heading of globalisation. This is the tendency to treat the world as the single unit of operation for human endeavour. We can see this at work in commercial activity, the environmental movement, human location and

---

58 Jameson, F, *Postmodernism, or, The Cultural Logic of Late Capitalism*, London: Verso, 1991, p 5.

migration and communications. Such globalisation is made possible by the development of multinational enterprises, trade and financial deregulation and technology.[59]

The consequences of these tendencies are the diminishing power of the nation state and the growth of international organisations. The corporation is the dominant institution in this global process because of the contemporary power of capitalism at the moment. The United Nations and aggregations such as the European Union represent alternative forms of wider and larger institutional arrangements. The more interventionist actions of the UN in recent times reflect this same tendency. These all point in the direction of the changed character of power and influence, power such as resources control and information management.

All of these issues affect Anglicans and thus Anglicanism. Changes in the character and form of the nation state, colonialism, capitalism and globalisation provide not only the challenges but also the opportunities for the reinvention of Anglicanism. These forces are both powerful and subtle and, as a consequence, the inherited tradition of Anglicanism might be enveloped by them. They have the capacity to shape the way we think and the options we readily imagine.

The power of these contemporary forces underlines the strategic importance of one of the dangers facing Anglicans in the present generation, namely a lack of informed critical awareness of the longer dimensions and strengths of Anglicanism. This lack diminishes the capacity of Anglicans to engage critically with the powerful forces at work in the environment. On the other hand, Anglicans have the great advantage that they belong to a tradition which in its theological profile should foster conversation and engagement. Its very openness provides an opportunity in the present environment which some other traditions have to struggle to obtain. Not only that, Anglicans have the opportunity to use the worldwide Communion as a resource in this cultural engagement. That Anglicans around the world are engaged in a similar interpretative challenge and that this challenge is located in discrete and discernibly different contexts means that the shared attachment to a common Anglican tradition facilitates significant synergy in the task of vocation and mission.

---

59 See the useful discussion of these issues as they affect Australia in Sheil, C (ed), *Globalisation: Australian Impacts*, Sydney: UNSW Press, 2001.

A thesis of transition and continuity

This introduction to the journey of Anglicanism provides the framework for the thesis of this book. That thesis can be set out in seven points. These points will emerge in the course of the argument, but they are set out here to indicate where I am going.

1. Anglicanism is at a major turning point in its history. For the first time its centre of membership and growth has moved out of the geographical and social roots which formed it in England.

2. Anglicanism has survived, as one of the discrete traditions within western Christianity, because it contained within it crucial elements of a theological kind which have made it resilient. Those marks are:
   - a conception of God who is participating in the human condition—an incarnational God
   - connectedness in its ecclesial conceptions—a real sense that God is present
   - an instinct about authority which derives from this and which is marked by qualities of open-endedness, porous borders, tentativeness, contingency awareness, and an authority experienced and exercised by the whole people of God
   - enmeshment in the social and cultural context and thus being guided by an awareness of both contingency and providence in regard to both ecclesial and social institutionality
   - a particular way of dealing with origins in relation to Scripture which sets it in a context of continuity with the early church.

3. The current 'moment' which faces Anglicanism is one of a series in its history. Some of the earlier moments include
   - the Saxon Celtic interface, marking out a tradition of influence and a monastic presence
   - the Roman invasion of Augustine, marking out a conception of territory and organisation
   - the Norman conquest, marking out a pattern of control and for the church legal separation and some institutional independence
   - the Tudor triumph, marking out a tradition of nationalism and statutory control which went along with a religious revival

- and the imperial colonial phase, marking a tradition taken to foreign parts in the clothes of empire, redolent of the domestic imperial conceptions of Tudor nationalism.

Each of these moments has carried with them cultural influences which have shaped the particular presentations of the tradition and provided the opening point for subsequent generations. They have contributed to the accumulation of memory, of the furniture our predecessors lived with and which now occupies various rooms in the house of Anglican community memory. The earlier moments are mentioned here by way of illustration. The last two will be more fully dealt with in the course of this discussion.

4. The current situation is marked by two predecessor paradigms.

   - Domestic national imperialism. The Reformation monuments are cast in the language and institutional assumptions of Tudor imperialism, and these distort the religious perception.

   - Colonial imperialism. Here institutionalities in the church, such as law, property and the means and power to decide, are influenced by the assumptions of overseas imperialism.

5. To imagine what Anglicanism might be like in the future requires not just re-conceptualising but also gaining some critical distance from these predecessor paradigms. This is in fact a classic example of contextualised theology. The reinvention has to struggle with mental and institutional paradigms inherited from variations of British imperial notions going back to the sixteenth century. That struggle is complicated by the widespread attachment in Anglicanism to the sixteenth-century Reformation monuments, which are clothed in Tudor political conceptions.

6. The underlying key issues in such a reinvention of Anglicanism are confidence to act in environments which are not always sympathetic, the nature of ecclesial community life in a voluntarist situation, and the pattern of engagement with the host society. These three issues constitute the key challenges in the reinventing of Anglicanism.

7. The particular example of Australia highlights these questions with remarkable clarity. The strong continuing influence of the past, especially the

Tudor Reformation monuments, can be seen in the constitution of The Anglican Church of Australia and this use in the rhetoric of church politics and power relationships. Colonial imperialism was only slowly shed; indeed, the consequence for Anglicans of its going have only become manifest in the last forty years of the twentieth century. In Australia, second-wave de-colonisation is sharpened by the Aboriginal issues, which are different from those in Canada and New Zealand, where there are greater numbers and more cultural consonance between the colonists and the colonised.

This book offers a different interpretation of Anglicanism, which locates the formation of its pedigree much earlier in time and sees the Reformation not just as a religious and theological movement but as a transition of political dimensions. As a consequence, the Reformation provides very particular ambiguities for modern Anglicanism because of the continuing importance of its defining politico-legal monuments in the sentiments and institutionalities of modern Anglicanism.

These particular issues in interpreting modern Anglicanism can be very clearly seen in the example of Australian Anglicanism. Its constitutional commitment to the Reformation formularies is particularly strong, and the social and political transitions in Australia have generally been slower and later than in other cases. There remains a strong political and institutional continuity, and at the same time within Australian Anglicanism strong regional differences are embedded in the diocesan structure. Australia thus provides a useful example to illustrate the interpretative task of reinventing Anglicanism in the modern world.

CHAPTER TWO

THE AUSTRALIAN EXPERIENCE

In this elaboration of the journey of Anglicanism the influence of the social historical context of this tradition is clear. I have argued that Anglicanism is best characterised as a discrete Christian tradition and that the origins of that tradition should be traced back at least to Bede in the eighth century. Furthermore, I have argued that this tradition is characteristically enmeshed in the social context. That means that the present 'moment' of Anglicanism, looked at in a post-colonial global context, is not only historically significant for the tradition itself but also that the identification of the particular location of the tradition takes on added importance. Since we are taking the Australian experience as an example to highlight the issues in the present 'moment', it becomes important to identify some of the particulars of that Australian experience.

First there was Valium, then came Prozac. Valium made millions of dollars for its manufacturers and subdued the rising tied of anxiety for millions of people in the western world. Prozac is in the process of making large profits for its manufacturers, and it is continuing the task of overcoming depression for millions of people by chemically induced change in the way they look out on the angst of the modern world.

What is true in western society is also true in Australia, and indeed there is a particular edge to the Australian experience of anxiety and social concern. Two of Australia's most acute social commentators have written at length on our present circumstances. In 1992 Paul Kelly published *The End of Certainty*,[60] and in 1993 Hugh Mackay published *Reinventing Australia*,[61] the first chapter of which was entitled 'The Big Angst'.

Paul Kelly is a political writer. He worked for many years in Canberra as the chief political writer for the *Australian*, the *Sydney Morning Herald* and the *National Times*. He has written a number of books on modern Australian political life, and he is currently the International Editor of the *Australian* newspaper. Hugh Mackay is a social researcher who has developed a 'listening group' technique to tap into the concerns and interests of Australians. Both writers confess to optimism, but both write of Australia in the 1990s in terms of anxiety and uncertainty. Mackay's book is the result of extensive social research across Australia, and Paul Kelly writes from the standpoint of a close observer of day-to-day politics, combined with time to stand back and reflect on the overall patterns of the last twenty years. Mackay's book is analytical and filled with illustrations of particular themes. Kelly's book is a narrative.

These two books provide a valuable window into the present condition of Australian society and flesh out the statistics which flow across the newspapers about a society which has the highest youth suicide rate in the western world, the highest use of VCRs and an obsession with mobile telephones. In different ways they provide a window into the inner anxieties that Australians experience at the turn of the millennium.

The end of certainty

Paul Kelly argues that the 1980s 'were a milestone in the redefinition of the ideas and institutions by which Australia is governed'.[62] Kelly argues that from the beginning of the century five key ideas have constituted together what he calls the Australian Settlement. This is not the settlement of Australia which occupied the

---

60 Kelly, P, *The End of Certainty: The Story of the 1980s*, St Leonards: Allen & Unwin, 1992.
61 MacKay, H, *Reinventing Australia*, Pymble: Angus and Robertson, 1993.
62 Kelly, p ix.

whole of the nineteenth century but rather the Australian Settlement which took hold upon the country after the formation of the Commonwealth. The five elements of this Australian Settlement were the White Australia Policy, tariff protection, centralised arbitration of the labour market, state paternalism and imperial benevolence.

That Settlement, according to Kelly, lodged itself in the Australian psyche soon after Federation. Both the Liberal and Labor parties were constructed according to this paradigm of Australia. In the 1980s, however, the fundamental divide in Australian politics was not between the Liberal and Labor parties. Rather, the real divide was between what Kelly calls 'internationalist rationalists', who he says know that the Australian Settlement of the previous eighty years is no longer sustainable, and 'sentimentalist traditionalists', who struggle to retain that Australian Settlement.[63]

From the beginning the White Australia Policy was intended as a statement of national identity. Australia was to be a bulwark against the rising new states in Africa and Asia. In the second half of the twentieth century, that attitude was focused more particularly on Asia, a focus which was sharpened by the war against Japan. It has been a continuing question. In 1928 the future Labour prime minister, Ben Chifley, won election to parliament with a direct appeal to the White Australia Policy against non-British European immigration. Late in 1948, as prime minister he appealed to the same policy against 'Asiatics',[64] just as the Liberal conservative John Howard in 1994 cautioned against Asian immigration and as prime minister in 2001 made a stand in the name of national sovereignty against a relatively small number of asylum seekers who were mostly of Asian origin.

While both major political parties have declared against racially based immigration and against the White Australia Policy, it would be a brave conclusion to say that the underlying issues have disappeared. Kelly is probably right in saying that the process of integration with Asia and the development of a more multicultural society in Australia are inevitable, but it is not yet by any

---

63 See the use of this idea in Hirst, John, *The Sentimental Nation: The Making of the Australian Commonwealth*, Oxford: Oxford University Press, 2000 and, by way of contrast, Birrell, Bob, *Federation: The Secret Story*, Sydney: Duffy and Snellgrove, 2001.
64 Day, D, *Chifley*, pp 231–33, 493f.

means universally secured. According to Kelly, the question at stake is how the traditional Anglo-Saxon Judaic Christian value system of Australia's history is to be reconciled with this Asian enmeshment and ethnically diverse population.

Tariff protection was the curious consequence of the formation of early federal governments, which enabled Alfred Deakin to secure the protectionist point of view in the first government. When the Labour Party came around to this point of view during the 1920s, protection became an almost unchallenged commonsensical point of view.[65] It was claimed that protection would build industrial strength. By an irony of history the late-nineteenth-century free traders of New South Wales found themselves fulfilling the key political role which led to the formation of the Commonwealth, but, in the event, their philosophy of free trade was eclipsed from Commonwealth activity for nearly a century.

Protection inevitably went along with centralised arbitration of work agreements. Justice Higgins gave full expression to this principle in the Harvester Judgment in 1907 and established in the social, legal and political tradition the idea of fair and reasonable wages which should be insisted upon centrally.[66] This one decision had a dramatic effect on the acceptance of the idea of a 'basic wage' which would be based on need.[67] Labor prime minister Ben Chifley used troops in the coal strike of 1948 in order to defend the authority of this central arbitration system.[68]

According to Paul Kelly, state paternalism derives from the earliest arrival of the Europeans on this continent. The governors were supreme in the colony, and during the course of the nineteenth century the state came to have an intimate involvement in social laws ranging from employment to education and health. All of these social advances were achieved on the basis of advancement of the power of the state. The end of the nineteenth century was a high point in 'statism'.

The final strand in the analysis of the Australian Settlement is imperial benevolence. It draws attention to Australia's dependence on the power of the British navy and, more recently, on the power of the United States.

---

65 See the struggle on this issue in the early Commonwealth in Bolton, G, *Edmund Barton*, St Leonards: Allen & Unwin, 2000.
66 For a brief discussion in the context of the development of the federation see Birrell, B, *Federation: The Secret Story*, p 258.
67 See Macintyre, S, *The Succeeding Age*, pp 102ff.
68 Day, D, *Chifley*, pp 489–92.

Paul Kelly asserts that by 1991 every one of these pillars of the Australian Settlement was in irreversible stages of collapse or exhaustion. This is, in my view, an overly optimistic assessment, but it is one which certainly is moving in the right direction, and his analysis is acute and perceptive.

The Australian Settlement has sat on the Australian landscape like a gentle fog, shielding a relatively wealthy country from the realities beyond its shores and defending it from the challenge to grapple with fundamental questions of social value and identity. It has also enabled Anglicans to persist with an 'establishment' picture of themselves while the social and religious realities of that establishment were disintegrating around them. The decline of the five pillars of the Australian Settlement to which Kelly refers has blown that fog away and brought an end to the certainty which it conveyed both for Australians generally and for Australian Anglicans.

Paul Kelly's *End of Certainty* is about political and economic institutions. It is about institutional change and the uncertainty which that brings. The degree to which that change affects the individual and social 'nerve' depends very much on what other changes are taking place and what elements of human life remain the same. The fact is that other institutional changes have been taking place in Australia. These changes intersect with some of Paul Kelly's 'pillars'. Women have entered the work force in vast numbers in the last forty years. This has changed the dynamics of family life, and the institution of marriage has been reshaped dramatically.

Living arrangements have changed for this and other reasons, and the institutions of leisure have changed out of all recognition. Women have not started going to work simply because the domestic economy demanded it. They wanted to go to work and they wanted careers like the men. The women's movement brought attitudinal and values changes which worked sympathetically with the economic possibilities. These changes in values inhabit the hinterland of Paul Kelly's picture of the political and economic landscape. In Hugh Mackay's account of the social institutional changes of Australia's recent past these values questions stand clearly in the foreground.

The big angst

Hugh Mackay writes from a quite different perspective. He begins his book by telling a story of listening to a group of women discussing the issues that were important to them. These women, he discovered, were not depressed but angry. They reflected a sense that everything was changing. They wished they had more control over their lives. They felt as if they were making it all up as they went along.

That story introduces the principle thesis which Hugh Mackay argues in his book.

> Largely by accident, Australians in the last quarter of the twentieth century have become a nation of pioneers; some heroically, some reluctantly, some painfully. We have been plunged into a period of unprecedented social, cultural, political, economic and technological change in which the Australian way of life is being radically redefined.[69]

Hugh Mackay speaks of an epidemic of anxiety. People feel as though they are living on a short fuse. They have a sense that the latest incident is the last straw. He draws attention to issues of drug abuse, domestic violence, high levels of stress, the use of medical resources and the need for counselling. The 1990 Mackay report, entitled *The Australian Dream*, showed that Australians were concentrating on surviving, not dreaming about the future, and in this respect they appeared to be remarkably different from their predecessors.

According to Hugh Mackay, the seeds of this anxiety go back at least thirty years into the last century, and they arise because of change. It is the change which brings anxiety. The anxiety therefore is a symptom of the age of redefinition .

> Since the early 1970's, there is hardly an institution or a convention of Australian life which has not been subject to serious challenge or to radical change. The social, cultural, political and economic landmarks which we have traditionally used as reference points for defining the Australian way of life have either vanished or been eroded or shifted.[70]

The age of redefinition can be seen in seven areas of social life, and Hugh Mackay devotes a chapter to each of these topics: gender roles, marriage, the value of work, the use of invisible money, the disappearance of economic egalitarianism, multiculturalism and the nature of the political system. In 1991, 62% of Australians expressed little or no confidence in the political system. Their anxiety

---

69 Mackay, *Reinvent*, p 6.
70 Mackay, *Reinvent*, p 17.

and loss of confidence arose from the radical changes that had taken place in the political system and cynicism about the adversarial nature of two-party politics. Underlying the cynicism about that adversarial system was a growing belief among Australians in the last twenty years that the difference between the parties did not relate to substantial policy or philosophical differences. It was more of a charade.[71]

Mackay's own suggestions about ways of coping with the 1990s arise out of his survey of the way in which people do in fact respond. They have to do with escape. Different kinds of retreats appear in the leisure agenda. Australians have discovered the country, the domestic enclave, the information club or the serious educational holiday. These are therapies in Mackay's terms and are only effective when they have not become addictive. Alas, in the age of anxiety sometimes these escapes have indeed become addictive for Australians who have allowed themselves to be locked out of the reality of ordinary life.

Australians also look around to try and find their bearings to reflect upon where they are going. The 'me' generation of the baby boomers reaches its mid-life crisis, when it is time for a second journey. However, often out of a sense of nostalgia, many Australians turn again to so-called traditional values. In the midst of all of this the appeals of authoritarian security in the form of various kinds of fundamentalism make their appearance. Hugh Mackay also draws attention to the desire for community to be found among Australians in the last two decades of the twentieth century. However, the rediscovery of the tribe, to which he refers, will have to be different from the kind of tribe which existed in the middle of the century. In the previous generation Australia was a homogeneous community. It was characterised by a high level of sameness. Now, at the beginning of the third millennium, Australia is much more diverse in style, character, culture and religion. This diversity is now a fact of life, and any move back to community will have to take into account that diversity. That, says Mackay, will force Australians to ask what it is that they genuinely have in common.

What Mackay reveals in his analysis is the inner side of the analysis which is revealed by Paul Kelly. Kelly concentrates on the public institutional political

---

71 For a perceptive discussion of the changing pattern of party politics in Australia see Marsh, I, *Beyond the Two Party System*, Cambridge: Cambridge University Press, 1995.

aspects. His stated area of concern is the way in which Australians are governed. Hugh Mackay is more concerned with the personal values and aspirations of Australians. But there is an uncanny echoing in these two analyses of anxiety, uncertainty and openness. That openness is sometimes discussed under the general heading of post-modernism, or a revival of liberalism. Here these terms are intended to convey a group of ideas which emphasise the creative characteristics of the individual, the individual's capacity to make their own truth. In another context Hugh Mackay has called a strident form of this 'truth by assertion'. It has to do with a continuing theoretical assault on notions of the power, value and the significance of institutions and of tradition.[72] Post-modernism in this sense is simply a title for a number of impulses which also appear in the analysis of both Kelly and Mackay. The two pictures given by Kelly and Mackay flow together at certain points to reveal a great tide of disaffection among Australians. The deregulation of financial markets and systems in the name of the market has led to many feeling disempowered and vulnerable. A decade of high unemployment has only magnified that feeling. The changing social landscape of multiculturalism in the name of being part of the global environment, and the impact of market forces on social institutions have also affected attitudes to political leaders and those thought to have some responsibility for these changes. In 1983 56% of Australians trusted the federal government, but in 1995 only 26% did so.[73] Despite the success of the Olympic Games and the celebration of Federation in 2000, the end of the twentieth century brought not only angst but also, for many Australians, disaffection with which to enter the new millennium.

That we are dealing here with long-term forces is shown by the fact that a similar pattern of change is revealed by Gregory Melleuish's characterisation of Cultural Liberalism.[74] He describes a tradition which emphasises the autonomy of the individual, a belief in the power of reason, a view of humans as being essentially spiritual and ethical, creatures of faith in evolution through which the world

---

72 See the philosophical interpretation of this phenomenon by Rorty, R, *Contingency, Irony, and Solidarity*, Cambridge: Cambridge University Press, 1989.
73 Christian Research Association, *Pointers*, June, 1998.
74 Melleuish, G, *Cultural Liberalism in Australia: A Study in Intellectual and Cultural History*, Cambridge: Cambridge University Press, 1995. See also his *The Packaging of Australia: Politics and Cultural Wars*, Sydney: UNSW Press, 1997.

might become more enlightened, rational and spiritual. He draws his picture of this tradition from 1880 to 1960.

The protagonists of this tradition mainly came to it as a result of university education. It is for that reason that the discussion of the role of universities in Australia looms large in his story. He distinguishes this cultural liberalism from the revival of liberalism in the 1990s and particularly from that liberalism which is associated with economic rationalism and the market mentality. The contrast has some echoes with the contrast made by Judith Brett between Robert Menzies' liberalism and the liberalism of John Hewson when he was leader of the Liberal Party.[75] According to Judith Brett, Robert Menzies asserted the importance of individual liberty in the context of service to the community, whereas John Hewson emphasised the importance of the individual in the context of choice for consumption. The tradition Gregory Melleuish is describing is not the radical political market mentality which has appeared in the 1990s in Australia but is a more broadly conceived tradition of culture, whose starting point is the integrity and dignity of the individual, conceived of in terms of a religious dimension.

Melleuish's picture of cultural liberalism touches on the theses argued by Paul Kelly. He is able to demonstrate that cultural liberalism was able to accommodate the terms of what Paul Kelly has called the Australian Settlement. Cultural liberals included both free traders and protectionists. At the end of the nineteenth century free trade liberalism, more prominent in New South Wales, was very successful in shaping the character of the federal Constitution. The assumptions about human nature and the place given to religion in the federal Constitution reflect a high point in the role of religion in the political domain. However, protectionism settled into the position of current orthodoxy soon after federation, and the Higgins model of bringing order to an otherwise amoral world through the instrumentality of government became not only the order of the day but also entered the pantheon of 'common sense' ideas. In this context Melleuish describes cultural liberalism as 'one segment within the burgeoning culture of rationalism'.[76]

However, cultural liberalism came from the humanities in general and often had a church background.

---

75 Brett, J, *Robert Menzies' Forgotten People*.
76 Melleuish, G, *Cultural Liberalism in Australia: A Study in Intellectual and Cultural History*, p 24.

> In denominational terms, Anglicanism and Liberal Protestantism predominated. What distinguished cultural liberalism from the other elements of the culture of nationalism was its concern with the spiritual side of human nature and the relationship of this spirituality to the dominant rational scientific spirit of the modern age.[77]

But not all Anglicans can be gathered into this tradition. At the turn of the century there were Anglicans who were drawn to a more internal and authoritarian kind of religion. This was the time when evangelicals, particularly in the Diocese of Sydney, became more intensely utopian or eschatological in their orientation and turned aside from the world, in order to look for the coming of the Kingdom of God.[78] Anglo-Catholics in the early part of the twentieth century, on the basis that they had captured that sense of the religious character of the human condition, focused it on the internal practice of the Divine presence in sacrament and ministry.[79] This latter gloss stumbled (along with the more liberal Anglicans, whom Melleuish sees as part of the tradition of cultural liberalism) as Australian society began to discover that the religious dimension of the human condition was more in the nature of an accessory or an add-on that you did not really need. The impact of this loss did not appear until after the passing blip of social and church growth following the Second World War. Due to the efforts of people such as Billy Graham, the evangelical tradition enjoyed a more extended revival after the Second World War,[80] but in time that tradition has found it hard to sustain a place in Australian society and now shows signs in some quarters of retreating into its turn-of-the-century privatism. That demise has come at precisely the commencement of the great angst and the age of uncertainty and provides the background for the desperate struggle that churches have been engaged in for the past two decades.

The Anglicans in Australia

During the 1990s the Bureau of Immigration and Multicultural and Population Research published a series of religious community profiles. The profile that dealt

77 Melleuish, G, p 24.
78 For a historical analysis of this see Lawton, W, *The Better Time to Be: Utopian Attitudes to Society among Sydney Anglicans 1885 to 1914*, and for a comment on its later significance at the close of the twentieth century see Lawton, W, 'Nathaniel Jones—Preacher of Righteousness'.
79 Hilliard, D, 'The Transformation of South Australian Anglicanism 1880–1930'.
80 Piggin, S, *Evangelical Christianity in Australia: Spirit, Word and World.*

with the Anglicans in Australia drew attention to a number of aspects of the situation of Anglicans at the end of the century. One of the questions which the report raised was the problem of the English origins of the Anglican Church.

> The Anglican Church of Australia often faces problems from its history of being the church of the British, of the ruling group, and of the privileged. While these perceived aspects are also great sources of strength, they can be great stumbling blocks in any attempt to reach out to an increasingly multicultural Australia.[81]

It was not only the attachment to a long-term British pedigree which sometimes presented a problem for Anglicans in Australia at the end of the millennium. Anglicans also had to confront dramatic changes in Australian society over the past one hundred and fifty years which have directly affected their position in that society. While Australia generally might be described as having come to the end of certainty and to be experiencing the great angst, Anglicans face those questions in a more particular and a more acute form than do their fellow Australians.

Making sense of it

This situation at the end of the century in which Australians generally, and Australian Anglicans in particular, find themselves can be presented in different ways. One could look at the statistical evidence of the last thirty years.[82] Those attending Anglican churches have tended to be older and those who have left the Anglican Church to join other churches have tended to be younger. One could point to financial difficulties and institutional tensions, which might help to account for the general sense of uncertainty in relation to the social and cultural environment in which Anglicans seek to work out their faith.

Both these approaches focus upon what might be called the ecclesiastical aspect of the question—what is happening to the institutional church? In this book I am more concerned with the position of Anglican Christians who are trying to live out their faith in modern Australia. The central concern is Australian Anglicans

---

81 Blombery, T, *The Anglicans in Australia*. This is also a theme in the various writings of Manning Clarke.

82 The best sources for this are the reports of the Christian Research Association (see www.cra.org.au) and of the National Church Life Survey, for example Kaldor, P, Bellamy, J, Powell, R, Hughes, B and Castle, K, *Shaping a Future: Characteristics of Vital Congregations*. Earlier work can be found through Mason, M, *Religion in Australia: A Bibliography of Social Research*.

living in a changed and changing society. I suggest also that the institutional questions which consume the energies of church politicians, lay and clerical, are not of great interest to the vast majority of churchgoing Anglicans. The factions which are created to be the vehicles of these church politics attract only a small membership and an even smaller active membership. Because factional conflict makes such good media material, this minority of Australian Anglicans—church politicians—gains wide publicity.

This book does not ignore these questions altogether, but its interest is elsewhere. I am interested in the challenge ordinary Anglicans face of making sense of their Christian vocation in contemporary Australia. I remember being at a consultation in a parish which was looking for a new minister. The facilitator asked those present to identify the things in the parish which could be celebrated. A list of items was compiled on the whiteboard of things like friendliness, concern, care and accessibility. This was clearly a church community which was easy to join and in which one could feel comfortable. Later people were asked to identify things which could be done better, and going out to others in mission was mentioned. In a revealing remark one person said he could not do this because he was not sure that what he believed and experienced in church would work or make sense 'out there'. It is precisely that person's anxiety and concern that I want to address in this book. The great strength of that parishioner's admission is that he saw the problem and had the courage to name it. Many of us do not quite see it or, if we do, avoid it with all sorts of stratagems.

This book is different from a number of other analyses because I do not approach the question in terms of sociological analysis or the statistics of decline. I want to approach this question by telling something of a story. Explaining things by telling stories has certain difficulties about it. It does not appear to be scientific. One wonders, in fact, how the story might be verified as to whether or not it actually happened that way and whether the story really has the meaning suggested. However, the advantage of telling a story of how we have come to the present situation is that it gives a framework which explains why we are where we are. A story does not necessarily explain how the present situation can be dealt with. The purpose of the story is to offer a framework which will illuminate what really are the issues that need to be confronted. It also helps to explain why Anglicans have such difficulty in engaging Australian society with their faith.

I am aware that history can be used for a variety of purposes and that what is true of history generally is true of Australian history. The urge to recite stories for the education and inspiration of later generations has given way in the last fifty years to a more critical use of history aimed at providing a basis for change in the present. Manning Clark is the most prominent example of this critical history in the Australian scene. Antiquarians stands in a different relationship to the future. They have turned their back on the future and seek to re-enter and re-create the past.

My use of story sees the past, the present and the future as dynamically connected. The future is not predictable on the basis of the past in any absolute sense. But an examination of the past provides an insight into the issues which are likely to be important in the present. Furthermore, the future lies before us as in some sense in our own hands. We can make decisions and do things which will change events and thus the shape of the future.

The story to be told provides the background and the framework for the critical appropriation of the past into the issues which emerge from the story and offer themselves in the present. It is this combination of continuity and discontinuity from the past into the present and the future which I call the 'tradition critical' approach. From this perspective I want to argue a thesis in this book about Anglicanism at the birth of the third millennium.

This 'tradition critical' approach is not simply story telling. It is also, and at the same time, an interpretation of the past for the present and the future. In that sense it is directly concerned with theology, the theology of Anglican Christian faith. However, in reality it is more than that. It is, in fact, theology. I approach the history as carefully and as accurately as I can, but I do so as a theologian and as a way of practising theology. The concern of this book is first and foremost the faith which Anglicans profess and seek to live.

A 'tradition critical' treatment must consider the spiritual, institutional and theological heritage which Anglicans have inherited. In particular, it requires a more radical interpretation of the heritage of the English Reformation, in relation to which I believe we have, to a significant degree, kept the bath water and thrown out the baby.

The present situation of Australian Anglicans is thus approached from the standpoint of a 'tradition critical' approach and by means of story in order to develop an argument, an argument that suggests that Australian Anglicans are on the back foot. Given what has happened, that is not surprising. Anglicans are caught up in the broad changing social environment which is Australia and which has been characterised by Paul Kelly and Hugh Mackay, but they have come to it significantly unprepared for the mental and spiritual effort needed to engage with their challenges.

The past period of contentment which characterised the general cultural circumstances of the Australian Settlement affected Anglicans as well. This was a period of natural growth and development. Certainly there were disputes within the church, and there were social crises which had to be addressed. The trauma of the First World War created great problems for the Anglican Church, as it did for the rest of Australian society. But the leadership of the church and the activity of church members was not so set back as one might have expected. Even the traumas of the Second World War did not diminish the confidence or the strength of Anglicans in Australia. On the contrary, it brought forth significant leadership and very considerable energy in the faith community. The period up until the 1960s was thus a time of contentment and natural growth of confidence and assurance. In this Anglicans were simply sharing in the post-war reconstruction energy of Australia. Anglicans benefited from this general social growth, because they were so clearly part of the 'Australian Settlement', which was enjoying its twilight splendour.

The angst of Australian society has been a more profound angst for Anglicans when it is put in the longer perspective of the association with the Australian Settlement, in which the Anglicans found such a congenial environment. Paul Kelly's analysis of the twentieth century needs, however, to be extended into the nineteenth century.

This story shows that, although Anglicans came as the church establishment, the position in Australia of Anglicans has been whittled away and undermined, so that, having once been top dogs institutionally and culturally, their church organisation and tradition is now merely one of a pack, barking at the outskirts of society. That institutional experience has had a significant affect on the confidence and vitality of Australian Anglicans, which the long sleep of the period of the Australian Settlement only disguised.

The broad story

In 1788 the Anglican supremacy came with the British settlement, because what came was essentially a colonial jail and the church was part of the military establishment. The Church of England provided the chaplains. When a church organisation was established in the colony early in the nineteenth century, it was a government-supported Church of England which was provided.

Throughout the nineteenth century, Anglicans found themselves step by step losing their dominant position in society, institutionally and culturally. Early in the twentieth century the broad central band of Anglicans came to an accommodation with the terms of the Australian Settlement described by Kelly and Melleuish. That accommodation has been falling apart in the last twenty years, just as the Australian Settlement has been falling apart.

The changed relationship with society for Anglicans has highlighted the internal differences within the Anglican community and has left them confused about their identity as Anglicans and, more particularly, as Australian Anglicans. The pathologies of the big angst are certain to be present among Anglicans as they are among Australians generally, and the temptations are clearly there: the temptation to escape, the temptation of social amnesia and thus of losing hope, the temptation of self-absorption, of avoidance of engagement with the wider culture and a preoccupation with internal affairs, flirting with authoritarianism in its various forms and the temptation to think that unity demands uniformity. These regressions to the particularities of the past remain as temptations for Anglicans in the twenty-first century.

However, this broad story needs to be teased out in more detail and given more flesh if its force is to be fully appreciated. There are three trajectories by which this story can be conveniently captured, namely church-state relations, education and the public culture. It is with these trajectories and the elaboration of the details of this story that we will now be concerned.

Church–state relations

On 26 January 1788 the Union flag was raised at Camp Cove in Sydney and Captain Arthur Phillip stood before the motley assemblage of convicts, soldiers and others and his commissions were read. On 10 February Phillip took his oaths of office. There were four customary oaths and a declaration which he had to make. After the first two oaths he made the following declaration.

> I, Arthur Phillip, do declare That I do believe that there is not any transubstantiation in the Sacrament of the Lord's Supper or in the Elements of Bread and Wine at or after the Consecration thereof by any Person whatsoever.[83]

If we had been there we would have marvelled at such a declaration in such a context, but it was not strange to Arthur Phillip. He probably did not believe the doctrine of transubstantiation. He certainly understood that that was not really the issue. The issue was that this religious denial was the category by which he must assert his loyalty to the English crown. Loyalty to the English crown meant denial of the Roman Catholic doctrine of transubstantiation, because the crown and the reformed Church of England were bound together.

No clearer picture could emerge from our bore hole to show how much the Church of England was part and parcel of the new political power which had come to establish itself on the shores of Port Jackson. It was a point to which Bishop Broughton, the first bishop, could successfully appeal as late as 1839 in order to prevent the government changing the education system.[84]

Philip had clear instructions about the imposition of the religious rites and privileges of the Church of England. He was to see that the services were properly conducted and to provide for the needs of the chaplain. He was not especially zealous in the performance of these duties, but duties they remained.[85] The simple truth was that the new colony was a military prison and the Church of England was the appointed prison chaplain.

In due course the political character of the colony changed and so did the ecclesiastical situation. There was some gradual recognition of other churches and of Judaism, but the dominant position of the Church of England remained. All marriages had to be registered through the senior Church of England chaplain and later the archdeacon when one was appointed in 1824. The first archdeacon,

---

83 *Historical Records of Australia*, 4, A vol 1, p 21.

84 Broughton, W, *Speech of the Lord Bishop of Australia in the Legislative Council upon the Resolution for Establishing a System of General Education.*

85 This is remarked on in most general histories of Australia and in histories of this period. One of the most illuminating commentaries on it is provided in Atkinson, A, *The Europeans in Australia: A History. Volume One, The Beginning.*

Thomas Scott, had virtual control of ecclesiastical matters in the colony, and as visitor of schools to all intents and purposes was also responsible for public education in the colony.

All this changed on 29 July 1836 when Governor Bourke signed into law an 'Act to Promote the Building of Churches and Chapels and to Provide for the Maintenance of Ministers of Religion in New South Wales'. The Bourke Act totally changed the basis of life in the colony as far as religion was concerned. The archdeacon, William Grant Broughton, who had succeeded Scott, had tried in vain to prevent this move. He returned to the colony in 1836 as the new bishop of Australia only to find that the government would now financially support the Presbyterian and Roman churches alongside his own. It was a death blow to the Anglican monopoly.

The following year 'The Church of England Temporalities Act' became law, and this provided a range of regulations for the control of the assets and property of the church. It also attempted to set out a system of clergy discipline. Five years later the 'Constitution Act' (1842) set a limit on the amount of money available for churches. The inflation of the early fifties caused by the gold rushes meant that this limited money was not adequate to cover both building costs and clergy stipends. Broughton in New South Wales gave priority to clergy stipends, but buildings were given priority in Victoria.[86]

Dramatic changes were taking place in colonial society. The 'democratic spirit' grew and reached a climax with the coming of responsible government in 1856.[87] The discovery of gold brought new wealth and a wave of new immigrants. These social and political changes had the distinct effect of putting the churches right on the back foot. Opposition to these political moves was organised by the Church of England and the Roman Catholic churches, but, given the changes in social attitudes, it was a lost cause. The best that was achieved in the Act of 1862 in New South Wales, which abolished state aid to the churches, was a set of sunset clauses for clergy already receiving stipend support. This arrangement meant that the aged Dean Cowper of Sydney was still receiving state support in 1902 when he

86   See Quaiffe, G, 'Money and Men: Aspects of the Anglican Crisis in Victoria 1850–1865'.
87   See Hirst, J, *The Strange Birth of Colonial Democracy, New South Wales 1848–84*.

died. A similar process occurred in Victoria, where state aid to churches ended in 1870, though in Western Australia aid continued until 1895.

During the later part of the nineteenth century the churches campaigned on social issues and in particular those which they thought touched on the Christian character of society. Hence there were campaigns against the erosion of Sunday as a day of godly rest and against alcoholism and the opening of hotels on Sundays.

The depression of the 1890s brought new and difficult challenges for the churches, particularly the Anglican church. Anglicans had long been involved in welfare activities of various kinds to relieve the worst aspects of dislocation in society. However, the depression forced a more fundamental question upon them. Bishop Camidge in Bathurst contemplated an effort to 'put down clearly defined abuses, by manifesting large hearted sympathy in a practical way, by teaching the dignity of labour'.[88] The influence of Charles Kingsley and F D Maurice, with what were thought by many to be Christian socialist ideas, can be seen in the debates of the Bathurst synod. In Sydney the archbishop called a conference concerned with social and industrial questions such as hours of work, living wage, industrial cooperation and old-age pensions. The social thrust of the 1897 Lambeth Conference influenced at least the Bishop of Goulburn when he spoke about the church 'seeking to impress Christ's law of life upon social and industrial relations, upon literature, art, education, and by a hundred other agencies goes forth more vigorously than ever into the streets and lanes ...'[89] A branch of the Christian Social Union was formed in 1898 by a number of clergy recently arrived from England. The archbishop of Sydney (W S Smith) was president, and a journal entitled *Progress* was produced. It included articles on a wide range of social issues.

In Melbourne social questions were similarly addressed with vigour. Indeed, the general tone of life in Melbourne in the last quarter of the century was expansive and filled with excitement about social and intellectual matters. Melbourne was at this time the largest and most wealthy city in Australia, having 'rushed to riches' on the discovery of gold. The cultural life of Melbourne was filled with new ideas. This spirit of inquiry reached its peak in the 1880s, and it was into this turmoil

88 Bollen, J D, *Protestantism and Social Reform in New South Wales*, p 87.
89 Bollen, J D, *Protestantism and Social Reform in New South Wales*, p 88.

that James Moorhouse made his distinctive contribution to Melbourne Anglicanism. Moorhouse adopted a more open attitude to the new ideas and was able to convey his 'progressive orthodoxy' in a flood of pamphlets and articles and a series of lectures which were so popular that they were moved to the town hall in order to accommodate the crowds who wanted to hear him. His contribution was in large measure to open up theological and social ideas in Melbourne, which had been so long influenced by the conservative Bishop Perry.

Charles Riley, archbishop of Perth (1895–1929), similarly threw himself into public affairs. His involvement took a different form from that of Moorhouse. Riley was an activist, and he made friends with public figures. He energetically engaged in military matters and was Anglican Chaplain General of the Australian Imperial Force in 1916. He directly intervened in a number of industrial strikes, notably the Perth tramway strike in 1920/1921.

In Sydney the Christian Social Union soon began to wilt. It never commanded widespread support among lay people, and it found itself marching to a different beat from the growing influence of the theology of Nathaniel Jones at Moore College.

Nonetheless, at the broader public level church people in Sydney found that they were able to participate in the moves to federation with considerable energy and success. In no small measure churchmen, particularly clergy, were able to do this because of the social circumstances of the mid 1890s. The colonies were recovering slowly from the severe depression in the early part of the decade. In the middle of the decade a severe drop in demand for wool, some poor seasons on the land, and difficulty in raising finance overseas placed considerable pressure on the social fabric. For many this raised issues of the moral character of society and the solutions which were proposed for dealing with the social problems. Churchmen involved themselves in these matters. The argument that religion was the key to morality and morality was critical in dealing with social problems came to have weight in public debate. In that context churchmen were able to involve themselves in public matters, including the moves towards federation.

The organisers of the Bathurst convention, called in 1896 to promote the federation cause, were keen to involve churchmen, in part because it was thought the clerics would help to raise federation in the popular mind. The local Anglican and Roman Catholic bishops were vice-presidents of the convention, and a local

Methodist minister was the secretary. Throughout the convention these clerics kept a reasonably united front in order to press their interests.

However, the parties soon divided when Cardinal Moran stood as a candidate for the Federal Convention to be held in 1897. He thought of himself as a Christian candidate wishing to speak for all, but his action was seen as divisive and brought forth organised Protestant opposition, which in the end led to his defeat.

There was also division between Seventh Day Adventists and other Christians on the question of a recognition clause which acknowledged God in the preamble to the Constitution. Adventists feared that it would be used to enable the federal government to legislate on a uniform national observance of Sunday. Petitions on each side were organised. In the end the Adelaide convention excluded the recognition clause but did include a clause saying that a 'state shall not prohibit the free exercise of any religion'. These issues were discussed in various assemblies. In the end the recognition clause was included in the constitution, and a clause protecting religious liberty was also included. The recognition clause came first, and it succeeded in no small measure because of the support of George Reid, the free-trade premier of New South Wales who had been sympathetic to the churches in their social campaigns against alcohol and Sunday trading.

In the final analysis the new constitution came before the people in referenda with both the recognition clause in the preamble and the protection of freedom of religion clause within the constitution. The final form of the preamble and the religion clause are as follows:

> Whereas the people of New South Wales, Victoria, South Australia, Queensland, and Tasmania, *humbly relying on the blessing of Almighty God,* have agreed to unite into one indissoluble Commonwealth under the Crown of the United Kingdom of Great Britain and Ireland, and under the constitution hereby established.
>
> Section 116.
>
> The Commonwealth shall not make any law for the establishing of any religion, or for imposing any religious observance or forbidding the free exercise of any religion, and no religious test shall be required as a qualification for any office or public trust under the Commonwealth.

The churches supported the federation bill, and it eventually passed. The whole experience of the federation process might have led churches, not least the Anglicans, to think that they had come out of the decade well. Certainly in New South Wales the Anglicans' association with the premier, George Reid, and the federation bill looked like a promising sign for the new century.

Clause 116 of the Australian Constitution has been the subject of a number of judgments by the High Court. Those judgments have shown that the clause did not lead to a strict separation of church and state. The court has found in relation to federal aid to church schools that even-handed assistance is not unconstitutional. Similarly, in relation to payroll tax exceptions religious groups can establish their entitlement if they can show that they have a religion.[90]

On several occasions Anglicans have found themselves before the courts not in order to obtain aid but to obtain a decision on an internal matter. In 1943 the High Court rejected an appeal by the bishop of Bathurst from the New South Wales Supreme Court that the bishop had improperly authorised the use of a particular prayer book (the Red Book). The case turned on the question of whether the use of the book involved a breach of the trust on which the property was held, principally the cathedral and the churches in which the services were taken by the bishop. The court found that it did involve that trust property and that the book contravened the terms of the trust.[91]

In 1992 the New South Wales Court of Appeal ruled that the bishop of Canberra and Goulburn could not be prevented from ordaining women on the grounds that only those sections of the constitution of the Anglican Church of Australia which were justiciable were those which referred to church trust property. It has not always been noted that in this case the court was not asked to consider the question of whether any church trust property was actually involved; indeed, the parties before the court agreed to exclude that question from the case. Rather, the court was being asked to enforce the doctrine and discipline of the church. The court explicitly refused to do this. Had the use of church trust property been included in the question, there is little doubt that the court would have been

---

90   See Kaye, B, 'An Australian Definition of Religion'.
91   See the account of this case in Teale, R, 'The "Red Book" Case'.

obliged to rule on the question, which would indirectly, at least, have meant dealing with a matter of doctrine or discipline.

These cases make it clear that the connecting point between the internal discipline of the church and the operation of the courts is the trusts on which church property is held. It would not take too much imagination to construe almost anything to do with church activity in some way involving the use of church property. One only has to think of the reach of concepts of intellectual property or copyright or indeed simply the use of the name of the church itself.

The High Court rulings also make it clear that the constitution does not inhibit the government from assisting churches in such matters as education or even benefits for more directly religious activities, as long as that assistance is given in such a way that the government is not aiding or establishing any one religion rather than others.

This is a very long way from the early Anglican monopoly. Step by step Anglicans have been removed from their privileged position in relations with the state, so that now they are in a position no different from that of any other religious body.

Anglicans and education in Australia

The Anglican experience of education has many parallels with what we have just reviewed in church-state relations because of the long and intimate connection with education of both the Anglican Church and the state. Nonetheless, our bore hole into the past of education highlights different aspects of the experience of Australian Anglicans, both in respect of how they understand themselves and how they have conceived of their mission as a church community in Australia.

At each stage in the development of educational policy in Australia Anglicans have been compelled to engage in various types of compromises. These compromises have been significantly shaped by the compromises made by their predecessors as well as by the changing social environment. Each decision was value driven and certainly had social values consequences. It is remarkable how those values have changed so dramatically in the course of history. The process has gone through four decisive changes in philosophy and practice, from an Anglican monopoly to government sponsored privatisation of education.

The beginnings—Anglican Church education

As we have already seen, when the colony of New South Wales was established it was assumed that the political ecclesiastical establishment of England would simply apply, with the qualification, of course, that the colony was essentially a military prison. Education was therefore assumed to be the responsibility of the Church of England. The Bigge Report in 1815 led to significant changes in education. Under Thomas Scott the Church Schools Corporation was established with an endowment of one seventh of all the land in the colony. This pattern applied until the Bourke Act in 1836.

The first phase, therefore, of education in the colony was by way of an Anglican monopoly because it was assumed to be the established church. This education was not only conducted by the Anglican Church but was specifically Anglican in character.

Transition—church and state education

The Church Act of Governor Bourke provided for government grants to each recognised church (Presbyterian, Roman Catholic and Anglican) on a more or less pro rata basis. This pattern flowed through to the provision of church schools as well. By this Act the religious pluralism that existed in the colony was recognised and the Anglican monopoly was destroyed.

In 1839 Governor Gipps tried to introduce a system of government schools. Along with the other Protestant churches Bishop Broughton had opposed a similar scheme in 1836. However, in 1839 he stood alone in opposing a scheme which did not provide for the teaching of the Anglican catechism. He claimed that the constitution gave to the Church of England the right to special protection. 'I maintain, that under the constitution, she is entitled to look to the Government for the fullest measure of aid and encouragement.'[92] The foundation of the constitution , he claimed, was the union of church and state. This was an arrangement in the interests of the citizens. 'Their reason for connecting the throne so inseparably with this faith, was their persuasion, that this faith was most consonant with truth and most friendly to liberty.'[93]

---

92 Broughton, W, *Speech of the Lord Bishop of Australia in the Legislative Council upon the Resolution for Establishing a System of General Education*, p 11.
93 Broughton, p 12.

Broughton's dramatic speech in the Legislative Council in August 1839 forced the governor to withdraw his plans for comprehensive government schools. However, the tide was running against Broughton's conception of the state. Indeed, during the course of the 1840s he changed his mind completely and concluded that the Anglican Establishment in the form of the Royal Supremacy was dead and buried. Thus in 1848 he was willing to compromise and see a dual pattern introduced, with a system of national schools alongside the four main church systems. There would be a separate board for the national schools and another for the denominational schools.

In 1836 the Anglican monopoly had gone. Now, in 1848, the monopoly of the churches had gone, and there was a dual system of state schools and church schools. At each stage the Anglicans had made compromises on the previous position but had maintained their involvement in education. Broughton's High Church principles drove him incessantly to see education as a key instrument in the mission of the church.

During the next two decades, however, the balance of funding between the denominational schools and the national schools changed. Also during this period Roman Catholic and Anglican attitudes changed, albeit in different directions. These changes led to the effective state monopoly of education established by Education Acts in various states.

State education

In 1866 the Public Schools Act in New South Wales amalgamated the denominational and national schools boards under a Council of Education. The new arrangement had a built-in bias against the denominational schools. Public schools were to have non-denominational religious instruction. Special religious instruction along denominational lines would be given by visiting clergy on a released time basis. In the light of what was to happen next, it is important to notice that the denominational schools which continued under this arrangement were open to all children. While a school might be administered by a church, no preference was given to the children from that church's membership.

In the period 1860–80 the Roman Catholic Church dramatically changed its attitude to education. In 1864 Pius IX issued the Syllabus of Errors, which condemned any state monopoly of education. In 1867 the Catholic Association for the Promotion of Religion and Education was formed in New South Wales. In Ireland the Irish Roman Catholic bishops condemned the Irish National System, which was similar to what operated in New South Wales. In 1878 Archbishop Vaughan and the Roman Catholic bishops waged a campaign for more aid and more independence for their schools. At the same time there was a rising tide of liberal opinion in regard to social policies. All state aid to churches for church buildings and clergy stipends was stopped in 1862.

It was in this context that the 1880 Education Act was passed in New South Wales. Similar acts were passed in other states at about the same time. This act set up a Department of Public Instruction which would be responsible for a complete school system including the secondary level. Denominational instruction could be given by visiting clergy, and compulsory general non-dogmatic religious instruction would be given by the schools. All state aid to church schools would cease from 1882. The Act in Victoria did indeed provide for 'free compulsory and secular education'. In New South Wales there were to be school fees. It is important to notice here that the term 'secular' had not yet come to mean non-religious. Rather it meant not controlled by the church.

Here, then, we have, for funding purposes, a state monopoly in education. The participation of the churches was still possible but within a framework set by the state system.

The result was a determined effort by the Roman Catholic Church to establish and run their own system for their own people. The Anglicans sought to improve standards in a much-reduced system of church schools. These schools tended to be high fee and secondary and thus moved Anglican schools away from the working classes and concentrated them in the middle and professional classes of society. By and large, under the impetus of Barry in Sydney and Morehouse in Melbourne, the Anglicans sought to participate in the state system. However, they had now embarked upon a dual commitment to middle-class private schools and participation in the broader based state system. In the course of time the commitment to the private schools won out.

Privatising government-funded education

The Education Acts at the end of the nineteenth century dominated the Australian scene until the 1950s. In the last twenty years we have seen dramatic changes in education in Australia which have profound social and value implications.

The 1950s saw changing educational ideas, and the school population grew dramatically in this decade. The school leaving age was raised, and comprehensive schools were developed to give expression to a more social and rounded concept of education. The Roman Catholic parochial school system was overwhelmed by the increased numbers, added to disproportionately for them by post-war immigration. The demands of the new education syllabuses stretched their resources. The Roman Catholic Church mounted a campaign for state aid for their schools, and the whole situation cracked in 1962 with the strike of Roman Catholic schools in Goulburn, New South Wales.

At the same time, Anglicans were in the process of changing their minds about state aid. For decades it had been a point of sectarian distinction, but in a series of steps Anglicans adjusted to the new realities. In 1964 the synod of the diocese of Sydney had two opposing reports on this subject, while at the same time the Anglican schools in the diocese had gone ahead and accepted the new federal government grants without waiting for the synod to make up its mind.

What began as grants for science laboratories has now come to be an extensive system of federal government funding of private schools. The constitutionality of this process was tested in the High Court and found not to be an infringement of the 'establishment' clause 116 of the constitution, basically on the grounds that it was not preferential to any religion.

The consequence of this policy has been a huge proliferation of community schools, many of which have been established by religious groups. Many of these schools are designed to provide schooling for a tightly defined religious group. Anglicans have been very active in establishing new schools, but, on the whole, they have tended to be more open in their admissions arrangements.

From both the terms of the High Court judgment and the arguments in Anglican synods, it is clear that the whole notion of the role of the state in education embodied in the 1880 Education Acts has been completely overthrown. Anglicans justified their new attitude on the grounds that education was the responsibility of parents and that parents should have the opportunity to send their children to a school of their choice. A similar line of thought can be found in the High Court judgments.

So we notice an extraordinarily important consequence of this dramatic social change: that the government funded privatisation of education has the potential of radically advancing the institutional and cultural pluralisation of society.

What our bore hole into education demonstrates is that Anglicans have been required to struggle for and accept compromises in relations with the state over education. Each compromise was shaped by the preceding participation and compromise. In 1836 the issue was the Christian character of the state. In 1848 it was about Christian participation in a plural state. In 1880 it was also about Christian participation in a plural state, but this time a state which took to itself a monopoly of public funds for education. In 1962 it was about the relaxation of that funding monopoly for state schools. In that sense it was about the institutional privatisation of education at government expense. Because of the way it has worked out, it has been a giant step in the privatisation of institutional religion.

This pluralisation of education raises important questions for Anglicans. In a way which was not true before, almost everything depends on the openness and quality of these new Anglican schools. If they are not open in their admission but aim at serving a discrete and demarcated religious group, then they are likely to encourage the tribalisation of society in this country.

Our bore hole into the past of Australian Anglicanism has shown that until the most recent times a vital area of the Anglican mission strategy was taken away from the church. The weight of this historical experience has lain heavily upon the self-understanding of Australian Anglicans. The very recent changes which have allowed a small re-entry into the educational arena are only a very small relief in an overall experience of institutional diminishment.

Public culture

From the earliest days of the colony of New South Wales, not only was the Anglican Church dominant institutionally in the area of education and shared a privileged position in church–state relations, it also was a pervasive and powerful influence upon public attitudes and culture. The fact that as late as 1839 Bishop Broughton could appeal to a special relationship between the Church of England and the Crown, indicates that such a point of view was at least not rejected out of hand, and indeed in many parts it was accepted as fair comment.

However, times changed dramatically during the 1840s. A small group of people, who met at the back of Henry Parkes's shop in Hunter Street Sydney from 1848 onwards, formed a nucleus of a growing democratic spirit in the colony. 1848 was, of course, a tumultuous year in European civilisation. There were revolutions and disturbances all over Europe, and in England the Chartist campaigns for constitutional reform reached their highest pitch. In New South Wales there were no such public disturbances. The issues did not appear to be as intense as they were in Europe. Indeed, the new democratic group called themselves the Constitutional Association, since the word 'democracy' in many people's minds still had threatening connotations of civil disorder. These democrats in Sydney had contacts with the Chartist Movement in England and, in many respects, were inspired by what was happening on the other side of the world. The group began to publish the *People's Advocate*. Its editor, Edward Hawksley, had worked on a Chartist newspaper in England.

Moves for popular reform of the kind advocated by the new Constitutional Association were seen by many as a threat to the public influence of the Church of England. Indeed, in this period of change the Church of England appeared in most people's minds as a defender of the status quo, a bastion of conservatism. In the end, however, it was these movements of popular sentiment which shaped the new constitution for the colony. Although the Constitutional Association did not last long as an organisation, the sentiments which it represented marked a turning point in public culture.

In this period in the middle of the nineteenth century the notion of a secular society, and of public institutions as being secular, was given its particular Australian formulation. When the University of Sydney was founded as a secular institution, it was nonetheless established for the promotion of useful knowledge and of Christian faith and morals. It was secular in the minds of the founders, and of those in colonial society who took notice of it, in the sense that it was not controlled by the churches. One of the principle reasons given by the founders, in the early history of the university, was that any institutional involvement by the churches, principally in the form of the bishops, would lead to sectarian disputes which would undermine the coherence of the university and unity in society.

During the second half of the nineteenth century, the churches could still campaign as if they were the embodiment of the conscience of society and as if they were defending a Christian country. Changes during the second half of the nineteenth century in the institutional position of the churches in their relationship to the state, to education, and to public services generally meant that the notion that this was a Christian society with Christian institutions lost its force. Increasingly, the public perception was that this was a society developing its institutions for the benefit of the people, in the light of the values to which the people as a whole aspired. The churches increasingly became campaigners in a plural society. In this process overt religious imagery and argument was gradually eroded from public debate and public culture.

At the end of the century the churches gained a brief period of public recognition in the Federation movement. The 1890s began with a recession and the emergence of republicanism. The *Bulletin*, founded in 1893, began to give expression to a strong, even aggressive, form of secular social philosophy. At the end of the nineteenth century 'secular' came to have the connotation of being not religious. Clergy were the butt of cartoon jokes and arguments against the recognition clause in the Commonwealth Constitution on the basis that this would be the thin edge of sectarianism in public life in the Commonwealth. In New South Wales the Protestant churches found support from Premier George Reid in their campaigns for Sabbath observance and against alcoholism. Nonetheless, the churches, and particularly the Anglican Church, maintained an extensive connection with and membership among the widest cross section of the population. Even as late as the 1980s, nominal Anglicans were the group whose socio-economic profile was closest to that of the population as a whole, a statistical vestige of a time when being Church of England was the nominal religious commitment of the vast bulk of the population. That pattern began to be eroded significantly at the beginning of the twentieth century and had largely collapsed at the end of the century.

At the political level, particularly in New South Wales, the Protestant churches, including the Anglican Church, had associated themselves with the free trade premier, George Reid. They supported him because he had supported their social campaigns. The Protestant churches also supported the growing Labor Party, in so far as they supported these social campaigns. Two things happened in the period 1890–1910 which had the effect of eclipsing the public distinctive profile of Anglicans as compared with Roman Catholics. On the one hand, support for

George Reid and his involvement in the Federation Movement enabled Anglicans to support the place given to religion in the new Commonwealth Constitution. Along with other church leaders, it gave them recognition. However, this support increasingly alienated them from the growing force of the Labor Party.

On the other hand, during this period the Roman Catholic Church increasingly identified itself with Labor. The monumental task of establishing a Roman Catholic parish school system, largely on the basis of the sacrificial labours of the religious orders, meant that Roman Catholics were becoming a distinct sub-culture within the broader host society of Australia. The school system which they were creating was designed for Roman Catholics, had a Roman Catholic curriculum and was designed to produce Roman Catholic citizens. Not only so, it was also aimed at preparing people for work in the public service. In New South Wales, particularly, Roman Catholic schools directed their efforts to preparing people for the public service entrance examinations rather than university matriculation. Generations of Roman Catholics who came through this process did so conscious that they were special, that they were Roman Catholics and then Australians. Roman Catholicism from the beginnings of Federation grew as a discrete self-conscious community of people within the Australian nation.

Meanwhile, Anglicans settled easily into the emerging establishment culture of the new Commonwealth. They became the invisible partners of what Paul Kelly called the Australian Settlement. Active Anglicans, as distinct from nominal Anglicans, increasingly associated themselves with middle-class literary liberal attitudes. In broad social terms, Anglicanism in this period increasingly became a wallpaper culture of the social establishment.

A distinct exception to this generalisation in regard to Anglicans is to be found in Sydney. At the turn of the century a group of influential Sydney evangelicals accepted much of the teaching and impulses of the Brethren and the eschatological attitudes of the principal of Moore College, Nathaniel Jones. That tradition of conservative self-referencing dissent has been a continuing element in Sydney Anglicanism since that time. There is a greater sense that the church, like Christ's kingdom, is not of this world and that Christians are called to be dissenters for the sake of the gospel against the world, the flesh and the devil. In contrast to the Roman Catholic dissenting tradition, this tradition did not have any significant influence on the culture of the host society in which it was located and did not engage directly with the problems which that society was throwing up. Roman Catholics developed their own intellectual and cultural traditions and interacted with what was going on around them, producing an extraordinary line of artists and writers who contributed to Australian culture. Separating Anglicans did not. Furthermore, where that tradition has emerged from time to time, it has been a strongly dissenting group, not only from secular society but also from the wider Christian community. A similar tendency to dissent can also be seen in the overall effect of the Anglo-Catholic revival in the forty years from around 1890. This culture became more noticeably ritualist and less committed to the social engagement of some of the early leaders of the movement.

These developments at the turn of the century have had a profound impact upon the place of Anglicans in Australian public culture in the course of the twentieth century.

During the course of the twentieth century the Higgins liberal view of public life grew to have a powerful influence. Higgins was a very Victorian liberal deeply involved in the moves towards federation. He believed that the constitution which finally came into effect was rigid and repressive, and he was one of only two of the convention delegates to oppose the bill. It left him an isolated and controversial figure in his home state of Victoria. Higgins became attorney general in the commonwealth Labor government in 1904, and in October of 1906 was appointed to the newly established High Court. He soon took over the presidency of the commonwealth Court of Conciliation and Arbitration. It was from this position that he was to have his greatest influence on Australian public culture. In his famous Harvester judgment, in relation to a case brought against the manufacturer H. B. McKay, he had to decide whether the wages Mr McKay was paying were fair and reasonable. It was this case which provided the basis for the development of the centralised arbitration system which has been such a mark of twentieth-century Australian labour relations.

Looking back over the period from the First World War until the present, it is striking how public exponents of Australian culture and Australian historians have so systematically ignored the religious dimension of Australian life. It is difficult to ignore the Roman Catholic tradition in this matter, because it has been such a distinct cultural sub-group. It was much easier to ignore the Anglicans, because, by a series of compromises and through political and cultural movements, they had eased into the background and become part of the furniture.

The present diversity in Australian culture and of the nature of the Australian body politic can be seen in the way minority groups have been treated since World War II. After the war the Australian government pursued a policy of assisted immigration. That policy and the way in which immigrants came to be treated has gone through several significant changes. Up until the late 1960s immigrants were expected to assimilate without much change on the part of the host culture. They were to become part of the 'weird mob' by themselves changing.[94] During the late 1960s and early 1970s immigrants were people with problems or people who caused problems because of their inadequacy or difference. From the early 1970s they became a pressure group looking for rights. From the middle 1970s governments pursued a policy of multiculturalism. However, this policy has itself gone through various stages. During the Hawke government (1983–1991) diversity was given considerable priority, though this was drawn back in policy formulation under Mr Keating (1991–1996). This was done by an increasing emphasis on citizenship and commitment to Australia. This emphasis lacked the precise legal and institutional focus of earlier policies, but it was clearly an attempt to find ways of handling the issue of social coherence and identity in a way which enabled maximum difference. This policy balance was set out in the government's statement *Our Nation. Multicultural Australia and the 21st Century*, published in 1995.[95]

Despite this re-evaluation of the role of citizenship and the re-emphasis upon core values in government policy, public culture has moved during the 1990s in a more individualist direction,[96] though that conception is not embedded in the fabric of Australian society to nearly the same extent that it is in the United States of America. Caught up in the culture and dynamics of a globalised civilisation, Australians have increasingly been told that it is more and more an individualist society. In the spirit of post-modernism we have been told that old institutions are no longer significant, that we are separated from our predecessors, as indeed we are from our children.

94 For a fictional evocation of these issues see O'Grady, J, *They're a weird mob: a novel*.
95 Australia, *Our Nation: Multicultural Australia and the 21st Century*.
96 See Sheehan, P, *Among the Barbarians: The Dividing of Australia*.

In this process, public culture is an arena in which Anglicans have not been expected to play a part and are studiously ignored by the leading protagonists of the cultural debate. It is hardly surprising that Anglicans have not ventured very much into this field in any self-conscious way.

The difference can be illustrated by the purposes for which the University of Sydney was established and how this was described at the opening ceremonies, and the kinds of assumptions implicit in modern discussions about civil society in Australia.

The official opening of the University of Sydney took place on 11 October 1852. Sir Charles Nicholson addressed the assembly and first of all explained the character and functions of the new university. The preamble to the bill setting up the university declared (as indeed the charter of the university does to this day) that 'it is expedient for the better advancement of religion and morality, and the promotion of useful knowledge, to hold forth to all classes and denominations of her Majesty's subjects resident in the colony of New South Wales, without any distinction whatever, an encouragement for pursuing a regular and liberal course of education'.[97] He deliberately set out the relation between the secular character of the university and religion.

> Indirectly, we believe, but in no small degree, will the secular teaching of the university subserve the cause of religion and of revealed truth. For it may safely be affirmed that a mind disciplined and enlarged by habits of study, and by the acquisition of knowledge, must be better prepared for the reception of divine truth, than one that is uncultivated and uninformed . . . Whatever tends to enlarge the domain of thought, to make us acquainted with the things that have gone before us, and the things that are beyond us, serves but to impress us the more deeply with sentiments of humility and reverence for the Great Author of all things.

In a later section of his speech he declared that the training which the student will receive at the university will enable him to fulfil his responsibilities 'in the particular station in life in which God's providence has placed him'. Further he declared that 'the foundation of the faith can never be finally impaired by knowledge'.

97 *Sydney Morning Herald*, 12 October, 1852.

My point here is not to highlight something about the origins of the University of Sydney but rather to draw attention to what these remarks reveal about the assumptions which could be counted on in a public address about the place of religion in society. What people did in society was a station to which God had called them. Knowledge and faith are allies not enemies, and a secular university was secular only in the sense that it was not controlled by clerics or the church and because it did not teach theology. It was supported by public funds and therefore could not support any sectional church interest, but in no sense did that mean that it had no interest in Christian faith; on the contrary, it served exactly to support and promote that faith.

In contrast to these tacit assumptions in the public domain we may note the 1996 Boyer Lectures, an annual series of radio lecture broadcasts on the Australian Broadcasting Corporation (ABC).[98] The lecturer, Eva Cox, devoted five lectures to the question of a civil society without once referring to any constructive role that religion, let alone Christianity or Anglicanism, might play in the creation of that civil society. She did not even discuss the question. My point is not that Eva Cox has non-religious views on this subject; that may or may not be the case. My point is that in a series of public lectures on the ABC the question of the role of religion was not thought worthy of discussion. That, I think, is not especially odd on the part of Eva Cox; on the contrary, it fairly represents the assumptions which prevail among public commentators in modern Australia.

Similarly, in a collection of essays recently published under the title *Creating Australia: Changing Australian History*, the editors expressly state their intention to draw attention to points of interaction in the creation of Australian identity, but they never discuss religion or Christianity in that context.[99]

At the start of the twenty-first century in Australia the public culture is not shaped by Christian assumptions as represented by the churches. Religion is certainly present in the public culture as a life style choice for individuals to make. The conversation is conducted on more pluralist assumptions.[100] This perception of the public culture by its principle participants is essentially secular and in the mass

---

98 Cox, E, *A Truly Civil Society.*
99 Hudson, W and Bolton, G, *Creating Australia: Changing Australian History.*
100 Compare the situation in the USA as presented by Carter, S, *The Culture of Unbelief.*

media represents the commercial values of business corporations. This is a far cry form the early days of the colony and even from the assumptions about the Christian character of society in the middle of the nineteenth century. The assumptions about the British character of the society survived well into the twentieth century, and this carried along with it a certain kind of Anglican mentality.

Conclusions

So what do these three bore holes back through history indicate? They point to a story of Australian Anglicans under pressure on a number of fronts. They reveal areas of previous strength for Anglicans in Australia in the early nineteenth century; indeed, they were areas where Anglicans had their hands on powerful levers of influence. These Anglican levers no longer move the points.

In the arena of church–state relations Anglicans have moved from a position of patronage, privilege and power through succeeding defeats and compromises to confusion and uncertainty. There is internal debate within the Anglican community as to just how far even the state, in the form of the courts, will or should adjudicate on disputes between Anglicans. It appears that the courts will only do that in relation to property, in the same way in which they would for any other voluntary association.

Given the story of the Anglican Church's relationship with the state and the community memory of that past position, it is understandable that the church should use images about its own internal organisation which are drawn from the state and government. So one hears talk of synods as parliaments, of the resolutions of synods as legislation and of the use of parliamentary practice in the synods. All these things are part of the memory of a past situation. It is as if, in some sense, what previously was an external relationship between the church community and the institutions of the state has been internalised into the inner life of the church community.

The time has come, however, for new images and new understandings, a different notion of what it is to gather as a community of Christian people to make decisions. Better images are needed that are drawn from the Christian theological tradition, with some sense of the Spirit of God among the people of God. Such a sense of the providence of God in the quest for decisions by Anglican Christians seems long overdue, as is some sense of an encounter with fellow Christians which is also, and at the same time, an encounter with the living and guiding presence of the Spirit of God.

This Anglican memory of a previous time, fossilised in the imagery of current internal arrangements, is, at one level, a memory about a good thing. It was about the openness of Anglicanism to the society around it through its principal institutional expression, the state. The intimate connection between the state and the church in the history of Anglicanism came to expression at a time when the society was thought of as Christian, and indeed Anglican. The church was the spiritual and the state the temporal aspect of that one Christian society.

That is not the case in Australia, though church and state are not totally separated by our constitution as interpreted by the High Court. That changed situation does not mean that Anglicans should refuse to be open to the society in which God has placed them. On the contrary, that openness is part of their spiritual heritage. The time is now for creative thought and experiment to be applied to the shape and character of that openness.

Such a process should not be guided by the present attitudes or so-called 'common sense' of society, though they provide the context within which such an openness might be practised. Rather, what we are concerned with here is the way in which a community of people shaped by the gospel in its Anglican expression might relate to their fellow Australians.

In the experience of education, Anglicans have gone from a monopoly situation through nineteenth-century statism to a growing but uncertain free market. In that story Anglicans have followed the policy of cooperating with the state arrangements once they had overcome the shock of having lost their monopoly position. That cooperative policy has meant that, on the one hand, the broad spectrum of Anglicans who have supported the policy of sending their children to state schools have had a very different experience of the identity-forming process of their education as Anglicans. On the other hand, those who have sent their children to private schools have had their Anglican identity formed in such a way that it has become almost impossible to distinguish it with clarity from the elite socio-economic stratas of the Australian society which those schools have in large measure come to represent. Even at the beginning of the twenty-first century, when Anglicans are pressing on with the establishment of low-fee schools, the interface balance between state paymaster and the mission-identifying purposes of Anglican schools still remains a tension.

The precise identity-forming role of Anglican schools is yet to be fully analysed. The history of Anglican involvement in education has not prepared Anglicans with either a tradition of thought or a set of categories which easily enables them to address this question effectively. The role of Anglicans in religious instruction in state schools is even more ambiguous. The terms of the various state education Acts have varied somewhat, but in general terms they provided for general religious education in the school, with dogmatic or specifically denominational religious education conducted on a released-time basis. This distinction has had a seriously detrimental effect on the understanding of Anglican education. The system required a division in thinking which made it difficult to sustain systematic thought about the nature of Anglican educational philosophy. With the demise of general religious education in the state schools in recent decades, the special education has become more general in character and, in the process, less specifically Anglican for those Anglicans who teach it and those Anglican students who participate.

The truth is that by the end of the twentieth century the categories for this area had changed significantly. The way in which education is thought of in contemporary Australia has changed so fundamentally that the challenge to develop an approach to this area which fosters and encourages the emergence of a discrete Anglican identity is, to say the least of it, an opportunity yet to explored.

In relation to public culture the establishment position of Anglicans was rebuffed by democratic statism in the early history of Australia. The collapse of the Australian Settlement and the recent so-called 'cultural wars' demonstrate how our national identity is itself an arena of conflict and disputation. The difficulty that Anglicans face is that they do not appear to have readily to hand workable categories that enable them to interpret modern Australian pluralism.

I have tried to highlight the historical background to the present Australian Anglican situation by three 'bore holes'. Another way to highlight the issues would be to show the general emerging position from 1788 to the present. I think that position has emerged in steps which can be in very general terms be seen at certain points in the story. Giving specific dates for changing trends is always dangerous and usually regretted afterwards. Nonetheless, on the basis that the following dates are taken as general indicators rather than specific points of change, the following pattern seems to me to be fair and also suggestive of the character of the historical situation at the end of the twentieth century.

1788–1836

The Anglican dominance. Control of all religious activity at first and then a monopoly on all government support for religion.

1836–1882

Collaborating with a Christian state.

A culture of individual liberalism in a Christian state loyal to Britain and the British race.

1882–1910

Defending the idea of a Christian society in a plural environment, with the help, especially in the 1890s, of political allies of convenience.

A culture of a liberal, that is democratic, state, loyal to Britain and the British race.

1910–1960

Anglicans maintaining humane values in the liberal society of the Australian Settlement.

New liberalism, that is egalitarian fairness in the state, and the erosion of the imperial connection.

1960–1995

Anglicans struggling with the new pluralisms.

Society moves away from the corporatist values of the Australian Settlement, to which Anglicans had attached themselves.

1995–

Confusion of Anglicans in their social position apparent.

The demise of the 'new liberalism' and its social values. Social and institutional values become problematic in favour of pluralism defined in terms of the individual.

The story of how Anglicans have come to their present situation in Australia is at once encouraging and sad. It is encouraging because individual Anglicans and groups of Anglicans have not only tried to be faithful through this period but have also succeeded. It is sad in that what has happened in the past has led us to a situation where Anglicans are distinctly on the back foot. The story reveals a situation where both individuals and Anglican institutions encounter great difficulty as they struggle to find their own characteristic Anglican role in a confusing social situation.

This story has also shown up an important element in the situation of Australian Anglicans which is not always so obvious but is nonetheless very significant. We are able to take part in social interaction because we share certain assumptions about what is sensible or reasonable. Our shared common assumptions of this kind facilitate conversation and understanding. They shape what we commonly regard as plausible. The story of Anglicans in Australia has shown that the geography of these shared assumptions has changed in all sorts of ways, but most particularly they have changed in regard to the way Anglican assumptions relate to these common tacit assumptions in modern Australia. These value assumptions have not changed totally—nothing like it. One of the remarkable features of Australian social values over the last hundred years has been their relative continuity. But the story we have looked at has suggested that the changes in the last thirty years of the twentieth century have had a particular impact on Anglicans. There is for them a plausibility dislocation with many of their fellow Australians. One important social psychological consequence of this is that Anglicans do not seem able to speak with the same confidence about their faith and their values in the public domain as they once did. This plausibility dislocation affects important areas of life, not just private activities, what we sometimes call personal morality.

Also at stake is the role and function of institutions and why they should be shaped in the way in which they are, the style of leadership and of community life, the character of the communities to which people belong and the values and purposes of their inner dynamics. These are areas where Anglicans operating within their church community find themselves, at significant points, distinctively out of step with the way of thinking that those same Australian Anglicans confront in other aspects of their social life.

This detachment makes engagement with that society and those other aspects of the life of Australian Anglicans outside the realms of the church community both uncertain and ambiguous. It also makes Anglicans suspicious of their heritage to the point where some say that they have no specific beliefs as Anglicans. This syndrome is reinforced by the diversity within the Anglican Church, so that people rush to the conclusion that there is nothing which Anglicans share. It is said that the ties that bind are thin to the point of breaking and that we are only held together by our common interest in inherited church property and clergy superannuation funds.[101]

But these conclusions reflect more the confusion of the present situation rather than a realistic assessment of the religious heritage which is Anglicanism. It is in this context and with these kinds of questions that I wish to argue in this book that we need to re-imagine Anglicanism. Even that way of putting the matter is not adequate. I would rather say that we should be allowing the church to be re-imagined. I put it this way because I want to underline throughout this book, but particularly at this point, that reinventing the church is not merely a matter of social organisational change. Rather, reinventing the church is a matter of finding ways of attending to what God is doing with Australian Anglicans and their church. The primary point is that the renewal of the church is an activity of God.

In the light of this story what are we to say lies before us. Anglicans in Australia at the dawn of the twenty-first century are in a situation of considerable uncertainty. Many feel that they are on the back foot in relation to their fellow Australians and in relation to their mission in Australia. The difficulty, I believe, is that we very often have taken up the wrong aspects of our heritage and sometimes have not fully understood the seriousness of our position. It is not just that people are not coming to Anglican churches as much as they used to, nor is it just that the people who do come to Anglican churches tend to be elderly, nor any of the other things which are revealed in the National Church Life Survey or in the census material. The real problem for Anglican Christians in Australia is that it is not easy for them to know how they might live Christianly in this society. It involves not just what we do in church. It much more fundamentally involves

---

101 Compare Hilliard, D, 'The Ties That Used to Bind: A Fresh Look at the History of Australian Anglicanism'.

what we do as citizens, as members of social institutions, and as we participate Christianly in relationships outside the confines of the discrete church community. It is because these questions are so ambiguous that we struggle to reflect what it means to live a Christian life as an Australian Anglican. It is not lack of commitment. It is that we need in some sense to reinvent ourselves, and to reinvent ourselves as Anglican Christians and as an Anglican Church, in order that we might be enabled to live Christianly as Australian Anglicans in the society in which God has placed us.

The real uncertainties upon which such a reinventing church must focus have to do with the way in which we are able to make judgments in the kind of plural environment we have in Australia. Our first challenge is to find sufficient confidence in making those judgments to enable us to live actively and intentionally as Anglican Christians in Australia. It is a question of judgment, of understanding, of perception and of action.

Secondly, we have before us a challenge about the nature of the church community. It's a question of how we are to conceive of and foster the relationships which are appropriate within a Christian community whose internal differences are accented and whose boundaries with other groups are now changing and unclear. In a very important book published in 1995, Phillip Hughes, Craig Thomson, Roan Prior and Gary Bouma concluded their study of Australian spirituality and the churches in the 1990s, by saying:

> The major challenge is finding new ways of developing community in a society which is not at all sure what community is. The major challenge is identifying and naming the presence of God in our fragmented life, that the dynamic quest for faith might be sustained.[102]

There is an urgent necessity to reinvent what we mean by the church community.

Thirdly, there are real uncertainties as to how we may act Christianly and politically as citizens in this country and in our global environment. Sometimes

---

102 Hughes, P, Thompson, C, Pryor, C and Bouma, G, *Believe It or Not: Australian Spirituality and the Churches in the 90s*. This comment may be compared with David Tacey's 'The interaction between spirituality and religion is of necessity an explosive and emotional one, in which the progressive spirit of the new collides with the conservative spirit of tradition and its resistance to change'. Tacey, D, *Re-Enchantment: The New Australian Spirituality*, p 16.

discussion on this question is sharpened as if it is a choice between a Christendom mentality and a modern or post-modern mentality. But our own story as Australian Anglicans carries forward to the present situation complications which make that formulation far too simple and inadequate. There are deep ambiguities within our own understanding as to how we can commend and promote government, corporate and social policies and action in a way which is genuinely Anglican and genuinely Australian.

Each of these areas, which one might summarise as confidence, community and engagement, have deep and serious theological questions lying behind them. Those questions have to do with the way in which we interpret in the present the religious heritage of which Anglicans in modern Australia are not only the heirs but also the stewards.

In one sense both these questions, making sense of the present and interpreting the heritage, are secondary questions. The primary question is about the presence of God in this situation. How do we hear God? How do we see God? How do we feel the presence of God? How are our lives shaped, led, transformed, renewed by the living God? How shall we live so that we are able to pray, and how shall we pray so that we are able to live? This primary question stands behind and pervades the argument of this book. That argument is that we cannot properly confront our contemporary questions without going back to our tradition, but that in so doing we will need to rethink quite fundamentally the way in which that tradition has significance for us today. In the process of that reinventing, a re-examination of our tradition will, I believe, show that we have often neglected the baby and concentrated on the bath water. It is now about time for us to throw the bath water out and help the baby to grow to some contemporary maturity.

These challenges are not peculiar to Australian Anglicans. Anglicans throughout the world face similar questions. There are some shared elements in the stories of Anglicans around the globe, and there are common elements in the received heritage of Anglicanism. The issues illustrated in Australia have their parallels elsewhere. In that sense the fundamental theological task of interpretation needs to be conducted in conversation between Anglicans in these different locations around the globe if the necessary task of reinventing is to be effective or have an adequate level of integrity. It is to the development of that conversation in relation to the key issues of confidence, community and engagement that the next three chapters are devoted.

CHAPTER THREE

CONFIDENCE—PERSUASIVE RESONANCE

The issues of confidence

To this point I have argued that Anglicanism is best characterised as a tradition thought of as a conversation and rationality, a faith embodied in a community over time. Anglicanism has certain theological elements, one of which is a commitment to enmeshment in society. These qualities mean that the intersection with the contemporary social and cultural context is always a critical question. Because of the confused situation of the tradition, Anglicanism needs reinventing, and the issues most critical to that reinventing have to do with the nature of the community which embodies the tradition and their relationship to the historical realities of their lives. Their confidence to act and the pattern of interacting are critical. It is the issue of confidence to act to which we now turn.

Because I travel a good deal, I often find myself in social situations where I do not know the people. In these circumstances conversation is always tentative. Where it is clear that an extended conversation is likely to take place, where the participants are unknown to each other, or relatively unknown, people commonly ask questions in order to find points of connection. In many situations connections can be found, however indirect, and they encourage the conversation to develop and grow. It is only as we feel comfortable in the conversation that we gradually begin to reveal ourselves and those things which are important to us in terms of our opinions, values and beliefs. Our confidence to participate and speak about those things which are most important to us in our own lives often depends upon a sense of the acceptability of speaking about such things in the conversation. We wait to sense the tacit assumptions of the interchange.

Of course, that sort of conversation is not the only kind of conversation. We have all heard the radio interview where the journalist and the person being interviewed have quite different agendas. This is patently clear when politicians are being asked questions which they want to avoid. They simply have prepared what they want to say and, often without much reference to the question which has been asked, they say what they want to say. This is not really a conversation. It is a verbal encounter. In order to engage in that kind of encounter, the politician, or any person being interviewed, needs to be very determined and very confident, because they have to assert what they want to say in a context they see as unsympathetic, if not hostile. This kind of verbal encounter rarely persuades and is often simply part of an attempt to make a statement rather than actually have a conversation.

More relaxed interviews which are not necessarily about news items or public policy but are explorations about people's opinions, feelings and experience are quite different. During the 1990s Caroline Jones ran an extremely successful series of interviews on the Australian Broadcasting Corporation about the meaning of life. She interviewed prominent and interesting Australians in order to try and elicit from them what was important in their lives, what they believed, what they felt and what they were committed to. Those interviews were genuine encounters, to which many listeners responded. It was an exceedingly popular program. What was going on in the program was not simply the uncovering of the inner convictions and beliefs of prominent Australians but a mental conversation between the listener and the interviewee, because the life experience of the interviewee and the listener resonated. It was this resonance which made the program so successful.[103]

103 Jones, C, *The Search for Meaning: Conversations with Caroline Jones.*

These ordinary experiences of life illustrate the importance of the tacit assumptions in our social encounters. Indeed, such assumptions often cannot easily be articulated, yet they provide the basis for confidence in conversation. It is the disjunction between such tacit assumptions which causes hiccups and misunderstandings in our conversations with others.

The confidence with which a conversation can be conducted between people who disagree is directly related to their perceived sense of commonality, the degree to which they think of themselves and respect each other as fully human persons. Stephen Carter's *The Culture of Disbelief* (1993) analysed how in American public discussion, especially in law and politics, religious belief and religious devotion was trivialised. The political tradition of the USA cherishes religion, as indeed all matters of private conscience. The First Amendment, which separated church and state in America, now operates to make religion insignificant. It is not that it does not belong in the human condition but rather that it does not belong in the public discussion about the nature of civic life. Many people, Carter says, have come to view any kind of religious element in public debate as simply part of some conspiracy of the radical right to take over American public policy.

> In our sensible zeal to keep religion from dominating our politics, we have created a political and legal culture that presses the religious faithful to be other than themselves, to act publicly, and sometimes privately as well, as though their faith does not matter to them.[104]

Because religion is trivialised in this way, one would not dispute a religious conviction. According to Stephen Carter's argument, religious belief, for the purposes of public debate, is of a similar order to questions of taste about chocolate or the colour of a tie. Consequently, people of deep religious conviction have to behave in public and speak in public and often in their more private relationships as if those deep convictions were merely trivial.

According to Stephen Carter, the tacit assumptions of public debate have ruled out the notion that religious convictions are a serious matter. This public culture is a culture of disbelief.

---

104 Carter, S, *The Culture of Disbelief,* p 3.

Australia has its own particular version of this syndrome. It is less aggressive, but it is much longer running. In the middle of the nineteenth century in Australia there were some who argued that, because religion tended to have a sectarian and therefore socially divisive effect when it was introduced into politics or public life, it should not be the subject of public policy. That point of view has never really prevailed in Australia, and our laws and constitutions in general provide a significant place for religion as part of institutional life. But at the level of public culture there has been a long-running tacit assumption that religion does not exist as part of our public culture.

Writing in 1963 at the height of popular attendance at church services, A L Mcleod declared that religion 'has been singularly absent as a cultural force in Australia'.[105] He identified several reasons: the origins of the country as a convict settlement, the poor quality of the clergy in Australia (unintellectual, poorly educated and either unable or unwilling to write and to preach on matters of concern with conviction or originality), the church has kept separate from the state and from the mainstream of ideas in culture in general, clergy are not usually university educated and there has been no notable Australian theologian. While it would be possible to refute some of these claims, Macleod reflects a common Australian attitude that religion is really not part of public life or the public conversation. This is not because there are not many Australians with religious convictions. According to recent survey reports, eighty per cent of Australians believe in God and around twenty-five per cent of the population go to church regularly, and most of those say that their religious beliefs affect the way in which they live.

In Australia, the tacit assumption of public conversation is that religion is not really part of that conversation. By and large that tacit assumption has been accepted by religious people. The situation which Stephen Carter describes in the United States of America as a novel and unpleasant recent development is, in a lower key, a long-standing tradition in Australia.

Such tacit assumptions affect the way in which we come to interpret the role of social institutions. Social institutions assume connections between people. The

105 McLeod, A, *The Pattern of Australian Culture*, p 6.

institution of the family assumes certain kinds of connections between husband and wife and children. Those relationships have been changing in recent years. Because different kinds of assumptions are brought to bear, the relationships are presumed to have ethical values which in a previous generation they did not have.

The ethical values which the institutions once assumed and fostered are often forgotten because of the changed assumptions. Incest was once a significant and powerful taboo within the context of a set of assumptions about close and long-running family relationships. In a changed situation where family relations are much looser, incest becomes a question of sexual assault. Its taboo status and power has changed. Our recent preoccupation with paedophilia and the sexual harassment of children is a symptom of confusion about the kinds of assumptions which ought to operate in institutional kinship and nurture relationships. Institutions perform many functions, but one of the most important is to flag the assumptions which can be made in the activities that take place within the institution. Because it is clear that this is the way things are done, we are able to relate to others with some confidence. We can count on reasonably secure expectations.[106]

The difficulty in our present circumstance is that many of our shared assumptions are changing. Much of the discussion which goes under the heading of post-modernism has to do with rearranging these tacit assumptions which have previously been thought to hold our community together and provide the basis for our public conversation. In such a situation, people speak not just of one or two plausible arguments which could be identified and accepted in a conversation but rather of a plurality of plausibilities.[107] Thus the reason one might hold a particular conviction can be justified by a multiplicity of reasons, many of which will not be shared, because the assumptions which underlie them are not shared in modern society. In this context it is not surprising that people speak of truth being deregulated. What is really happening is that the shared tacit assumptions which enable us to conduct public conversations with confidence are changing. It is these changes which create much of the uncertainty which marks contemporary Australian society.

---

106 Nicolaus Luhmann has made this a central point in his major analytical work, *Social Systems*.
107 See the discussion in Biemer, G, 'Religious Education—A Task between Divergent Plausibilities'.

In such a circumstance it is easy to think that a public conversation which encompasses a large cross section of those who live in Australia is simply not possible, and so be tempted to withdraw into a discrete and narrow group. Sub-groups define themselves in this context by an increasingly narrow range of interests and values. People select into interest groups whose qualities are uni-directional and focus on the interests of that group. That tendency is a very considerable concern, not just for religious people. In her Boyer Lectures for the Australian Broadcasting Corporation, Eva Cox was preoccupied with this question. She spoke about social capital as being the residual power of the connections which we have among us as citizens. Bowling along on our own in a multiplicity of single-issue groups diminishes that public capital and creates a different kind of society.[108]

In such groups, which are singular in their interest and determinedly focused in their activities, the authority, power and confidence that is exercised is different from that which can operate in a more plural multi-directional public conversation. It is not surprising that religious groups are affected by this tendency and become sub-groups with this sort of authority, an authority which becomes singular, more focused and assertive. Such authority may be that of the teacher who preaches the word, the priest who administers the sacrament, the counsellor who defines experience, or the expert who has the secret knowledge which constitutes the basis of the group's integrity.

A great temptation in the age of uncertainty is to withdraw into such discrete groups. That process leads to an effective authority in group life which is more singular and authoritative than that which can effectively apply in a more plural interactive public conversation. That process magnifies social differences and individual incoherence.

Furthermore, when a church community allows itself to move into that mode of existence, it establishes a more profound dualism between the religious experience of its members on the one hand and the public and social life which those same people lead in other contexts. It is what Parker Palmer described as the loss of a capacity to cope with the company of strangers.[109] The process involves

---

108 Cox, E, *A Truly Civil Society*.
109 Palmer, P, 'The Company of Strangers: Christians and the Renewal of America's Public Life'.

not just a 'dumbing down' of our social skills but an erosion of the tacit assumptions upon which public conversation can be conducted.

If Australian Anglicans arrived at the end of the twentieth century already in some sense on the back foot because they found themselves relegated institutionally from a position of dominance and leadership to being just players in important areas of social life like education, relations with the state and public culture, then the temptation to withdraw is very powerful. In any withdrawing mode a significant conflict arises about the nature of authority for Australian Anglicans. If the style and mode of authority of the withdrawing group takes hold among Australian Anglicans, then the challenge to participate, let alone be effective in the public conversation of a modern plural society, becomes exceedingly difficult.

The constitution of the Anglican Church of Australia directs Australian Anglicans back to the Book of Common Prayer and the Thirty-nine Articles for their inherited notions of authority. These notions of authority relate not just to personal issues—indeed, not even primarily do they relate to these. The formularies are more concerned with institutional authority, including of course the institution of the biblical canon. Furthermore, these formularies were shaped in sixteenth- and seventeenth-century England in order to be instruments of a political enterprise. The political clothing of these formularies relates not just to what they say at various points about political matters, such as Article 37 on the civil magistrate. The conception of society, uniformity and the status of institutions are necessarily caught in the warp and woof of the political and social conceptions of the rulers. The issue for Anglicans since the Reformation, and certainly in Australia at the beginning of the twenty-first century, is how to deal with this tradition so as to be critically aware of the centralised top-down authority conceptions which have shaped these centrally important formularies. How can Anglicans avoid taking over the political ideology rather than the more considered religious and theological qualities which made the Reformation so significant. When we go beyond the sixteenth-century English Reformation to the New Testament, we do not find such a precise and narrow understanding of authority. That point is reinforced by recent theological work on the doctrine of the Trinity.

The New Testament and the English Reformation formularies are central to the history of Anglicanism, and Anglicans have been participants in the theological tradition. This means that they have been part of the formation of the Anglican tradition of Christianity. Furthermore, for the purposes of understanding the present situation of Anglicanism and its challenges, these are key appeals in the rhetoric that marks out the debate in contemporary Anglicanism and to which people look to defend their position. In seeking to revisit the Anglican tradition with a view to reinventing Anglicanism, I shall touch on each of these elements. It is not possible to revisit these elements in their entirety, but I have chosen aspects of them in order to highlight the issues before Anglicans at the present time. I want to conduct this visit in a 'tradition critical' vein. It is out of the tradition of their faith that Anglicans will find the tools and inspiration for reinventing, but they will only do so if the visit is critical and creative.

The New Testament—Paul in a plural society

Anyone reading the New Testament would quickly become aware that Jesus, Paul and other authors appeal to different considerations in different circumstances. The gospels describe Jesus as teaching with authority which was different from the authority of the Scribes and the Pharisees. Jesus' authority was marked by miraculous events. The actual content of his teaching was expressed in parables, stories and brief aphorisms. He declined to settle disputes but made statements which hung in the air waiting to be appropriated by those to whom they were often only indirectly addressed.

If one is to judge by results, Jesus was not particularly successful as a teacher. The disciples did not understand the miracles, failed to comprehend the parables and did not understand his intentions in going to Jerusalem. The gospel stories underline and repeat the difficulty which many people had in understanding the point of what Jesus was saying. However, all of this evidence cannot gainsay the fact that Jesus' teaching was nonetheless persuasive and compelling in a curious and almost uncanny fashion.

The difficulty is that Jesus often expressed himself according to assumptions which were not readily shared or understood by those with whom he spoke. His utterances on the family fall on uncomprehending ears not because they are not clear but because they are based upon assumptions which are different from those of his hearers.

Similarly with Paul, the arguments which he deployed in his letters often appealed to assumptions, principles and traditions which were not immediately either understood or shared by the recipients. We see Paul trying to overcome this problem in his letters. For example, when he wrote to Colossae, a place he had never visited, he sought to make connections. He passed on greetings to as many people as he could in order to establish his personal links with the Colossians. He also tried to establish common ground for his argument by expounding at the beginning of his letter what was almost certainly a common and shared Christian tradition about the person and work of Christ. As the argument in the letter proceeded he drew upon that shared material.

Much scholarship has been devoted in recent years to what has been called the rhetorical style of Paul's letters. One Christian group with which he spent a good deal of time and with whom he exchanged a number of letters was the Christian group in Corinth. Paul's letters to the Corinthians provide an admirable example for us, because in many ways the social circumstances of first-century Corinth resonate with the plural and cosmopolitan character of much of western society, including Australia.[110]

Old Corinth was destroyed by the Romans in 146 BCE, and it was not until 144 BCE that Julius Caesar ordered the city to be rebuilt as a Roman colony. It was populated by Caesar's veterans and Roman freedmen, who together constituted the citizen body. Greeks who remained in Corinth after it was rebuilt were resident aliens in the city and could not hold public office. Buildings in new Corinth followed the Roman pattern. It was a great centre of trade because its location gave it a pivotal role in the east–west trade of the Mediterranean world. There was some manufacturing in Corinth and many visitors. The Isthmian games were held there every two years and the Imperial games every four years. The Romans incorporated many of the Greek gods in their buildings in Corinth, and there was a profusion of cults and temples as a result. In Paul's time it was a bustling prosperous city with a population of some 70,000 or 80,000 people, with

---

110 On the social circumstances of Corinth at the time of Paul's mission see for example Witherington III, B, *Conflict and Community in Corinth: A Socio-Rhetorical Commentary on 1 and 2 Corinthians*, Marshall, P, *Enmity in Corinth: Social Conventions in Paul's Relations with the Corinthians*, and Vos, D, *Church and Community Conflicts: The Relationships of the Thessalonian, Corinthian, and Philippian Churches with Their Wider Civic Communities*.

rampant prosperity, social and religious diversity and confusion, and divisions of political and economic privilege. It was in many respects a difficult environment for the new Christian group.

Paul's first letter to the Corinthians is clearly a response to information which Paul had received from Corinth, probably by letter and probably also through some oral communications.[111] Throughout this letter his strategy clearly is that the Corinthian Christians should live a Christian life in the world but not be of it. That was a very risky strategy in Corinth because of the morally and religiously hostile environment of the city. However, that policy can be seen in Paul's approach to sexual matters, to family and marriage, and to civil relationships. His approach in this letter, as indeed in his other letters, is to engage with the context in which his readers are set. As a consequence, he often engages in an extremely subtle but effective way with the problem with which he is dealing.

In the first chapter of 1 Corinthians he is dealing with dissension of one kind or another, and lying behind this problem is some pretence on the part of the Corinthians which Paul interprets as a form of pride. He thus introduces his letter with a set of variations on the theme of wisdom and foolishness, power and weakness. But he does this in a sophisticated and rhetorical manner which would have been recognised by those Corinthians who were trained in rhetoric and, it would appear, were making much of their skill in Corinth and significantly contributing to the problems in the Corinthian church.

In other words, Paul interacts with the other orders of the world which are causing the difficulties for his readers in Corinth.

Underlying Paul's strategy are a number of convictions. The world had been prepared by God for the gospel which was now being proclaimed throughout the Mediterranean, the gospel which turns the world upside down. This gospel represents an order, a cosmos, which is different from the Roman and Greek cosmos in Corinth. Paul interacts with that other cosmos by the method of his writing. Further, Paul operates on the assumption that God is the agent of the faith of the Corinthians; there is nothing that they have that they have not been

---

111 See Hurd, J, *The Origin of 1 Corinthians for Various Partition Theories,* but see also Barrett, C, *A Commentary on the First Epistle to the Corinthians,* and Kaye, B, 'Paul and His Opponents in Corinth'.

given. The instruments of God's action are the gospel which Paul preaches, Paul's apostolic ministry, the ministry of Apollos, the Corinthian Christians themselves, the Corinthian group in its interactions, and the tradition which he himself has received and passed on to them. But at crucial points the decisive issue is the action of God in the lives of the individual Corinthians. Differences of capacity in the Corinthian congregation are not denied but rather affirmed by being described as gifts from God. The unity which Paul seeks in Corinth is a unity which is built upon the cohering presence of God in the diversity which God by his gifts creates and enables.

Underlying these instruments is something about the moral character of God and of his people: humility, faithfulness and wisdom enabling the Corinthian Christians to make judgments about their lives. In 1 Corinthians Paul is working out the meaning of belonging to Christ in the context of God's action in Corinth, and the touchstone of that action is clearly the character and presence of Christ.

If we stand back from this Corinthian situation and ask what the basis is of Paul's confidence in regard to his Christian faith in this plural environment in Corinth and how he seeks to deploy that in his letter to the Corinthian Christians, then the answer is certainly not singular and not even simple. There are clearly a number of interweaving considerations that provide Paul with a basis of confidence in his engagement with Corinthian society. He is confident about the wisdom of God as compared with the wisdom of humanity. He is confident about the moral values which he sees as being implicit in the Christian moral tradition in comparison to the values of the environment in Corinth. He is confident that the diversity in the Christian community in Corinth can be regarded as divine provision. He is confident that there is a hierarchy of value: love is more fundamental and more important than the gifts which are given, and therefore love should direct the exercising of those gifts. He is confident that the issue at stake in the Corinthian congregation is whether or not a stranger, when he walks in, perceives that God is present with them. In more general terms Paul's confidence appears to derive from a certainty about his connection with Jesus' death and resurrection through the tradition which he himself has received and through his own encounter with the risen Christ. He is similarly confident because of a sense of the present activity of God in his own life and in the lives of the Corinthians, whether that activity is described in terms of the gifts, the presence of the Spirit or the presence of the risen Christ. He is also confident that the Corinthian community is itself a mark of the presence of God.

These considerations operate on an axis between the past and the present and also on an axis between Paul, the Corinthian group and their fellow Corinthians. In the Corinthian correspondence there is an orientation to the future in terms of the development of the Christian maturity of the Christians in Corinth and also in terms of the behaviour that happens within the Christian congregation. The future is when all things will be fulfilled, and that fulfilment will incorporate Paul and the Corinthian Christians. It will be a time when Christ is all in all.

While there are clearly moral differences between the behaviour that is to be found in Corinth and the behaviour which Paul expects of the Christians in Corinth, there is no sense of a dualism between believer and unbeliever, between Corinth and the Corinthian church. There is no sense in which Paul wants the Corinthian Christians to withdraw from their engagement with the cosmopolitan and generally corrupt Corinthian society. Rather, this is a society in which God is yet at work, calling people to faith and sustaining the fabric of human society. The authority which Paul lives by and which he calls his Corinthian Christians to live by derives from an experience of the presence of God expressed in terms of Christ crucified and risen, and it is set in the light of the hope of the resurrection when Christ will be all in all. As well as that, there is a sense that the 'world' or cosmos in which Paul lived was a world which had been prepared for the gospel by the providential ordering of human history. Those twin principles provide the basis for commonality and differences between the Corinthian unbelievers and the Corinthian Christians, between Paul the Roman Christian and his fellow, unbelieving Roman citizens.

The elements which are highlighted by this cameo from the New Testament clearly raise fundamental questions about the central character of the Christian understanding of God and the nature of his sovereignty. It is with the issue of sovereignty that we now turn to the Reformation element in the Anglican tradition and rhetoric.

The Reformation

The English Reformation has been of continuing importance for Anglicans in Australia. This is clear not only in terms of their history, which saw Anglicanism established in Australia from the Church of England, but also in terms of the constitution of the Anglican Church of Australia. The Ruling Principles declare that the church is derived from the Church of England and 'retains and approves the doctrine and principles of the Church of England embodied in the Book of Common Prayer, together with the Form and Manner of Making, Ordaining and Consecrating of Bishops Priests and Deacons and in the Articles of Religion sometimes called the Thirty-nine Articles'. The Book of Common Prayer, which was created in the English Reformation, is regarded as the authorised standard of worship and doctrine in this constitution.

Apart from these historical and constitutional questions there is also the continuing personal perceptual connection. For many years Australians retained an attitude of respect and affection for things British because of the origins of the European settlement of Australia. Within Australian Anglicanism there is a similar strand of sentiment which attaches people to what has happened and what is happening in the Church of England. In varying forms these two elements appear in contemporary Anglicanism in many countries, and they present real ambiguities for the way in which we relate to the Reformation of the sixteenth century. It is in part for these historical reasons that Anglicans so often use the Reformation as part of their contemporary rhetoric, and for this reason it is important to see how relevant these Reformation formularies can be for the present situation of Anglicanism.

The context

In recent years the English Reformation has been the subject of intense historical scrutiny.[112] It is not my purpose to revisit the Reformation in general terms but rather the tacit assumptions of that packaging by which it has come down to Anglicans in the formularies. What was experienced in England in the sixteenth

---

112 There is a growing and substantial literature on this matter. Some introduction to it can be found in Haigh, C, *The English Reformation Revised*, Haigh, C, *English Reformations: Religion, Politics, and Society under the Tudors*, Collinson, P, 'The Elizabethan Church and the New Religion', Collinson, P, 'England', Guy, J, *Tudor England*, MacCulloch, D, *The Later Reformation in England*, MacCulloch, D, *Tudor Church Militant: Edward VI and the Protestant Reformation*.

century by the population, or by different sections of the population, is quite a different question. For example, in the mid-1530s Henry VIII established himself as the head of the church, and under that authority the spiritual government of the nation was to be in the hands of the bishops. They administered canon law, indeed Roman canon law, for the project to revise canon law was a much frustrated and delayed event. Those who were the recipients of the judgments of the bishops in matters of morals and other issues were not much affected by this transfer of power at the top. Monasteries, on the other hand, were dissolved but cathedrals were not. This may have been related to the retention of episcopacy for political and jurisdictional purposes, but its undoubted effect on the common was to remove the pastoral care exercised through the monasteries and chantries.

The common people were also affected by such innovations as an English Bible and changed liturgies. But even Cranmer's prayer book contained substantial resonances from the old services in the collects and prayers. True, the eucharistic theology was changed, as was also the funeral service. These changes in the prayer book clearly affected many people. After Henry's death the various institutional changes which he introduced undoubtedly influenced what Mary was able to do in seeking to reassert papal power in England. Similarly, what was done under Henry and Elizabeth undoubtedly affected the internalising of the reforming instincts into the more radical expression of the commonwealth period and under the later name of Puritanism. Even so, what the institutional changes almost certainly did was to make it impossible for Puritanism, or indeed papalism, to triumph. By a curious irony, these institutional developments almost certainly made it more likely that acceptable English religious practice would in the end be more comprehensive than Henry, Mary or Cranmer intended or imagined.

When Henry initiated his legislative changes in 1529, England had become a much more centralised state. Henry VII and Henry VIII had established a very significant degree of central control in English political life. That process echoed changes in Europe generally. Through the fifteenth and sixteenth centuries states and principalities were emerging which were more centrally controlled than previously.[113] This period prior to the Reformation witnessed an attempt to consolidate what Peter Brown has called mini Christendoms in western Europe

---

113 See the interesting comparison in the context of colonising the Americas in Veliz, C, *The New World of the Gothic Fox: Culture and Economy in English and Spanish America.*

into a more unified papal entity. The increasing ambition for centralised control on the part of the pope was itself part of a tendency reflected in the principalities of western Europe.

Many things in England inhibited the development of absolutism, even though Henry's policies clearly moved in that direction. Henry could not afford a standing army, a police force or a large standing bureaucracy. Communication within England hindered centralisation, and so local authority figures needed to be won to support the royal will. The common law tradition was still influential in England and constituted a significant brake on any absolutist royal authority. When Henry used parliament in his battle with the pope, in its turn parliament developed its own strengths. While it has often been remarked that Protestantism carried within it an assertion of individual responsibility and the power of an appeal to the individual conscience, that dissipating force was constantly held in check in England by the Reformation statutes and the actions of Henry, Edward, Mary and Elizabeth.

Tudor power was not as absolute as the political power of the prince in Castille. There a highly centralised political structure enabled the Reformation forces to be dispatched quickly. Tudor political power was also constrained by the influence of the northern humanist tradition and the conciliar movement. It is not surprising to find in the writings of Thomas Cranmer constant appeal for the principles of the conciliar movement to provide an alternative notion of church polity to the rising ambitions of papalism.

It is in this mixed context that Henry began his ambition to detach England from the power and reach of the pope.

The packaging

Many years ago Sir Maurice Powicke began his account of the Reformation in England with a famous statement:

> The one definite thing which can be said about the Reformation in England is that it was an Act of state. The King became the head of the church, the King in parliament gave a sanction to the revised organisation, formularies, liturgy, and even in some degree to the Doctrine of the Church. The King's council and ministers took cognisance over ecclesiastical affairs. The King cooperated with the

bishops, in the government of the Church, and he appointed commissions to determine appeals in ecclesiastical cases. All this amounted to a revolution.[114]

First made in 1941, this account would now need some different nuances in the light of recent historical work. Nonetheless, its bald statement of the point highlights a significant issue for us in regard to the kind of authority that is implied in the documents of the English Reformation. Of course, there were theological and religious impulses at work in the Reformation in England, and a good deal of those forces related the English Reformation to the religious revival which was going on in parts of continental Europe. However, in England the institutional changes were brought about by government. Those changes were not always introduced for purely religious purposes. Religion and politics mutually coalesced in a way which is hard to grasp for those nurtured in a modern plural culture. The methods by which the Reformation was effected through legislation have shaped the way in which the Reformation has influenced subsequent generations even to our own day. They are in fact embedded in the 1962 constitution of The Anglican Church of Australia by its commitment to the 1662 Book of Common Prayer.

It is often suggested that the action of Martin Luther in nailing his ninety-five theses to the door of the Schlosskirche at Wittenberg marked the beginning of the European Reformation. The following year Zwingli began work in Zurich, and in 1519 he publicly denounced indulgences. In 1520 Luther was excommunicated at the Diet of Worms, and a year later Henry VIII was made defender of the faith by the pope for his defence of what seemed to be orthodoxy against the teachings of Martin Luther. England and its king certainly were not early starters in the Reformation which began in German-speaking Europe.

In 1526 a reformation commenced in Denmark, and in the same year Tyndale published his new translation of the New Testament. Four years later in 1530 the Confession at Augsburg established a degree of collaboration among the reforming movements in continental Europe. It was in 1531 that things began to move in England in the direction which would lead to an English Reformation.

---

114 Powicke, M, *The Reformation in England,* p 1.

Legislation in England began in 1532. Throughout, the legislation of Henry VIII was directed primarily to the assertion of the supremacy of the crown in England over all authorities and jurisdictions, particularly external forces and powers. In 1532 the clergy submitted to the king and undertook to make no new canons in Convocation. They further submitted that the canons which had been previously made in the Convocation would go to a committee for revision. In that same year an Act to provide for the conditional restraint of Annates was passed. In this Act we find the first clear statement of a new doctrine of the Royal Supremacy. This Act sought to address what was portrayed as a problem of large sums of money being paid to Rome in connection with the appointment of bishops. Where a new bishop entered upon his bishopric, so-called 'first-fruits' of the income attaching to those bishoprics were paid to the pope. The Act refers to a sum of one hundred and sixty thousand pounds being paid in this connection since the time of Henry VII. The Act asserts that the king and all his subjects,

> as well spiritual as temporal, be as obedient devout catholic and humble children of God and Holy Church as any people within any realm christened.[115]

Nonetheless, the financial burden was too great, and the Act abolished the payments. Furthermore, authority was given to archbishops to consecrate in England those who had been restrained in Rome from gaining admission to their bishoprics. This Act authorised the consecration of archbishops in England by two bishops, as in ancient time.

In February 1533 an act for the restraint of appeals to the pope was passed. In the preliminary recital of this Act the full doctrine of the Royal Supremacy is expounded and justified. It is this Act which initiates Henry's unilateral declaration of independence from the pope. Clearly he had an interest in restraining appeals where it looked as if his divorce problem was not going to be settled in Rome. Just as clearly this Act reflects the growing political theory that motivated Tudor political life.

> Where by diverse sundry old authentic histories and chronicles, it is manifestly declared and expressed, that this realm of England is an

---

115 Gee, H and Hardy, J, *Documents Illustrative of English Church History*, p 180.

empire, and so hath been accepted in the world, governed by one supreme head and king, having the dignity and royal estate of the imperial crown of the same, unto whom a body politic, compact of all sorts and degrees of people divided in terms and by names of spirituality and temporality, be bounden and ought to bear, next to God, a natural and humble obedience: he being also institute and furnished, by the goodness and sufferance of almighty God, with plenary, whole, and entire power, pre-eminence, authority, prerogative and jurisdiction, to render and yield justice, and final determination to all manner of folk, residents, or subjects within this his realm, in all causes, matters debates, and contentions, happening to occur, insurge or begin within the limits thereof, without restraint, or provocation to any foreign princes or potentates of the world . . .[116]

The 'body spiritual' referred to here is the English church, which it is said has been sufficiently endowed and is sufficiently numerous and skilled to carry out all of the responsibilities that might fall upon an ecclesiastical body in England. The temporal is similarly described as having the capacity to try the property of lands and goods and to conserve the people of this realm in unity and peace. Both these authorities, spiritual and temporal, join together in the due administration of justice the one to help the other.

The theory is crystal clear from this Act. The body politic is an empire, the head of which is the godly prince, and within the empire there are two jurisdictions, temporal and spiritual, which together work for the administration of justice and the promotion of civil order. The Act says that only sentences in the king's courts can have effect in England, the king's courts, of course, comprehending both ecclesiastical and temporal matters. Clergy are to celebrate the services, notwithstanding any attempted constraint from the Bishop of Rome, and no appeals are to be sought to the Bishop of Rome. Indeed, all appeals are to be held within the realm of England, and there are various courts for dealing with such appeals.

The Act casts its net widely, as if there is more than one essential point at issue here.

---

116 Gee, H and Hardy, J, *Documents Illustrative of English Church History*, p 187.

All causes testamentary, causes of matrimony and divorces, rites of tithes, oblations and obventions (the knowledge whereof by the goodness of princes of this realm, and by the laws and customs of the same, pertaineth to the spiritual jurisdiction of this realm) already commenced, moved, depending, being, happening or hereafter coming in contention, debate or question within this realm, or within any of the king's dominions, or marches or the same, or elsewhere, whether they concern the King our sovereign lord, his heirs and successors, or any other subjects or residents within the same, of what degree soever they be shall be from henceforth heard, examined, discussed clearly, finally and definitively, adjudged and determined within the king's jurisdiction and authority and not elsewhere, in such courts spiritual and temporal of the same, as the natures, conditions, and qualities of the causes and matters aforesaid in contention, or hereafter happening in contention, shall require . . .[117]

In the following year an Act was passed in regard to the Submission of Clergy and the further restraint of appeals. According to this Act, a Convocation could only properly be assembled by the king's writ, and the clergy shall not enact without the king's consent. No canons will be passed by Convocation against the king's prerogative, and there will be no appeals to Rome.

The royal power was further consolidated in the same year with seven more Acts. Two concerned the Succession, one established the validity of Ann Boleyn as queen and declared void the marriage of Catherine, according to the judgment of the Archbishop of Canterbury, who was supported in this by the clergy and Convocation. It further established Elizabeth as the heir, failing male issue from the marriage. The second Succession Act confirmed these details. Two Acts concerned the appointment of bishops. The first was the Ecclesiastical Appointments Act, which forbad any archbishop being presented to Rome for any kind of confirmation or appointment, and further provided that the election of bishops and archbishops could only take place on the king's nomination. The second Appointments Act dealt with suffragan bishops. The clergy were obliged by a further Act to abjure any kind of papal supremacy.

117 Gee, H and Hardy, J, *Documents Illustrative of English Church History*, p 189.

From the point of view of political theory underlying this Reformation, the key legislation was the Supremacy Act, passed in November 1534. It declared that the king's majesty justly and rightfully is and ought to be the supreme head of the Church of England and is recognised by the clergy in this realm in their Convocations. However, in order to confirm and to remove any kind of doubt,

> be it enacted by authority of this present parliament, that the King our sovereign lord, his heirs and successors, kings of this realm, shall be taken, accepted and reputed the only supreme head in earth of the Church of England, called *anglicana ecclesia*.[118]

This Act went on to annex to the crown all the titles, privileges, jurisdictions and authorities associated with the church.

By these Acts Henry established his complete independence from the pope, established an entire system of appeals within England, and established himself as the supreme head of the country and the parts of the country, spiritual and temporal.

As if to confirm his total supremacy in all matters spiritual and temporal, Henry issued royal injunctions to the clergy in 1536 and 1538. When he did this in 1536, it was the first time he had acted without the consent of Convocation. The clergy were directly instructed by the king to observe all of the anti-papal laws and to observe the Royal Supremacy. They were told to explain the Ten Articles, which had just been passed by the Convocation. The second set of injunctions in 1538 carried on this tradition and, among other things, instructed that the great Bible should be set up in all the churches. Here was the king instructing the clergy in relation to religious matters as the head of the church.

While Henry's Reformation legislation may have been aimed at establishing independence from papal power, this dramatic change was carried forward according to a revolutionary political theory of Royal Supremacy in England. Previously in Europe princes and kings had often declined to accept the pope's authority on a number of matters. The pope had often sought submission from princes but by no means always successfully. Nonetheless, there had always been a degree of independence for the ecclesiastical domain in its relation to the pope.

---

118 Gee, H and Hardy, J, *Documents Illustrative of English Church History*, p 243.

Now Henry established a complete empire in England with the crown at the pinnacle.

The reign of Edward VI brought different kinds of problems, and the Reformation legislation under Edward was not so much about restricting papal power in England; that had been achieved by Henry. Legislation in the reign of Edward was about religion within England, and it is in this time that a Book of Common Prayer was produced and an argument for a new form of liturgical life in the Church of England was established. The first Act of Uniformity of Edward in 1549 was passed in January, and the prayer book to which this Act referred was established by subsequent Acts. Trouble was taken in the opening section of this Act to provide a rationale for this new approach. It declared that for a long time there had been different kinds of common prayer, commonly called the Service of the Church. There had been the uses of Salisbury, York, Bangor, Lincoln, as well as other diversities of form and fashion which had been used in the cathedral and parish churches in England and Wales. This diversity had applied both to morning and evening prayer and to the service of the holy communion and also in the administration of other sacraments of the church. Attempts had been made by public authorities to restrict innovations or new rites, but without a lot of success. Therefore the king expressed his clemency in not punishing those who had offended in this situation because of the good intentions of those involved. However the Archbishop of Canterbury was appointed with certain others to draw up one

> convenient and meet order, rite, and fashion of common and open prayer and administration of the sacraments to be had and used in his majesties realm of England and in Wales . . .[119]

The intention is not simply to honour God but also to bring about a

> great quietness, which by the grace of God shall ensue upon the one and uniform rite and order in such common prayer and rites and external ceremonies to be used throughout England and in Wales . . .[120]

The Act anticipates that the book will commend itself to many but nonetheless provides that all ministers after the next feast of Pentecost must use the book and

119 Gee, H and Hardy, J, *Documents Illustrative of English Church History*, p 359.
120 Gee, H and Hardy, J, *Documents Illustrative of English Church History*, p 360.

no other. Furthermore, no person shall speak against the book or anything contained in it. Offences would be subject to sanctions in the courts, and those sanctions are spelled out.

Edward's Act of Uniformity established a new principle, that all in the Church of England must pray in the same way and use the same words out of the same book. It was as revolutionary a principle for the establishment of 'quietness' as was the revolutionary political theory of the Royal Supremacy. However, it did naturally flow from that theory. Once a political entity was established on a supreme and singular authority, then the degree of diversity which could be tolerated within the realm must inevitably be drastically diminished. Where religion was so much part and parcel of the fabric of life, then diversity in religious practices, chiefly in public or open prayer, would necessarily need to be brought into some kind of uniformity.

The Second Act of Uniformity (1552) compelled people to go to church on Sundays and holy days on pain of ecclesiastical censure. Because doubts had arisen in some quarters in regard to the previous prayer book, a new 1552 Prayer Book was published, and clergy were required to explain the book and its meaning to people.

Henry established control over the church by a singular political theory of total royal supremacy. Edward established a uniformity within that supremacy in relation to the way in which people must practise their religion.

Of course, much of this was reversed in the reign of Mary but re-established under Elizabeth I. However, Elizabeth's legislation was aimed more precisely and distinctly at dissent. Very quickly after she came to the throne, Elizabeth issued a proclamation forbidding preaching other than on the set gospel and epistle for the day, clearly an attempt to constrain political preaching. A set of injunctions, which were probably prepared by Lord Cecil, was ready in June 1559 for visitors to take around to the churches. It was a very lengthy set of injunctions given directly from the authority of the crown.

Elizabeth's Supremacy Act in 1559 restored the situation from the time of Henry. All foreign authority in the queen's dominions was abolished. Spiritual and ecclesiastical authorities were annexed to the crown. The crown was declared to have authority to assign commissioners for various ecclesiastical and other purposes, and an oath of supremacy of the crown was required.

This section of the Act shows how, once uniformity is made the requirement of the political theory, then the criteria for orthodoxy within a Christian faith which has obviously broader and catholic connotations needs to be carefully established. The criteria identified in this Act for judging heresy were Scripture and the first four general councils or parliament with the assent of Convocation. Elizabeth's Act of Uniformity in 1559 re-established the prayer book of Edward VI, with some alterations and additions. As time went by, Elizabeth found it necessary to legislate against Jesuits (1585), Puritans (1593) and Recusants (1593). Elizabeth also had to take administrative steps to restrain prophesying. Indeed, she placed the Archbishop of Canterbury under close house arrest for not taking what she judged to be adequate steps to contain such activity. The point at issue was not an estimate of the religious value of such meetings but an awareness of the political potential of such religious justification for diversity and dissent.

The proclamation of James I for the Book of Common Prayer in 1604 incorporated the result of the Hampton Court Conference and proceeded along the same lines as Elizabeth. James was concerned to establish uniformity, particularly against Puritans from the north. However, in this case his instrument is not a tested orthodoxy but the office of the bishop. Barlowe, reflecting at least a contemporary perception, reported the king as saying of the Puritans

> that they aymed at a Scottish Presbytery, which, sayth he, as well agreeth with a monarchy, as God and the divell. Then Jack and Tom, and Will and Dick, shall meete, and at their pleasure censure me and my councill, and all our proceedings.[121]

And then, turning to the bishops, the king said, 'If once you were out, and they in place, I know what would become of my supremacie. No Bishop, no king.' Elizabeth would have sympathised with James.

The Reformation legislation again appeared in the time of Charles II after the Restoration following the eighteen years of Civil War and the Commonwealth. Charles's instrument, like that of James, was the institution of episcopacy. He

---

121 I Barlowe, *The Summe and Substance of the Conference*, London, 1604, p 83, quoted from W K Jordan, *The Development of Religious Toleration in England from the Accession of James I to the Convention of the Long Parliament (1603–1640)*, London, 1936, p 19. For a critical appraisal of these events see M H Curtis, 'The Hampton Court Conference and Its Aftermath', *History*, Vol. XLVI, 1961, pp 1ff.

ordered the Savoy Conference to be held in order to consider the prayer book. The 1552 Prayer Book was revised and changed on a number of points and then incorporated into an Act of Uniformity in 1662. Clergy were to take an oath to use only the Book of Common Prayer and to assert that there was no claim upon them from the solemn league and covenant from the time of the Commonwealth. A new element in the Act of Uniformity was introduced. It required that only episcopally ordained clergy were to hold office. Those in office who were not episcopally ordained or did not manage to obtain episcopal ordination would be deposed. None but episcopally ordained people were to be admitted to any office. The Act provided an exception for 'foreigners or aliens of the foreign reform churches allowed or to be allowed by the King's Majesty, his heirs and successors in England'.

Now, for the first time in the Church of England, an Act of Uniformity required that all clergy holding any office must be episcopally ordained. That, of course, does not mean that previously clergy were not episcopally ordained. It was clearly designed to deal with the consequences of the Commonwealth period. Large numbers of clergy declined to be so re-ordained and were ejected. The political character of this action can be seen in subsequent Acts dealing with the problem of dissent. The Five Mile Act (1665), the First and the Second Conventicle Act (1670) and a Test Act (1673) all moved in this direction. They were designed to enforce uniformity against 'the growing and dangerous practices of seditious sectaries and other disloyal persons who under the pretence of tender consciences, have or may have at their meetings contrive insurrections . . .' (Second Conventicle Act). [122]

The legislation of Henry VIII was aimed at papal power in England and sought to remove it. It did so by the establishment of a new and revolutionary theory of the Royal Supremacy. It placed the king in total control of both temporal and spiritual aspects of society. Legislation under Edward was directed towards uniformity of religious practice and the establishment of only one prayer book, which was legally enforced. The legislation under Elizabeth was aimed at re-establishing independence from the pope and at containing dissent. It repeated the political theory of Henry and provided an Act of Uniformity for a single prayer book. She acted in turn against dissenting groups such as Jesuits, Recusants

122 Gee, H and Hardy, J, *Documents Illustrative of English Church History*, p 623.

and Puritans but also against the practice of religious exercises which had the potential for encouraging diversity and dissent. In the seventeenth century the instrument used to maintain uniformity was a particular theory of episcopal ministry which sat comfortably with the singular notion of the authority of the crown. These various steps arise from and reflect a fundamental political theory of authority which was lodged in the institutional arrangements of the English Reformation by Henry VIII.

The basis of authority which is implied in these institutional arrangements contains a number of important elements, the most important of which was lay supremacy. Claire Cross has described the period up until 1660 in relation to church and people in England as the triumph of the laity in the English Church.[123] In the reign of Henry, the laity were represented by the godly prince. This was reflected in the legislation and in the Erastianism of Thomas Cranmer his archbishop. In his last days Cranmer even went so far as to admit that potentially Nero could in some sense have been regarded as in the position of a godly prince.[124]

The Reformation legislation under Henry did provide for spiritual power, and the king, of course, did not consecrate, ordain or conduct ecclesiastical tasks of this kind. However, Henry did directly intervene and instruct clergy with his injunctions, just as Elizabeth acted decisively against Archbishop Whitgift when he refused to restrain prophesying. The ideal of the godly prince was one tradition of thought which is reflected in these Reformation settlements. Another is that of corporate authority, which went back to the conciliar theory which was developed in the fourteenth century particularly over against the increasing claims of papal power. In 1543 Henry even entertained the possibility of a full ecumenical council being sponsored by the English Church.[125] The conciliar theory implied an authority which was more corporatist and dispersed in character than could sit comfortably with the Tudor notion of the authority of the prince, but it underlay much of English religious thought in regard to authority in the church and was a continuing theme in the developing opinions of Thomas Cranmer.

When the power struggles turned from the external opponent of the pope to internal domestic struggles, then a strategy of uniformity, enforced by means of

---

123 Cross, C, *Church and People 1450–1660: The Triumph of the Laity in the English Church.*
124 MacCulloch, D, *Thomas Cranmer: A Life*, p 577.
125 MacCulloch, D, *Thomas Cranmer: A Life*, p 346.

one prayer book in the reign of Edward VI, was employed. This stratagem was revisited in 1662 in more extreme form. A second strategy to maintain a singular royal power was episcopacy, which was seen as a more reliable institution of authority than Presbyterianism. It is well illustrated in the exchange between James I and the Puritans at the Hampton Court Conference.

The point of the king's remarks in this conference is not that he particularly favours the bishops for their personal or religious qualities but rather that he saw that, if his own authority was to be maintained in a singular form as the supreme governor, then he must have subsidiary authorities cast in the same authority mould. Episcopacy could fulfil that requirement. The same logic derivatively applied in the Restoration settlement when ministers who were not episcopally ordained were deprived of their livings.

While these political theories of singular authority and uniformity are the categories by which the English Reformation was effected, a previously existing and enduring theme was that of lay dominance in the affairs of the Christian community, that is to say, in the church. After the Restoration, lay control began to move from the crown to parliament. In the period 1640–60 lay domination of affairs secured itself, partly as a reaction to the experience under Archbishop Laud and partly from the experience of dissent and diversity during the Commonwealth period.

Thus a curious situation arose for the parliament of 1661. This was essentially a Protestant, or evangelical, parliament. However, even though the parliament passed the Act of Uniformity in 1662, they found that they could not control all, and a good deal of dissent remained after the 1662 Act. That process moved on in parliament after 1662, so Claire Cross is able to say:

> By 1714, if not by 1689, the triumph of the laity in the English church had involved the recognition in the counties as well as at Westminster, of the legality of diversity in religious allegiance. The laity had made good their superiority in the national church; some laymen, more precariously but as it proved permanently, had also established their right to live outside its bounds: an age of religious pluralism has begun.[126]

---

126 Cross, C, *Church and People 1450–1660: The Triumph of the Laity in the English Church*, p 242.

Indeed. However, it was not essentially a new age but rather a return to a former period before the impact of Tudor political theory.

In a sense, the English Reformation was an exercise in a political theory of singular imperial authority. It was also an experiment in a notion of conformity enforced by law, by the Book of Common Prayer and by an episcopal order of ministry. But in the end, this experiment did not work, and the issue returned to one of growing diversity and of lay control. Diversity meant, however, a change in the character of parliament, and this in the end demanded a reconception of the lay element in the life of the church. In England this was the struggle of the nineteenth and twentieth centuries. The settlement that exists in the Church of England today continues that unresolved dynamic.

But to return to the Reformation. What were the theological issues at stake in these various forms of the Reformation settlement in the Church of England? And how do they relate to the political legal instruments of the Reformation? The religious substance of the English Reformation, in the end, is not found in the political assumptions about authority, power, conformity or institutional absolutisms of the legislation. The real substance lies in the theological interpretation that is to be found in attempts to legitimate what happened during the Reformation and in the motivating convictions of ordinary people, because these arguments attempt to bring the Reformation novelties into relation with the enduring religious traditions of the English people.

The significance of the English Reformation

Among the key players at the time of the English Reformation there were manifestly different perceptions as to what was really going on and what was at stake. Thomas More was compliant to a great degree, but in the end even he could not accept the king as the supreme governor in the church, and he died for his faith on that point. Thomas Cranmer worked assiduously through the reign of Henry VIII and Edward VI but, in the end, at the hands of Queen Mary, died for the faith he had pursued. There were those who pursued a radical reformist interpretation and sought to go beyond anything that was proposed in the Tudor legislation. From their point of view the Reformation in England did not go far enough. There were those who sought to regard the changes as simply being a matter of shifting to the crown the power which had been inappropriately arrogated to itself by the papacy. Then, of course, there were the Roman

Catholics, particularly the Jesuits, who saw the English Reformation as a schism from the true church.

These different pictures of the English Reformation provide the context into which the most enduringly successful interpreter of the English Reformation addressed his writings. Richard Hooker published his *Laws of Ecclesiastical Polity* at the end of the sixteenth century, though the later books (6–8) were not published until later in the seventeenth century.[127] Book 8 is concerned with the Royal Supremacy. In particular, it is concerned to address those who claim that the power of ecclesiastical dominion, which the Reformation laws gave to the king, should not be given to a civil prince or governor. The law being referred to here is the Elizabethan Act of Supremacy of 1559, but it echoes the Supremacy Act of Henry VIII.

Up until the end of the sixteenth century most defences of the Royal Supremacy had been based upon an appeal to the tradition of a godly prince. Imagery was drawn from the Old Testament to claim that the godly prince was appointed to his position by God and that this justified the sort of power which Henry and Elizabeth took to themselves.

It is striking to put Hooker's interpretation of the Royal Supremacy in that context, for he does not base his understanding on that principle at all. Hooker assumes, with his contemporaries, an identity of membership between the church and the commonwealth. That point of view could have been accepted by those who supported an autocratic king, by those who stood for a papalistic interpretation and also by the disciplinarians, or Puritans. All of these could, and did, appeal to Scripture and church tradition. The problem was to show exactly how these two communities, religious, and civil, were indeed one. Hooker argued that the church was a species of a more general concept of body politic and that it was distinguished from others by being committed to the highest aim of all human associations, namely the glory of God. It was committed to true religion.

Hooker was of course aware that religious consensus within a commonwealth

---

127 The details are set out in the new critical edition, Speed Hill, W E, *The Folger Library Edition of the Works of Richard Hooker*.

could not always be assumed. He noted that in the Roman Empire before the time of Constantine there was no religious consensus in favour of Christianity. In that context, according to Hooker, the civil ruler had no legislative authority in religious matters. In this, however, Hooker was clearly addressing himself to the situation in front of him and seeking to develop an interpretation which enabled him to justify the claims of the Royal Supremacy from a theological point of view. His argument is essentially that the society in which that claim was being made was a Christian society, and for that reason the ruler of that society had a proper role in authority over both the civil and spiritual subsets within the commonwealth.

However, having said that, Hooker then goes on to list a series of qualifications which brings his commitment to the Royal Supremacy in any enduring sense into the most substantial doubt. In chapter 2 of Book 8 he mentions three limitations on this religious supremacy. It is obvious to him that the king must be subject to God, 'For what man is there so brainsick as to except in such speeches *God* himself, the King of all the kings of the earth?' (3:332.9–19). More than that, Hooker declares that the Royal Supremacy is not a matter of divine appointment.

> As for supreme power in ecclesiastical affairs, the word of God doth nowhere appoint that all Kings should have it, neither that any should not have it. For which cause it seemeth to stand altogether by human right that under Christian Kings there is such dominion given. (3:335.5–9)

Hooker contrasts the authority of the king with the authority which Christ has. First, the king's authority is subordinate in order to the authority of Christ. Second, the king's authority extends no further than a particular time or space; it only operates within the realm over which the king rules. That is not true of Christ's headship. Third, Christ rules inwardly by grace, whereas the Christian ruler exercises a purely external and instrumental headship.

According to Hooker, the king's rule is also subject to law. 'The grant of any favour made contrary to law is void' (3:342.20–21). It is not easy to tell at this point in his argument whether Hooker is describing what he thinks is actually the case in Tudor England or whether he is seeking to interpret and influence that situation by a rhetorical description. On balance, it seems to me that Hooker is probably trying to change the way in which his contemporaries understand the

Royal Supremacy. Either way, what Hooker clearly believes is that the royal authority is subject to law.[128]

The Royal Supremacy is also qualified in relation to the community, which, according to Hooker, is the original subject of political power. 'God creating mankind did endue it naturally with full power to guide itself in what kind of societies it should soever choose to live' (3.1:3:334.8–10).

It is manifest from this interpretation of the Royal Supremacy that Hooker is prepared to legitimate the Reformation legislation but is not prepared to indicate that he believes that is the way—and certainly not the only way—in which a Christian might approach such matters. Indeed, it is a very clear example of applied theology. He addresses a specific situation and seeks to provide a theological rationale. That theological rationale, however, makes it clear that in the long term he is not absolutely committed to the Royal Supremacy as it was expressed in the Tudor legislation. The fact that he includes the whole community as the source of the authority makes his account of supreme political authority, in the words of A S McGrade, 'Progressive in the long term but in the short term conservative'.[129] I would put it this way: Hooker thought that the Elizabethan settlement in its place was theologically defensible, but he did not believe in it in any fundamental sense.

Hooker touches on issues of authority in a number of contexts throughout the *Ecclesiastical Laws*. In Book 1, in his treatment of providence, he gives authority to history and tradition. There he argues that what pertains should be regarded as having *a priori* an assumption in its favour unless there are good reasons to show that it 'works to the ill'. The strong emphasis on consensus and continuity gives to Hooker not only an apparently conservative point of view but a point of view which, in its underlying theoretical terms, yields only a contingent authority to any particular example. No single authority in a historical context could ever claim to be absolute or permanent or universal.

There is a strong theme throughout the whole of the *Ecclesiastical Laws* on the grace of God, and particularly the grace of God in relation to worship. The

---

128 See the commentary by A S MacGrade in Speed Hill, W E, *The Folger Library Edition of the Works of Richard Hooker*, vol VI, Part 2, p 997, and MacGrade's introductory essay in vol VI Part 1, pp 364ff.

129 Speed Hill, W E, *The Folger Library Edition of the Works of Richard Hooker*, Vol VI, Part 1, p 380.

incarnation is a statement of God's saving of human beings. Because Hooker conceives of salvation as being in Christ, the sacraments take on a very significant role. They represent the incarnational principle of salvation to which he is committed. It is at this point that he comes closest to John Calvin's notion of salvation as being in Christ.[130]

This attitude towards tradition, understanding and law lies behind his constant appeal to public argument as a way of resolving differences. It is in that spirit that he appeals for debate with the Puritans to take place in the universities. In the universities there is the occasion and the opportunity for informed scholarly public argument. Steven McGrade suggests that Hooker's belief in the possibilities of education 'suggest active sympathy with renaissance assertions of the dignity of human nature'.[131]

Hooker is a very good example of the kind of tradition critical approach which I wish to espouse in this book. He clearly seeks to address the actual historical situation of his time and to do that in a way which is properly theological. He is committed to the authority of Scripture, to the early church's examples and to tradition. He is committed to the authority of the church community as a whole and therefore seeks for consensus. But what is justified in one particularity does not necessarily mean that it will be justifiable elsewhere or at a subsequent time or in a preceding time in the same locality. Where, for example, the religious consensus had broken down, then Hooker clearly would have taken the view that the civil authority ought to have no authority in religious matters in the community. In his only briefly published introduction to Hooker's edition, Pusey tried to deal with the problem of the mid-nineteen-century problem of a supreme parliament which was no longer a Christian body and yet retained the form of political supremacy over the church. He tried to deal with this by reference to an absolute and continuing place for the office of episcopacy, and he had the greatest difficulty enrolling Hooker to his cause—not surprisingly, since Hooker did not share such a view of episcopacy. If Pusey had concentrated on the contingent justification of the Royal Supremacy rather than the office of episcopacy and apostolic succession, he would have been able to enrol Hooker in his cause, but

---

130 For a discussion of Calvin in this respect see McGrath, A, *Iustitia Dei: A History of the Christian Doctrine of Justification.*
131 Speed Hill, W E, *The Folger Library Edition of the Works of Richard Hooker*, Vol VI, Part 2, p 380.

he missed this really radical aspect of Hooker's theory and it is not surprising that his introduction was not reprinted in subsequent editions.[132]

Conclusions

What, then, are we to make of the English Reformation and the continuing impact of the Reformation documents in Anglicanism? Whatever the Reformation in England was, it was a very mixed event. At the political level it was marked by the ambition of the monarchs. That is true of Mary, Henry and Elizabeth. Each in their own way sought to establish what they believed to be right. The ambitions of each were put in place by legal measures. In the case of the Reformation of Henry and Elizabeth this involved legislation which provided for independence from the pope for Royal Supremacy within the realm, and for uniform worship.

These legislative moves implied very particular ideas about authority and ecclesiology. Authority in this legislation is singular, coercive and top down. In other words, it mirrored the kind of authority to which it was opposed in the rising papalism that was emanating from Rome. In terms of ecclesiology it supported episcopacy, because it was an office capable of expressing the same kind of singular authority and because of the political need for control. Religious orders and monastic houses were abolished, not just because they were said to be corrupt. Perhaps some were, but the political problem was that they provided an alternative idea of Christian community and authority to episcopacy and to the diocesan organisation which was the expression of episcopal rule. The ordained ministry eventually was narrowed as a matter of legislative principle to episcopally ordained priests.

Church membership in this legislation was of course co-terminus with citizenship, because England was conceived of as a Christian country ruled over by a godly prince. The church was therefore national and, furthermore, self-reliant. It had the resources to sustain its own life. Control in the church belonged in lay hands, whether in the first instance with the king and crown or later, in the seventeenth century, in the parliament. At the political level, therefore, there is a very clear profile on issues of authority reflected in the legislation and the Prayer Book, Articles and Ordinals which are attached to that legislation.

---

132 Pusey, E, *The Works of That Learned and Judicious Divine, Mr Richard Hooker: with an Account of His Life and Death by Isaac Walton.*

However, the social reality was something different. There was always some diversity in England, even throughout the whole of the Reformation period. There was always some connection beyond the borders of England. Contact was maintained with continental churches before, during and after the Reformation. There was continuing residual appeal throughout the Reformation period to conciliar notions of ecclesial authority; one sees that not least in the writings of Thomas Cranmer. There was pastoral care in spiritual life outside the organisational lines of the diocesan and parish system, principally through the religious orders. So the legislation does not tell the whole story by any means at all. More than that, the significance or legitimation of the terms of the legislation, such as is offered by Richard Hooker, is vastly more open-textured than the political theory implied in the legislation.

This complex situation creates a significant problem for Anglicanism. This is especially so for those parts of Anglicanism which are constitutionally committed to the Reformation formularies which have come down to us via the legislative model. Subsequent Anglican polity has been significantly influenced by the Elizabethan settlement in attempts to understand how the church might arrange its affairs. This is particularly so in Australia. At their conference in 1850, the Australian bishops struggled with the Royal Supremacy and tried to understand their situation in terms of spiritual and temporal affairs in the church. Effectively they were internalising into the church community the terms and categories which had been used to describe the nation of Tudor England in the Reformation legislation.[133]

Of course, the Royal Supremacy did not and has not existed in Australia. It had been put aside by force of social circumstances. Nonetheless, its categories of imperial authority have been imported into the life of the church community. We have imagined that the synods are supreme governing bodies with coercive power, or that the ordained ministry in its forms has monarchical or imperial authority, or that the lay members should act in councils and committees like power brokers in an imperial game. We have not been helped in all this by our commitment to the formularies of the English Reformation as expressed in their legislative form,

---

133 For a discussion of the influence of political contexts on ecclesiastical changes see Kaye, B N, *The 1850 Bishops Conference and the Strange Birth of Australian Synods*, Kaye, B N, 'Broughton and the Demise of the Royal Supremacy'.

which form has brought with it the assumptions of imperial categories. The difficulty is also that the legislative form does not reflect the broader social reality of the dynamics of the English Reformation. Further, it does not convey the theological interpretation of the sixteenth-century Reformation which provides a better continuity with the longer tradition of Anglicanism, both before and after the Reformation.

In other words, in its constitutional framework and commitment to the English Reformation monuments Anglicanism has been traditional but not adequately critical.

The challenge, therefore, is to identify the real significance of the Reformation to which the formularies only ambiguously point. That significance belongs in the religious and theological impulses which legitimated the practice rather than the political theories of the sixteenth century. But those theological issues did not and do not demand that the precise political and authority structures implied in the Reformation legislation should have any necessary claim upon modern Anglicans. What we need to do in our contemporary situation is look beyond the form to the substance, thus making possible a reconsideration and reinventing of the Anglicanism in its polity and constitutionality. By far the most important contribution to that discussion is the interpretation offered by Richard Hooker. In many respects it presents a conservative picture if one looks at it simply in terms of the sixteenth century to which it was addressed. However, if we look at the theology which underlies the legitimation of the Royal Supremacy, then we will see, as Steven McGrade has pointed out, that it is a highly progressive, radical and transforming interpretation of providence in history and of consensus in the Christian community. It is those issues highlighted by Hooker which provide the keys to open up our understanding of authority and to enable a better provision of confidence for Anglicans. That kind of approach can be seen more generally in some recent work on the doctrine of the Trinity.

Theological tradition—the doctrine of the Trinity

The doctrine of the Trinity holds an important place in Anglican formularies. It stands prominently in the Thirty-nine Articles and, until very recently, dominated the character of the annual church calendar by the long season of Trinity. But the doctrine has had a varied history in Christianity. In the early church it became a critical issue because of what was at stake: the nature of the faith which Christians experienced. The gospel narrative of Jesus as apparently divine, cast in the context of the tradition of Jewish faith in the one God of Israel, and the promise that Jesus would send a divine Spirit after his departure, created questions that needed to be resolved by the early Christians as they sought to come to terms with the meaning of their faith in their social and philosophical intellectual context. The understanding of God as one and three was a vital faith question.

The doctrine remained for centuries, even though the issue was not as contested as it was by the end of the fifth century. Michael Servetus (1511–1553) twice published books denying the doctrine of the Trinity. He was denounced to the Roman Catholic inquisition and imprisoned. However, he escaped and fled to Geneva, where he was arrested on the instructions of John Calvin and, refusing to recant, was burnt as a heretic. Whatever else may be said, Servetus's experience showed that the Roman Catholic Inquisition and John Calvin were alike in their commitment to the doctrine of the Trinity.

I remember being present at the opening of a seminar conducted by Karl Barth in 1968 which was supposed to be on Schleiermacher. However, Barth began with a ten-minute statement on the importance of the doctrine of the Trinity. He began the seminar by saying, 'Do not despise the doctrine of the Trinity. It is the finest creation of Christian theology.'

Barth represented something of an exception at that time. Across the channel in England John Robinson confessed to not liking to preach on Trinity Sunday because he did not know what he should say. A popular perception has developed in recent times that the doctrine of the Trinity is in some sense a theoretical question of no great consequence. In general, since the eighteenth century the doctrine of the Trinity has been marginalised in Christian thinking and experience, because it has been set within realms which are purely theoretical and rational rather than having to do with the living experience of the Christian community. The impact of Enlightenment conceptions which moved God aside from, or above, public knowledge meant that the doctrine of the Trinity became something of an embarrassment. The new mode of conceiving of transcendence was a way of moving God out of the way.[134]

---

134 Placher, W, *The Domestication of Transcendence.*

However, in the last thirty years theologians have become concerned with the question of God as Trinity. This revival of interest among theologians was stimulated, in no small measure, by the work of Karl Barth and his continuing desire to relate the revelation of God to Israel, focused on the nation, the law and the temple, and to the church, which is focused on Christ. The Trinity was thus a way of reading the Bible to make sense of the discontinuities in the revelation of the one and the same God. Jürgen Moltmann, in a series of publications, has focused on the interaction of God with history and hence has given emphasis to social categories. He reunites the idea of God as Trinity with notions of revelation. These theologians resort to the gospel narrative for the power and force of their appeal to the Trinitarian character of God.

Feminist work on the Trinity

The new attention to the doctrine of the Trinity strongly emphasises the notion of relationality. This is often portrayed in contrast to a unity of substance. Clearly the dominance of theism as the principal vehicle for speaking about God in western theology, particularly in the last two hundred years, is being challenged by these theologians. It is not surprising that the Enlightenment and philosophical underpinning of western culture is also at the same time being challenged.

The interplay between contemporary culture and the formulation of the doctrine of the Trinity can be seen in the struggle to find suitable language for the doctrine. Feminism in the western world has changed the way language is used and has drawn attention to the male-specific and patriarchal character of language. The history of the doctrine of the Trinity is full of gender language; central, of course, is the language about God as Father and Son. This issue has also affected the language of liturgy. Modern Anglican liturgies now strive for more inclusive language in order to meet this problem. The issue is not that the worship is being changed or a new God invented but is rather the inescapable influence of the hearer upon the effective meaning of the words used. Janet Martine Soskice has made this point.[135] This cultural context has raised important issues about the way we properly speak about God so as to more adequately reflect the very character of that God rather than the language about God being itself an attempt to secure

---

135 See Soskice, J M, *Metaphor and Religious Language.*

unexamined social interests. It is an example of the classic challenge of whether the religion serves or challenges the social interests of participants.[136]

Considerable appeal has been made to the Eastern Orthodox tradition of theology, and especially the writings of the Cappadocian fathers from the early church, to understand the relational character of God. New language is often sought so that one does not speak about the unity so much as about 'the three', as indeed did Gregory of Nazianzus.[137]

All of this resonates with late-twentieth-century interest in pluralism and the challenges of social connection.[138]

Colin Gunton underlines a point made by Karl Barth, that the church is the community from which theology begins.[139] He also claims that worship is a relational activity and, furthermore, that worship is a paradigm case for what happens in other dimensions of life. He seeks to cast theology in this framework of Trinitarian activity. He speaks of the possibilities of Trinitarian theology and how it helps us to understand that the church is an echo of the Divine and therefore relational, and not collective or individualist. He says it enables us to see better how we should understand our human responsibility to the world and our understanding of the kind of world in which we live.

These writers all draw attention to important aspects of the doctrine of the Trinity as it was experienced and as it emerged in the early church.

It is often hard for us to get behind the intellectual tradition which we have inherited, not least because we are not always conscious of the categories we use in trying to understand the faith we experience. Some of these theologians speak of the doctrine of the Trinity as having practical significance, and consequences which need to be worked out. I want to emphasise that the doctrine of the Trinity

---

136 The contrast in response to feminism can be seen in Kimel, A F, *Speaking the Christian God: The Holy Trinity and the Challenge of Feminism*, and Duck, R C, *Gender and the Name of God: The Trinitarian Baptismal Formula*. Interestingly, Karl Barth used Paul's references to the man as 'head' of the woman (1 Cor 11:3) to develop a theory of female subordination. See Barth, K, *The Doctrine of Creation: Church Dogmatics, Volume III,4*. See the critique of political and clerical monotheism in Moltmann, J, *The Trinity and the Kingdom of God: The Doctrine of God*.
137 Zizioulas, J, *Being as Communion*.
138 Vanhoozer, K, *The Trinity in a Pluralistic Age*.
139 Gunton, C, *The Promise of Trinitarian Theology*, and Gunton, C, *The One, the Three and the Many: God, Creation and the Culture of Modernity*.

is something which arises out of the practical experiences of Christian faith. It is not an inherited doctrine which needs to be applied. It is a way of explaining and interpreting the experience of God which is the common coin of all Christian people in any particular historical circumstance, and it provides a valuable service for them in that situation.[140]

However, for the purposes of the discussion in this book in relation to Christian confidence, I want to suggest that the doctrine of the Trinity is best thought of as a tool which enables us to moderate and understand our experience of God. Living in an increasingly plural environment where plausabilities multiply and truth appears to be deregulated, what we require is not so much principles to apply but guidelines to help us find our way through this confusing changing plural environment. We need guidelines and parameters, mechanisms and governors which will enable us to see how we may live and speak with due confidence in a plural environment. A revived notion of the Trinity helps us in that respect. It underlines the importance of the gospel narrative, the past, present and the future, Israel, Jesus and the Spirit. But these are not watertight compartments; each of them has its own continuity and discontinuity with the past and the present. The idea of Trinity helps us to hold together the diverse and different experiences of God that are portrayed to us in the biblical narratives. Not only so, the doctrine of the Trinity speaks about the way in which we ourselves experience God, both in our own personal and social lives. God comes to us as Lord, Creator, Saviour and Redeemer, as Comforter and Convictor. The doctrine of the Trinity works as a heuristic device for interpreting in a faithful way the experience of God which is ours today. The doctrine of the Trinity thus also implies that there are appropriate Christian practices which the presence of this Triune God might produce in the lives of Christian people. Among these David Cunnigham identifies peace-making, pluralising and persuading. It is the last of these which I am concerned to emphasise here.

The doctrine also provides us with a way of understanding how God is at once present for us and also in the lives of our fellow human beings and in the created order, and yet is not fully present in any. There are what Augustine called the

---

140 See the excellent discussion in Part Three of Cunningham, D, *These Three Are One: The Practice of Trinitarian Theology*.

'vestigia' in the created order, which provide the possibility of echoes or resonance between the faith community, the family of humanity, and the natural order.

Thus the doctrine of the Trinity speaks of wholeness and diversity, of faith as walking in trust, because there is yet openness. The doctrine speaks of an order of authority as gently persuasive, never complete and always yielding a contingent result. It speaks of argument as grounded in resonance, not shaped by logical rigidity. It is this character of this God that provides the confidence for Anglicans to believe, to act and to speak. For Anglicans this part of the theological tradition draws attention to the diverse and different ways in which God is present. In doing so it also draws attention to the multifaceted character of the divine persuasion which draws people to God, and thus also to the nature of the confidence we have in believing and with which we persuade.

The baggage which Australian Anglicans bring with them to the question of authority and confidence in modern Australia is thus rich and varied. The theological tradition, the biblical tradition and the Reformation tradition are all capable of speaking to our situation. But all need to be critically reappraised. Because the Reformation formularies are so much a part of the mental furniture of Anglicans, they need to be subjected to radical reappraisal. They need to be critically reconstructed so that we identify the Tudor political categories of the Reformation legislation. These imperial categories not only do not reflect the broad range of the Anglican tradition but also are singularly unhelpful in the current social context in which Anglicans are called to live out their faith.

On the issue of authority, or confidence, each of these traditions points to different ways in which we might live in a plural society, ways which acknowledges the truth of the gospel which reveals the God and Father of our Lord Jesus Christ and the power of the Spirit, and enable us to resonate with the presence of that same God in the lives of our fellow Australians and in the structures of our Australian society.

Persuasive resonance

I began this chapter by talking about the kinds of tacit assumptions that are necessary for real conversation and then drew attention to some assumptions in modern American and Australian society which inhibit real conversation about Christian faith. I have already tried to show in the first two chapters how

Australian Anglicans at the present time find themselves somewhat on the back foot for a variety of historical reasons. What they need to discover is not a renewed version of the old authority which they had in Australian history as top dogs. Rather, what is needed is the development of a kind of authority which is appropriate to the present circumstances and yet is faithful to the Christian tradition of which Anglicans are heirs and stewards. What we are looking for, therefore, is confidence which is enough to engage with our fellow citizens in word and deed, a kind of confidence which is enough to enable us to make commitments and to live our lives, a confidence which is discriminating and enables us to make judgments about which things are important, which things are better and which are worse. Such a confidence will enable an engagement with our fellow Australians; it will be a confidence to engage and to persuade. Such a confidence is in significant contrast to the sort of truth by assertion or the exercise of coercive power which is often resorted to in the present uncertainties. Such a confidence can be discovered from the inner substance of the tradition of which Anglicans are the custodians.

In this chapter I have reviewed three elements of the Anglican tradition: the Reformation Settlements, an example from the New Testament (Paul in Corinth), and the revived interest in the doctrine of the Trinity. The political legislative language of the Reformation documents does not help us in our present circumstances, and, indeed, it is a positive hindrance. A critical appropriation of the Reformation tradition is better found in the interpretations and the experience of English people at the time of the Reformation. We took Richard Hooker as an example of such an inner interpretation and drew attention to his way of justifying, yet not being committed to, the Tudor political notions of Royal Supremacy and the notion of authority that went with those legislative enactments. In his analysis he draws to the surface a conviction about the providence of God while yet wanting to test what Providence has created in the present by whether or not it works to the 'ill'. In other words, value judgments are to be made, but there is a privileged position for what Providence has created.

The combination of that judgment and that Providence creates an environment in which it is clear that the Christian lives in a contingent condition and thus by faith. Hooker's underlining of Christ's authority as being supreme and inward, rather than external and coercive, correlates with that notion of contingency and walking by faith. In his analysis, the Christian community is responsible for itself, and hence there is an authority of consensus within the Christian community, both contemporary and historical. Once again, such an argument is never absolutely final, it is always open. There is always a sense in which the consensus is a part of the pilgrimage of the Christian community. It is in the context of that pilgrimage, contingency and faith that Hooker's emphasis upon the grace of God in Christ becomes so critical as a touchstone for what he has to say.

A critical appropriation of the Reformation tradition will look to these issues of Providence, Christ's authority, community consensus, the grace of God and the contingent faith character of the Christian pilgrimage. It is these issues which a critical use of the tradition will want to discover in modern Australia.

The example taken from Paul's dealings with the Corinthians shows similar issues to be at stake. Paul believed the world had been prepared by God for the gospel which was then being preached. He underlines that God is the author of the Corinthians' faith. What they have, they have because they have received it. In his action God uses the preaching of the gospel, the ministry of Paul and Apollos, the Corinthian Christians themselves, individually and as a group, and the tradition which they have received from others through Paul. The action of God among the Corinthians and through Paul reveals something of the character of God and his action. It is moral in character, marked by humility, faithfulness and the gift of wisdom (in order to make judgments), and pre-eminently by love. The touchstone again is the presence of Christ. When the stranger comes into the Corinthian assembly the question is, do they perceive that God is present? In all of this Paul in no sense withdraws these Christians from the hostile plural environment which is Corinth. On the contrary, he sees their vocation as located in the midst of their neighbours. He therefore interacts with the orders and tacit assumptions in Corinth in relation to which the Corinthian Christians are to live out their Christian lives.

The theological tradition is picked up in relation to the revived interest in the doctrine of the Trinity, and its origins in the early church. In early Christianity it was an attempt to give expression to the experience of God which had come about through the revelation of God in Christ and the continuing guidance of the Spirit after the resurrection of Jesus. The recent revived interest in the doctrine of the Trinity emphasises relationality in the Godhead, in contrast to the theism which has been so dominant in the period of modernity. It also underlines the doctrine of the Trinity as an interpretation of the Christian experience of God.

However, the particular point I wish to draw from this theological tradition is that the doctrine of the Trinity is not something to be applied in Christian life as if it were external to it, but rather that it is a tool to moderate and understand our experience of God. This Trinitarian influence draws attention to the ambiguity of God's presence in the world and in the lives of Christian people. In one sense God is present, at work in the lives of Christian people. In the words of the letter to the Hebrews, Christ is the radiance of God's glory, the stamp of God's very image, and he sustains the universe by his word of power. Yet that presence is not constantly and unvaryingly visible. There is a clear and important sense in which God is absent, and the life of the Christian is not a path in the light in absolute terms but is a path of walking by faith. Even though later we may see clearly, at this point we see through a glass darkly.

Christians are thus constantly called to work out the meaning of the presence of God in their lives and in the created order. The confidence of the Christian is therefore an act of faith, a life of faith, which seeks to resonate with the presence of God in the created order. Critically appropriated, this tradition provides the basis for an engagement by Australian Anglicans with their fellow Australians which has the marks not of assertion but of persuasive resonance, a resonance with what God is already doing in the lives of our neighbours.

Confidence to engage thus arises from the inner substance of the Anglican tradition when critically appropriated in this way. Paul's Corinthian example is a key point of reference from the New Testament and illustrates the way in which the grace of God finds an echo in the hearts and lives of the Corinthians. The Reformation experience certainly presents significant language problems for Anglicans because of the political and legal terms in which the Reformation tradition has been retained in our formularies and in our institutional understandings and habits. Yet the inner substance and significance of that experience is about the providence of God pointing to faith, just as the renewed interest in the doctrine of the Trinity points to the life of faith in God's world and thus is about God's character in relational terms.

All of these moments in the tradition, critically appropriated, speak of the moral character of God and point to the possibility of a rebirth of confidence for

Anglicans. The confidence which it speaks of is a confidence to be participants in a persuasive resonance in the human conversation.

Such a notion of confidence as persuasive resonance is in many senses in our modern situation counter-cultural in that it is against coercion and against self-originating assertion, but it is nonetheless pro-human and pro-gospel. It enables a portrayal of the human condition which makes sense of it and challenges its problems yet leads on beyond it. It enables a portrayal of the whole of the human condition and hence enables Australian Anglicans to experience and to present a fully human expression, articulated in words and actions, art, community and institutions, which resonates with the continuing presence of God in the hearts and lives of modern Australians.

Persuasive resonance is a way of speaking about a confidence which arises in the context of living in the modern Australia which is inhabited by our fellow citizens, and which enables Australian Anglicans, out of their faith tradition and their experience of God, to interact with their fellow Australians with confidence.

CHAPTER FOUR

COMMUNITY—
INTERDEPENDENT DIVERSITY

Given the quality of Anglicanism as a community-embedded tradition of Christian faith which has grown in English soil over more that fourteen hundred years and the present dispersal of that tradition in recent centuries to many different social and cultural contexts around the globe, the essential qualities of this community is an important issue. I have argued that the confidence Anglicans need to relate to their fellows should be shaped by attending to the doctrine of providence, which has been a characteristic strand in this Christian tradition. We therefore must turn now to the community question in the tradition.

When the fourth-century-BC Greek philosopher Aristotle opened his essay on ethics by relating the good in human life to politics, he was drawing attention to something which is quite fundamental in the human condition. As humans we inevitably live with other people. Thus Aristotle's claim that the end of politics is the 'good for man' immediately leads him into the relationship between the good of the individual and the good of the community. 'For even if the good of the community coincides with that of the individual, the good of the community is clearly a greater and more perfect good both to get and to keep. This is not to deny that the good of the individual is worthwhile. But what is good for a nation or a city has a higher, diviner, quality.[141] The dialogue between the individual and the community is endemic in the human condition and raises the challenge of relating constructively to others.

Human beings have never been able to be alone and yet have wanted to be independent. The balance between these two forces has been quite varied. For itinerant hunter gatherers that relationship takes on a particular profile of teamwork, which is different from what is required where life is sustained in an agricultural or an industrial society.

In their imperial expansion the British faced the great problem of how to relate to the occupants of the lands which they discovered and colonised. In New Zealand they were more readily able to understand the tribal social structure of Maori people, because it was more consonant with their own understanding of social structure. The more subtle and nuanced kinship relationships among Australian Aborigines entirely defeated them. In the course of time they sought to impose their own pattern of social relationships among Aborigines by creating kings and queens, a notion hardly commensurate in any sense with the existing powerful lines of connection among Australian Aborigines.

Not all connections we enter are similar, let alone the same. People are drawn together on the basis of common interests, and often those combinations are transient. In ancient Israel there was no standing army. When there was an external threat, such as from the Philistines, people had to be called out for battle. Once the enemy had been defeated or repulsed, the association for common defence dissolved.

In the course of social development different kinds of relationships have evolved in order to sustain continuity in social life. Such relationships are often coloured by differences of power. Some become masters of servants, and societies institutionalise that relationship in an attempt to make it more permanent and enduring. Again in ancient Israel, there were restrictions on slavery among Israelites, but an Israelite could have non-Israelite slaves. Furthermore, in ancient

---

141 Aristotle, *Ethics*, I, 2 (p 27).

Israel institutional mechanisms, such as the year of Jubilee when debts were forgiven, inhibited permanent imbalances in social relationships. Similarly, there was no provision for adoption, because the kinship connections were assumed to be sufficiently extensive to cover every eventuality.

This area of human experience is, of course, the subject of incessant analysis and reflection. One of the most powerful modern contributions to that reflection was Ferdinand Tönnies's 1877 book *Gemeinschaft und Gesellschaft* (Community and Society). Tönnies was reflecting upon the circumstances of European society in the second half of the nineteenth century. In particular, he was reflecting upon the processes which led to the unification of a number of German states and the position of local communities in the development of larger political entities. He drew a contrast between community and society.

> All intimate, private and exclusive living together is life in *Gemeinschaft*. *Gesellschaft* is public life . . . in *Gemeinschaft* with one's family, one lives from birth on, bound to it in weal and woe. One goes into *Gesellschaft* as one goes into a strange country . . . *Gemeinschaft* is old . . . *Gesellschaft* is new. *Gemeinschaft* should be understood as a living organism, *Gesellschaft* as a mechanical aggregate and artefact.[142]

He wrote in response to the unification of the German states under Bismark. He also wrote in the light of the Enlightenment assertion of the mathematical character of public knowledge. Tönnies thought that European society was inevitably moving away from the intimate relations of community to the external relationships of society. It did not mean that all community, in the sense of local and enduring contact over time, was disappearing. Rather, what he meant was that these two ways of looking at our connections were beginning to form more on the side of society than on the side of community.

John Kingdom's critique of the Margaret Thatcher program in Great Britain, entitled *No Such Thing as Society? Individualism and Community*,[143] analysed the way in which Margaret Thatcher diminished the role of government and accentuated the role of the individual in the formation of social policy and in thinking about

---

142 Tonnies, F, *Community and Society*, Michigan State University Press, East Lansing 1877, pp 37–39.
143 Kingdom, J, *No Such Thing as Society? Individualism and Community*, Open University Press, Buckingham 1992.

the nature of life in Britain. His title picked up Margaret Thatcher's own declaration that 'there is no such thing as society'. The very terms of John Kingdom's analysis reflect the kind of distinction which Tönnies had made a hundred years before. Kingdom tries to balance the way in which individuals find connections in society and in community. His analysis is cast in the categories of Tönnies but is set in late-twentieth-century Britain.

Of course, the particularities of his analysis are different from those which were important to Tönnies. German society in the second half of the nineteenth century was quite different, in terms of its balance, its occupations and its power structures, from late-twentieth-century Britain. On the other hand, there are enduring concerns in both analyses about the nature of social organisations, the nature of society and the way in which individuals exist in more intimate connections which, when taken together, can be talked about in terms of community.

The classic statement of these issues in the twentieth century was Robert Nisbet's 1953 book *The Quest for Community*. It was republished in 1962 under the title *Community and Power*, the publisher obviously trying to capture the spirit of the post-war early 1960s. However, in 1969 the book was republished as *The Quest for Community*, and it has been published again in 1990 under the same title. It is a book of enduring importance. In 1990 Robert Nisbet wrote a preface to the book indicating emphases which, if he could rewrite the book, he would have liked to have included at that time. The 1990 edition contains a foreword by William Schrambra which relates the themes of the book to political life in the United States in the previous twenty years.

Nisbet begins his analysis with a description of what he sees in 1953 as the loss of community, particularly in the western world. His opening statement is dramatic:

> One may paraphrase the famous words of Karl Marx and say that a spectre is haunting the modern mind, the spectre of insecurity. Surely the outstanding characteristic of contemporary thought on man and society is the preoccupation of personal alienation and cultural disintegration.[144]

144 Nisbet, R, *The Quest for Community: A Study in the Ethics of Order and Freedom*, Institute for Contemporary Studies, San Francisco 1990, p 3.

Nisbet's book is divided into three parts, the first of which deals with community and the problem of order. Beginning from this analysis and his identification of the loss of community as the great issue of his day, he looks at the various images of community. The themes of Tönnies's argument echo in his claim that the problem is principally that the small traditional associations founded upon kinship have lost their place in the large economic and political decisions of western societies. This leads him in the second part of his book to consider the state and community. He speaks of the emergence in the sixteenth century of centralised political jurisdictions in the form of the state and the emasculation of intermediate groups and associations between those centralised government powers and individuals. In that sense, he says, 'The state is revolution in that it overcomes and undermines the commune and the community which had been such a mark of the local existence which characterised the medieval period'. The sixteenth century was the great turning point. 'This is pre-eminently the century of the beginnings of secularism, religious dissent, economic individualism, and of political centralisation.'[145]

The third section of Nisbet's book is concerned with the problem of freedom in relation to community. He argues we can only discover freedom in the interactions between authorities which shape and frame the life which we live in our connectedness with others. This he contrasts with mass society, which is inimical to freedom. He quotes with approval from Louis Mumford, who said in his *Culture of Cities*, 'With overgrown institutions, overgrown colleges, overgrown corporations, overgrown cities, is it any wonder that we easily become the victims of propaganda machines, routineers and dictators?'[146]

In his summary conclusion Nisbet contrasts two kinds of states. On the one hand there is the state which seeks to extend its administration of powers and functions into all realms of society in order to preserve freedom, that is to say, freedom from want. On the other hand there is the kind of state which seeks to maintain a 'pluralism of functions and loyalties in the lives of its people'.[147] This second state, he says, 'is inherently pluralist and its power will be limited by associations whose

145 Nisbet, R, *The Quest for Community: A Study in the Ethics of Order and Freedom*, p 78.
146 Nisbet, R, *The Quest for Community: A Study in the Ethics of Order and Freedom*, p 245.
147 Nisbet, R, *The Quest for Community: A Study in the Ethics of Order and Freedom*, p 251.

plurality of claims upon their members is the measure of their members' freedom from any monopoly of power in society'.[148]

Nisbet claimed that western society was poised in the middle of the twentieth century between two worlds of allegiance and association. On the one hand is the historic world in which

> loyalties to family, church, profession, local community, and interest associations exert, however ineffectively, persuasion and guidance. On the other hand is the world of values identical with the absolute political community—the community in which all symbolism, allegiance, responsibility, and sense of purpose have become indistinguishable from the operation of centralised political power.[149]

Twenty years later, in 1970, Nisbet reflected that there were a number of things which he would rather have emphasised more than he had in 1953. He would have emphasised that his book was not a lament for the old and nostalgia for the village or the parish but rather a call for the establishment of new forms. He would have liked to have made more of the theme of alienation, not just alienation from things or places or nature but from people, from the social bond which is community. He would have emphasised more the nature of authority, which is different from power. Power, he claims, is external and based upon force; authority is a form of constraint but is based 'ultimately upon the consent of those under it; that is, it is conditional. Power arises only when authority breaks down.'[150] He would have liked to have given stronger and clearer emphasis to 'the wide diffusion of the ideology of centralised power in contemporary society'.[151]

This is surely one of the most powerful analyses of the issues facing twentieth-century civilisation. He shows how our individuality and our connectedness are both important elements of our humanity. In the foreword to the 1990 edition of Nisbet's book, William Schambra claims some developments in the United States exemplify the theses which Nisbet argued. He refers to the emphasis in the Reagan political program on intermediate associations. He contrasts that with J F Kennedy's new frontier and Lyndon Johnson's great society, with their

---

148 Nisbet, R, *The Quest for Community: A Study in the Ethics of Order and Freedom*, p 252.
149 Nisbet, R, *The Quest for Community: A Study in the Ethics of Order and Freedom*, p 249.
150 Nisbet, R, *The Quest for Community: A Study in the Ethics of Order and Freedom*, p xxvi.
151 Nisbet, R, *The Quest for Community: A Study in the Ethics of Order and Freedom*, p xxviii.

tremendous expansion of the national state through the 1960s. He claims that the importance of the community to be found in intermediate associations, for which Nisbet argued, had been grasped by social policy in the United States.

That was not a point of view shared by Robert Bellar and his associates when they wrote *Habits of the Heart* (1985). They argued that the associations in the Nisbet sense were being undermined as a result of the combined influence of big government and big corporations. The great difference between the time when Nisbet wrote and the end of the twentieth century in western culture has been the changing balance in power in western societies from governments to large business corporations. This is one aspect of the multiplication of the tendencies towards the mass society which are being formed around us and are in turn becoming part of our internal mental and emotional furniture.

In the United States there are many large cities and the population is spread more widely than in Australia. The two largest cities in Australia (Melbourne and Sydney) contain 39 per cent of the total population, whereas in the United States of America the two largest cities (New York and Los Angeles) contain 12.6 per cent of the total. The absence of a significant number of large cities in Australia implies, on Nisbet's analysis, that we are more susceptible to being manipulated. That is one of the marks of a mass society. A similar contrast can be seen in volunteer involvement. Whereas in the United States not-for-profit organisations and voluntary activity in not-for-profit and community organisations is one of the fastest growing sectors of activity, in Australia it is diminishing. Community groups are finding it increasingly difficult to attract members. This applies not just to groups such as the Boy Scouts, the churches or other voluntary community groups but also to the political parties, whose membership has diminished significantly in the last twenty-five years.

Susceptible to all of the dynamics of late-twentieth-century social forces, Australia finds itself increasingly in a vortex of the issues which Nisbet analysed in 1953. Hugh Mackay's recent analyses of Australia highlight the eclipse of the influence of the neighbourhood and the dramatic way in which the entry of women into the work force has changed the structure and dynamics of families. The point is not that families of the past somehow are lost and should be restored but rather that these social changes have not yet led to effective reflection upon the values of a human kind, which the old patterns were supposed to sustain. In the new environment such values appear unrecognised and unaccounted. When politicians speak of traditional values, more often than not they are speaking of traditional structures. In Hugh Mackay's analysis the local and the immediate— what in Nisbet's terms would be called community—are in the Australian environment in a period of dramatic change, and the values which are necessary for human integrity and dignity are not yet visible on the horizon.

Because these questions are cast in a national environment of a particular kind, we can learn something from recent discussion of the social significance of nations and nationalism. There has been a significant modern debate about the nature and emergence of nationalism. Benedict Anderson has argued that the notion of nationalism arose as a consequence of the American War of Independence. This war created the possibility of believing and feeling that one could belong to a nation. What has been called the modernist analysis of nationalism believes that such a conception arose in the late eighteenth century as a consequence of the emergence of the nation state and the attempt to find some basis for coherence among the population in those nation states. So Eric Hobsbawn[152] begins his analysis of nations and nationalism in 1780. Similarly, Ernst Gellner[153] coordinates the transition to an age of nationalism with the rise of the industrial society.

Adrian Hastings has recently challenged this approach in his book *The Construction of Nationhood.*[154] He is in line with much historical work that has been done in the last twenty years in relation to the transition from feudalism to the modern era. In this context the sixteenth century becomes a critical turning point, as it did for Nisbet. In Hastings's view it is the high point for the notion of nation. Nationhood, he believes, arises out of ethnicities. Religion plays a vital role in it, particularly Christianity. Because of the authority of the Bible and the tradition of the story of ancient Israel, he believes Christianity plays a powerful role in forming concepts of belonging to a nation. He thinks England is the forerunner, indeed the prototype, of the nation, and he traces not only the lexicon of nationalism and nation but also the concepts back to the writings of Bede in the eighth century.

---

152 Hobsbawm, E, *Nations and Nationalism since 1780.*
153 Gellner, E, *Nations and Nationalism.*
154 Hastings, A, *The Construction of Nationhood: Ethnicity, Religion and Nationalism.*

Hastings's central theses are that nationhood emerges from one or more ethnicities and that it is dependent upon the development of a vernacular literature. An ethnicity, he says, is a group of people with a shared cultural identity and spoken language. A nation, however, is a more self-conscious community. 'Formed from one or more ethnicities, and normally identified by a literature of its own, it possesses or claims the right to political identity and autonomy as a people, together with the control of a specific territory, comparable to that of biblical Israel and of other independent entities in a world thought of as one of nation states.'[155]

A nation state is a state which identifies itself with such a nation. But nationalism may be a theory, namely that each nation should have its own state, or it may be a practice, such as the cultivation of nationalistic feelings in the nineteenth century. Religion, Hastings claims, is integral, and in his view the Bible provides an original model for the nation.

However, according to Hastings, there is always a tension in Christianity between the local and the universal. It is the working out of the dynamics of those two contrary tendencies which marks the rise of Christian influence on notions of nation and nationalism.[156] This point echoes the distinction between community and society elaborated by Tönnies in the nineteenth century.

Even this brief review shows that any attempt to consider the nature of community in the reinvention of the church necessarily involves us in a number of critical issues in our present condition in western civilisation and in Australia in particular. These issues raise for us important presenting questions as we try to formulate the context in which the church might be reinvented in Australia. There are four principal questions which claim our attention: difference, connection, direction and institutions.

Difference

Robert Nisbet drew attention to the importance of the individual being able not simply to connect with others in intermediate associations but also to be able to connect with others in different kinds of intermediate associations. Furthermore,

---

155 Hastings, A, *The Construction of Nationhood: Ethnicity, Religion and Nationalism*, p 3.
156 He returned to this theme in Hastings, A, 'Chrtistianity and Nationhood: Congruity or Antipathy?'.

it was important not only that individuals should be able to connect with other individuals but also that different groups of individuals should be able to connect. It was for that reason that in his concluding chapter he opted for a form of the state which allowed for a plurality of associations and sub-groups.

Pluralism has been an important point of discussion among political scientists throughout the whole of the twentieth century. At the beginning of the century, English political scientists raised the issue within a European context. The Anglican cleric David Nicholls has been a continuing exponent of the issue in more recent years and has drawn attention to the difference between the kind of pluralism espoused in North America as compared with the English model of pluralism. North American pluralism has tended to be a pluralism of individuals within the state, whereas in England pluralism has tended to take much more account of what Robert Nisbet was subsequently to call intermediate associations. David Nicholls has consistently expounded his point in relation to theology, drawing attention to the correlations between conceptions of God and the sovereignty of God on the one hand and the social realities within which those conceptions were developed on the other.[157]

Within the Australian environment, there is a very particular slant on this issue of pluralism. In the nineteenth century, as the colonies tried to emerge out of the Anglican hegemony, what came to be called the sectarian move was adopted to deal with what was seen as religious conflict between the denominations. An attempt in 1836 by Governor Richard Bourke to develop a tripartite religious hegemony in the colony essentially failed. By the end of the nineteenth century particular religious convictions—what were called denominational dogmas— were removed from the arena of public financial support.[158]

However, the sectarian move, as it was initiated in the middle of the nineteenth century, presumed a Christian society. The University of Sydney was established on this principle. It did not contain theology in its curriculum when it was established, and the bishops and clergy were excluded from its governance. Yet it

---

157 Nicholls, D, *Deity and Domination: Images of God and the State in the Nineteenth and Twentieth Centuries.*

158 See for example Bollen, J, *Religion in Australian Society: An historian's view*, Border, R, *Church and State in Australia 1788–1872: A Constitutional Study of the Church of England in Australia*, Austin, A, *Australian Education 1788–1900: Church, State and Public Education in Colonial Australia.*

was established to promote Christian religion and morality.[159] There was a clear assumption that the particular denominations were not entitled to public support financially through the instrumentality of the new university. Yet, nonetheless, the university represented the community, and that community was thought of by the founders as a Christian community with basic Christian religious beliefs.

This Australian sectarian move took on a different character later in the nineteenth century. That is reflected in the recent report of the Equal Opportunity Commissioner entitled *Free to Believe*.[160] Belief is here conceived of not as public activity but as private practice and thus is eliminated from the public domain. It represents a complete transformation of the nineteenth-century sectarian move.

Since 1972 there has been a multicultural dimension to Australian pluralism. This has arisen because of political decisions to assert the principle that people who come to Australia ought to be able to retain important elements of their cultural and ethnic heritage. The policy has gone through a variety of stages. It was certainly conceived of as a way of building on the rejection of the White Australia Policy. Nonetheless, under different governments it has moved in an oscillating way, giving greater or lesser emphasis to what, in the Keating years, were described as core values, mostly discussed under the heading of citizenship and commitment to Australia on the one hand and the support of ethnic diversity on the other.

Ethnicity is not the only category of plurality in Australia. Paul Sheahan has argued that 'Australia at the end of the twentieth century is divided more by principles and theories than by anything else'.[161] At the same time, these value distinctions have been conceived in terms of individual choices. Just as in the second half of the twentieth century the privatisation of religion became part of the 'common sense' of Australian culture, so ethical values were increasingly privatised matters. Thus the ethical values tacit in the inherited public institutions were eclipsed. It is not surprising that this period saw an explosion in civil

---

159 Turney, C, Bygott, U and Chippendale, P, *Australia's First: A History of the University of Sydney, Volume I, 1850–1939.*

160 Commissioner, H R, *Free to Believe? The Right to Freedom of Religion and Belief in Australia.* On the general question of sectarianism in Australia see Hogan, M, *The Sectarian Strand: Religion in Australian History.*

161 Sheehan, P, *Among the Barbarians: The Dividing of Australia*, p 284.

litigation and the development of codes of conduct for professions and organisations. Any evacuation of ethical values from the public domain inevitably changes the assumptions about difference, and the basis of relationships moves in an authoritarian direction.

In Australia since the middle of the 1980s there have been a number of efforts to promote research and debate on the question of social values. Increasingly, those values are tending to be seen as values which belong to the individual and to individual choices and behaviour. These moves tend to eclipse the critical issue of the values tacit in the shape and operation of institutions and feed the different construing of pluralism to which Sheehan draws attention.

The first presenting question for our consideration of community is that of the existence of difference and diversity and the necessity, therefore, for some kind of pluralism within a social entity such as Australia.

Connection

The second presenting question is the other side of the first, namely, in what manner and how can connections be made between people and groups who have different allegiances and different senses of belonging? It is a commonplace to observe that no significantly complex society can function without trust. Trust is fundamental not just to intimate personal relationships but also in the more casual relationships of commerce. Societies where there is a high level of trust, such as in a small community, may not need as high a level of external constraint to secure acceptable social behaviour. Commitment to agreed behaviour patterns provides the basis for what Luhman has called reliable expectations. Where expectations about other people's response cannot be relied upon, other constraints are necessary. Thus, in a mass society higher levels of institutionalised violence, such as incarceration in prisons, will inevitably be necessary. The patterns of connection will be different in an interdependent society from those in a conformist society with a strong leader.

Belonging is fundamental to the human condition. The way in which it is construed in a differently characterised plural environment is an important presenting question for any attempt to reinvent one of the communities that exists within Australia, namely the Anglican Church.

Direction

In such an environment, if one takes a longitudinal view, then the way in which societies move or achieve some sense of direction becomes crucial. This is particularly true in a fluid environment, such as exists in Australia today. As many analysts have pointed out, we have been going through a period of significant and profound change. What has been changing most of all has been the institutional framework and organisational arrangements. Tacit in those institutions and organisations are values which are also subject to change and adjustment. However, as Robert Nisbet pointed out in 1953, 'change is always, at bottom, the reaction of individuals to new circumstances and the consequent effort of individuals to comprehend these new circumstances, to make them meaningful, and to build them into new values and new systems of allegiance'.[162]

It is in this context that discussion about leadership should be located. Leadership is one of the mechanisms which enables a community of people, large or small, discrete or otherwise, to gain some direction in its affairs. Leadership always takes place within the framework of some institutional sense, whether it is conceived of very loosely (national, public, political) or as the much more structured framework of a business corporation.

In that sense Alistair Mant[163] is entirely correct when he says the leader signifies a commitment on the part of both the leader and those led to the values of the institution within which that leadership is taking place. He speaks about binary relationships and ternary relationships. A binary relationship, for example, is one between a master and a servant. It is essentially a power relationship. A ternary relationship is a relationship which exists within a framework shaped by and presupposing agreed values, whereby one person serving those values leads and influences another also committed to those same values. Max De Pree's conception of leading without power is an exploration of this area. He points towards the important issue of ethical values that relate to direction and leadership for communities of people.[164]

However, Mant and DePree are dissenting voices in a culture which in its public self-manifestation has been moving in a more individual and pluralistic direction.

162 Nisbet, R, *The Quest for Community: A Study in the Ethics of Order and Freedom*, p 80.
163 Mant, A, *Intelligent Leadership*.
164 De Pree, M, *Leading without Power: Finding Hope in Serving Community*.

'Leadership' is more popularly used for strong leadership, by which is meant a leadership which is more authoritarian. A move to this kind of leadership is understandable in a uncertain environment, and it is reflected in the attraction of Wyart Earp CEOs for major corporations under threat. However, it is not a good model for any long-term or sustained institutional life, because it inevitably undermines the legitimacy of institutional authority and encourages relationships based on the exercise of power.[165] These social forces inevitably affect Anglicans and thus any project of reinventing the church.

Institutions

The fourth presenting question is inevitably institutions. Human societies of the twenty-first century are vastly complex, with multitudes of interlocking organisations and systems. It is not immediately easy to provide conceptual clarity about these institutions, and I want to refer to just three of the many authors who write on this area in order to sharpen up the conception of institution I have in mind, especially in relation to Anglicanism.

One of the really great Australians of the twentieth century was H C Coombs. 'Nugget' Coombs, as he came to be known, was one of Australia's most distinguished civil servants. He played a leading role in post-war reconstruction and, as a consequence, was a very significant figure in rebuilding civil institutions after the ravages of the Second World War and also in the design and creation of new social institutions. All of that life experience was brought to bear in his Boyer Lectures,[166] where he discussed the nature of social institutions. We are, he said, an institution-creating species. It is institutions which enable us to be, indeed make us, human. By institutions Dr Coombs did not mean mechanical organisations. He meant those patterns of association between people which endure through time. He was referring to institutions such as marriage and the family, governmental institutions, such as those associated with parliamentary democracy, institutions of a kind that he helped to forge in post-war Australia. These institutions, Coombs claimed, were necessary to human flourishing and were subject to and shaped by moral values.

---

165 For a helpful analysis of power and authority see Pfeffer, J, *Power in Organizations*.
166 Coombs, H, *The Fragile Pattern*.

The second person I want to refer to is David Schnarch, whose extraordinarily interesting book entitled *Sexual Crucible*[167] describes a long-term intimate relationship as a crucible of virtue. What he meant was that marriage was an enduring relationship, an institution, which required the parties to sustain a relationship through all of the vicissitudes of close sustained loving contact. Inevitably that meant learning to deal with conflict. It meant learning to deal with disagreement. It meant learning to deal with failure and forgiveness. It meant learning to give and learning to receive. Schnarch said these are virtues. They are the moral values which help to make us truly human, and we are better able to learn them because of the experience of marriage as an enduring monogamous relationship.

These two authors draw attention to key elements in an understanding of institutions. Institutions have to do with relationships, relationships that endure through time. They can refer to relationships between roles which may have changing inhabitants. They refer to matters of behaviour which are not only necessary for the operation of the institutions but also are properly described in moral terms. They are virtues. In this sense institutions are not morally neutral but imply and foster moral values.

Alastair MacIntyre has addressed this question from a philosophical point of view in his recent project to present a different reading of the good life. He develops that project in the face of the collapse of the attempt to create our own moral values, what he calls emotivism. MacIntyre argues that we learn to behave well and that we do so within the framework of a tradition which is exemplified in a community. He develops a notion of institution in relation to a particular conception of 'practices' and their goods. Practices are socially established cooperative human activities which lead to the realisation of 'internal goods' as participants strive to achieve standards of excellence in the activity concerned. Thus, chess playing is a practice and, as excellence is achieved, the internal goods which make the practice possible are also realised. These goods are internal because they are specific to the activity of playing chess and because they can only be appreciated by those who have so learned to play chess.

167 Schnarch, D, *Constructing the Sexual Crucible: An Interrogation of Sexual and Marital Therapy.*

MacIntyre then argues that virtues are what help us to achieve these internal goods. Virtues are the way we define our relationships to others with whom we share the purposes and standards of practices. That relationship is not only with the contemporary practitioners but also with their predecessors, and so practices are set in a tradition.

Such practices cannot survive through time without institutions. In the case of chess playing, the sustaining institution would be chess clubs. Such institutions are concerned with external goods, that is, acquiring material resources to sustain the practice. This commitment to external goods inevitably can corrupt the practices and its internal goods. The role of the virtues is thus clearly defensive: 'Without justice, courage and truthfulness, practices could not resist the corrupting power of institutions'.[168]

On this account, institutions are arrangements to sustain certain kinds of activities by providing the material possibility for those activities. This analysis places institutions in a derivative position and, although MacIntyre underlines the close connection between practices and institutions, the institutions are construed in that relationship as necessarily malign because of their single commitment to external goods.

This is a striking and helpful analysis. It advances the issues in a number of respects. It underlines the passing of time in conceiving of institutions. It underlines thereby the tradition narrative within which institutions are likely to emerge. It underlines the tradition framework of practices and thus of virtues. However, by locating the nexus between relationships and virtues in practices, it necessarily gives an activity framework for the virtues. Dispositions to behaviour and behaviour are clearly learned in sustained relational activity, but the mental imagined activity which arises from that relationship and its relevant area of activity also shape and foster capacities and likelihood to behave well. This is true not only in relation to the imagined activity but also the ongoing profile of the relationship.

It makes more sense to me to bring the conception of institutions into the arena of relationships and, further, not only relationships with people but with things. This move means that the treatment of material things is brought more directly

---

168 MacIntyre, A, *After Virtue: A Study in Moral Theory*, p 194.

into the arena of the virtues or the arena of habituated good. It also has the effect of making them more susceptible of a moral account.

The corruptibility of institutions, on this analysis, is in no way a different case from the corruptibility of relationships, or 'practices'. All are subject to the corrosive influence of sin in its multifarious forms. The institutional law of self-defence at the expense of others is in principle the same as the operation of that law by the inhabitants of institutions and by individuals. The formal aspect of an institution may provide a façade behind which to hide ambition, greed or envy, but that is in principle no different from the personal façade we call hypocrisy. Such a move as this overcomes the dualism which appears to be opening up in MacIntyre's account.

I propose, therefore, to regard institutions as patterns of sustained relationships between people and/or things which exist through time. These relationships necessarily imply moral values, good or evil, and they also foster those moral values. When we come to the specific issue of community in the tradition of Anglicanism, its institutions can only be considered within the framework of the values of that tradition, and, as a consequence, those values will always be theological in character.

These presenting questions are important in any attempt to reinvent the Anglican Church as a discrete community of Christian people within the Australian environment. They are questions about difference, about connection and allegiance, about direction and leadership, about institutions and values through time.

Tradition revisited

In attempting to discuss these presenting challenges for the reinvention of the Christian community in modern Australia, we shall look again, as in the previous chapter, at the tradition which is the heritage of Australian Anglicans. This revisiting will be along tradition critical lines so that we appreciate the strengths which that tradition has reflected in its past environment, in order to try and discover what the faith might look like in a new situation with new challenges and different issues. As in the previous chapter, we will look at the New Testament, the English Reformation and the more recent theological tradition before seeking to draw together what this visit might yield.

Community in Corinth

We have already had occasion to look at the Christian community in Corinth in terms of its situation in a very plural and commercial city. The Corinthian Christians were a small group and faced a variety of difficulties as they sought to live out their Christian life in a fairly hostile environment. Their difficulties were of a social and moral kind, and they also had the natural problems of a developing community in the first generation of the new faith of seeking to shape and discover the nature of the gospel and Christian belief. The challenge for Paul and for the Corinthians was faithfulness in their Christian vocation in Corinth.

The two letters which we have from Paul are our principle sources of information about the Corinthian community. Of course, there is the account in the Acts of the Apostles which provides some background. The two letters are clearly not the only letters which Paul wrote. Paul refers to other letters, and he also refers to a letter which he has received from the Corinthians, or at least some of them. As a consequence, the two letters which we have are not the entire story about Corinth, but they do provide very interesting and valuable information about the nature of this emerging Christian community.

The two letters are very different in terms of what they seek to deal with and in their orientation and style. The first letter to the Corinthians is taken up with some introductory matters to do with Paul's relationship with them, their allegiance to him, their relationship to Apollos, and certain other social and moral questions. This then leads on to a series of responses to questions which have been raised in written form to Paul from Corinth. The questions in 1 Corinthians have to do with moral questions and how to live faithfully in Corinth. They are about the nature of the faith and aspects of the dynamics of the life of the Christian community when it meets together as an assembly. In the second letter to the Corinthians the questions are much more focused on the nature and significance of Paul's apostolic relationship to the Corinthians. Clearly there were people who opposed Paul, and that is addressed particularly in 2 Corinthians.[169]

The different concerns of these two letters can be seen in their introductions. Characteristically, Paul addresses the people to whom he is writing with some

---

169 See Marshall, P, *Enmity in Corinth: Social Conventions in Paul's Relations with the Corinthians*, and Kaye, B, 'Paul and His Opponents in Corinth'.

ascription and prayer. So, in 1 Corinthians he says that he is writing as an apostle of Jesus Christ by God's call and by his will and that he is writing, with his colleague Sosthenes, to God's church at Corinth. That church is characterised as dedicated to God in Christ Jesus, called to be his people. Paul then goes on in prayer-like form to give thanks for the Corinthians for the grace given to them in Christ Jesus, the enrichment that they have come to in Christ and the knowledge and gifts which they have, and he expresses his confidence that God will keep them firm until the end without reproach.[170]

Paul begins the second letter to the Corinthians by describing himself as an apostle of Christ Jesus by God's will, and he associates Timothy with himself. But he addresses his letter to the Church at Corinth together with all the people throughout the whole of Achaia. Achaia was the province to the north of Corinth. It encompassed quite a large area and a significant population. In prayer like-form Paul then goes on to praise the God and Father of our Lord Jesus Christ, the all-merciful Father whose consolation never fails. Paul immediately begins to talk about the way in which God consoles us in our troubles and how this consolation enables us to console others. That enables him to go on and refer to the troubles that he has had in Asia, where he nearly despaired of his life. He is confident that God will deliver him and will continue to deliver him. The many people who were praying for him in Corinth meant that there would be many to give thanks for his deliverance. This opening prayer in 2 Corinthians is much more orientated towards Paul's relationship to the Corinthians and the intimate spiritual bond which exists between them.

The difference between these two documents helps us make better sense of the emphases on community that we find in the two letters. In both of them there are issues to do with the Corinthians' relationship with Paul, relationships among themselves, and the moral character of the community life which was emerging among the Christians in Corinth. We can see this in each of the four areas which are of concern to us in our revisiting of the Corinthian situation, namely questions of connection and allegiance, difference and diversity, direction and leadership, and the emergence of institutions as vehicles for the maintenance of values within the community's life.

---

170 O'Brien, P T, *Introductory Thanksgivings in the Letters of Paul.*

Connection and allegiance

The very fact that Paul writes to the Corinthian Christians is evidence of a relationship between them. He was the apostle who first preached the Christian gospel in Corinth and whose work led to the emergence of the Christian community there. It is in that sense that Paul is able in 1 Corinthians 4:14 to speak about the Corinthian Christians as his dear children. It is a significant claim in the context, because he is seeking to establish his position as apostle in relationship to others who might come in later and contribute to the Corinthian Christian group, people such as Apollos. He goes on to say in 1 Corinthians 4:15, 'You have many tutors in Christ but you have only one father, for in Christ Jesus you are my offspring and mine alone through the preaching of the gospel. I appeal to you therefore to follow my example.'

The Corinthians, therefore, are in a very particular relationship with Paul. He has founded the Christian community by preaching the gospel in Corinth. That primary basis of the Christian community gives Paul grounds for an appeal to special consideration. He wants them to pay particular attention to him. In a certain sense they are his offspring. Thus people come from Corinth to Paul with questions. He enjoys a natural relationship as teacher and founder with this Christian community. Apart from the comparison with Apollos, this all seems quite natural and accepted in 1 Corinthians.

However, in 2 Corinthians the situation is very different. Here Paul's position as apostle, the founding preacher of the gospel, appears to be contested. In 2 Corinthians he makes a similar point to the one made in 1 Corinthians 4 and refers to the letters of recommendation that other people produce. He counters this by claiming that the Corinthian Christians themselves are his commendation. 'You are all the letter we need, a letter written on our hearts. Anyone can see it for what it is and read it for himself' (2 Corinthians 3:2).

Paul thus takes a strong view of his relationship to the Corinthians. He declares that what he did among the Corinthians was a work of God. It is plain, he says, 'that you are a letter that has come from Christ, given to us to deliver, a letter written not with ink but with the spirit of the living God' (2 Corinthians 3:4). Later, in 2 Corinthians 5:20, he describes himself as Christ's ambassador: 'It is as if God were appealing to you through us. We implore you in Christ's name to be reconciled to God.'

It is clear that there is some question in the minds of some of the Corinthians about Paul's reliability, particularly in relation to his travel plans. In both letters he has to defend his decisions about travel and also some of his actions in writing to the Corinthians. He justifies his change of plans on the basis of his particular and extraordinary love for the Corinthians and his transparent sincerity towards them. He claims that he has related to them throughout with godly sincerity (1 Corinthians 1:12). His appeal to them is open before God (2 Corinthians 5:11). He says that he has opened his heart to the Corinthians in this letter, and he appeals to them to open their hearts to him (1 Corinthians 6:11–13). 'Make a place for us in your hearts', he says (1 Corinthians 7:2), and he appeals in gentleness to them (2 Corinthians 10:1).

It is quite apparent that relationships between Paul and at least some of the Corinthians have been difficult, but he does not yield an inch on the basis which had been established when he wrote 1 Corinthians, namely that he is their apostle, he is the founder of this community and they are his spiritual offspring. Furthermore, he has been the instrument of God, and continues to be the instrument of God, as their founding preacher.

These two letters also reveal contact with others who belong to God. In 1 Corinthians 10:1 Paul speaks about 'our ancestors' being under a cloud. 'Our ancestors' here may mean the ancestors of Paul and his fellow Jews—indeed, it probably does refer to that (Exodus 13:21). But at least some of the Corinthians were Jewish and would have been incorporated in that characterisation. In 1 Corinthians 16 Paul talks about the collection for the saints and asks for the involvement of his readers. In his opening to the first letter to the Corinthians, Paul speaks about those who invoke the name of our Lord Jesus Christ, wherever they may be. Paul's second letter to the Corinthians is addressed to all God's people throughout Achaia. He refers again to the collection in 2 Corinthians 8 and the contribution being made by the churches in Macedonia. In 2 Corinthians he also refers to Titus and Timothy as his colleagues, as well as some others who are going to Corinth.

All of these people, scattered throughout Achaia, located in Macedonia, even with Paul in Asia, have a common cord of connection: they belong to Christ. Not only so, they all have a common destiny in their belonging to Christ, namely that God will raise them all together into his own presence. Indeed, Paul looks forward to a great gathering of thanksgiving in this resurrection scene. Just as God raised Jesus to life, so God will bring us to his presence.

However, there is another group who are alienated from the Corinthian Christians, or at least are distinguished from them. These are the non-believers. In a previous letter Paul had apparently told the Christians not to associate with immoral people, and in 1 Corinthians 5:9 he had to correct a misunderstanding of his statement. He had not meant the immoral unbelievers but immoral believers. He was referring to a disciplinary question within the Christian community. This distinction not only identifies moral difference between belief and unbelief but also underlines the moral character of the Christian community in Corinth. Sexual immorality is out of place in this community, and the immoral brother is to be disciplined. Paul reminds the Corinthians that bad company ruins good behaviour.

This moral community has within its membership the resources to sustain its life. Paul uses the image of the body to speak about their different gifts. This was a well-known image in political circles in the ancient world, but here Paul applies it to the Corinthian community and calls them the body of Christ. That includes the idea that they are a Christian body, just as the Roman empire might be thought of as a political body.

The connections between the Corinthians are profound and religious in character and therefore are also moral in character, for what binds them together is their common belonging to Christ. For this reason the ultimate argument for the way in which they should interrelate to each other in the context of exercising their different gifts is love, for love is the very expression of the character of God as demonstrated in the gospel. Paul appeals to the Corinthians as sensible people (1 Corinthians 10:14), and he calls upon them to exercise their judgment. He asks rhetorically, 'Examine yourselves. Are you living the life of faith? Put yourself to the test. Surely you recognise that Jesus Christ is among you. If not, you have failed the test.' The Corinthian Christians are therefore bound in a community by their common allegiance to Christ and by their shared experience of the presence of God in their own lives and among themselves as a Christian community.

The same community has extensive connections not only with Paul (connections which are very particular and precise because of him being their founding apostle) but also with Christians elsewhere in the Mediterranean world and, indeed, in an imagined sense, with their predecessors in the history of Israel. These connections and these allegiances are created by the activity of God. This Christian community is a community being brought into existence by the activity of God through the preaching of the gospel and the work of the Spirit.

Difference and diversity

The truth that God is bringing this community into existence is further underlined by the way in which Paul explains difference and diversity in the community. We have already noticed that members of the community are quite fundamentally different from the immoral of this world. There are also differences between Paul and others from outside Corinth who visit Corinth; he is their apostle and therefore enjoys a special and privileged relationship with them. Apollos has a different role, and each of those roles is a gift from God. There is no suggestion that calling and gift imply sameness; on the contrary, difference and diversity are manifest.

Paul treats the individual contributions the Corinthians make to the life of the Christian community in a way which underlines the diversity in a most powerful and extraordinary way. He does not simply draw attention to the differences: one speaks in tongues, one prophesies, one makes this or that contribution. Rather, he speaks of these different contributions as being from God. They are gifts not just to the individuals who exercise them but to the Christian congregation. Of course, these gifts do not all have the same importance for the life of the community, but they and their diversity are validated as gifts.

This point is underlined by the progression of the argument in 1 Corinthians 12 and 13. In chapter 12 Paul offers the body image as a way of understanding the unity and diversity created by the gifts. However, such an image is actually too static for the dynamic operation of the community. He therefore goes on in 1 Corinthians 13 to show them a better, more excellent way of dealing with this matter. That better way is for the Corinthians to behave towards each other, in the exercising of their gifts, according to the central gospel character of love.

The difference between the dissension in the early part of 1 Corinthians and the diversity of gifts, even divisions of opinion, in the later part of 1 Corinthians is quite marked. The dissension involves allegiances which speak about distance and animosity rather than a diversity which speaks about mutual service and interdependence. Paul is at pains to reprove the dissension and affirm the diversity of gifts.

In 2 Corinthians Paul speaks about this dissension in more explicit terms. He fears that he might find quarrelling and jealousy, angry tempers, personal rivalry, backbiting and gossip, arrogance and general disorder. These things have to do with the way in which people regard each other and whether they see Christ in their fellow Christians, whether they act according to love towards their fellow Christians. These kinds of divisions are of a moral character and are excluded by the terms of the gospel upon which this Christian community has been founded.

However, it is a community which not only fosters difference but also contains some who are able to make wise and sensible judgments about difficulties which arise within the community. The community has the capacity to deal with its problems. Thus, when Paul calls for unity among the Corinthians, he is calling for a restoration of moral attitudes rather than eclipsing or flattening difference. The unity which Paul looks for arises from the common belonging to Christ in the gospel, a gospel which itself creates diversity. That is the character of the gift of God. So any uniformity beyond the essential moral qualities of the gospel is a contradiction of the gospel upon which the Corinthian community has been founded.

Direction and leadership

Clearly this was a dynamic community. In that sense it was a community on the move. It was a community finding direction, and that raised issues of leadership. Leadership is a mechanism whereby direction can be achieved. In the Corinthian situation it was quite understandable, in the first flush of its foundation, that it should look for leadership from Paul, the founding preacher. Paul and Apollos were stewards, each providing different kinds of contributions, each providing different kinds of leadership.

While Paul claimed a unique position as apostle, that unique position was not the only exercise of leadership which was felt in the community. Paul's leadership claims were very substantial. He claimed that he was an ambassador for Christ and that his appeal was before God—indeed, God was making his appeal through him. He was God's minister. At the same time, his position among the Corinthians grew as the faith of the Corinthians grew. His role was to enable the Corinthian community to flourish.

Others also have an influence in the Corinthian community. Apollos has already been mentioned, and he figures especially in 1 Corinthians. But Timothy and Titus come from Paul's group and exercise an influence in the Corinthian community. There are people in Corinth itself who influence the direction the community takes. Paul reminds them of the family of Stephanas, who were the first converts in Achaia and who have devoted themselves to the service of God's people. He urges the Corinthians 'to accept the leadership of people like them, for anyone who labours hard at our common task' (1 Corinthians 16:16).

It is clear that the Corinthian community has many leaders, each exercising their gift, each providing direction and each fulfilling their calling. Certainly, some are mentioned, such as Stephanus or Pheobe, who seem to emerge as having particular influence on the Corinthian community. But the leadership which is envisaged here is a leadership which belongs to the community, is exercised from within the community, and is achieved through the gifts of the members. Leadership is not a narrow concept; it is a particularly discriminating concept, and different people exercise different kinds of leadership in this community. It is in this way that the community finds direction, and the direction that it finds is a direction towards maturity in Christ and hope in the resurrection.

Institutions

With the passing of time, any Christian community will establish habits, customs or traditions. What is remarkable about the Corinthian community is that it was founded upon traditions, and it established rules and habits and customs very quickly. The gospel, which was the foundation of this Christian community, was itself a tradition which Paul himself had received. In 1 Corinthians 15:1 he describes how he preached to them what he himself had first received. He also mentions another tradition which he handed on to the Corinthians, namely a recollection of the last supper.

First Corinthians 11 is one of the most tantalising sections in the whole of the Corinthian correspondence. It has two sections to it. In the first Paul says that he commends the Corinthians for always maintaining the traditions which he handed on to them. He then goes on to add to this tradition certain things about the relationship between men and women and also some comments about whether or not women should be bareheaded. He appeals to a number of considerations, including what the Corinthians might learn from nature.

However, the argument seems to run into the ground somewhat, because he says that, if anyone still insists on arguing, there is no such custom among us or in any of the congregations of God's people. It is, unfortunately, not clear what custom he is referring to. However, this sentence clearly implies that certain customs were beginning to emerge generally among the Christian congregations in the Mediterranean area.

Paul then goes on to talk about things for which he does not commend the Corinthians. When they come together, there is dissension. They appear to have had the habit of some kind of communal meal, which Paul says is in no sense the Lord's supper, that is to say, it is in no sense a supper which belongs to the Lord. It is not Christian in character. In order to provide a powerful example to lay upon the Corinthians, Paul relates to them the tradition which he had handed on to them about the last supper of Jesus and his disciples. It is that institution, that repetitive pattern, which is here laid upon the Corinthians as a basis for their proper behaviour at their communal meal. That is the tradition which Paul uses to constitute the institutionality of the Corinthian fellowship meals.

Such patterns of behaviour which are repeated over time constitute the beginnings of the institutions of Christianity.

Paul also deploys rules which are less well formed than these traditions. He has a rule about marriage and remarriage, and there is a wider rule in the churches of the saints that women should not speak in the church assembly (1 Corinthians 14:33,34). Similarly, there is a rule Paul has in all the churches that people stay in the position in which they were called as Christians. When dealing with the contributions of prophets and those who speak in tongues to the assembly, he sets out clear guidelines, and he then declares his authority on this point to be superior to any inspired utterance because what he writes is a 'command of the Lord' (1 Corinthians 14:37). These are socially conservative rules, understandable in a movement which had the appearance of being revolutionary.

It is clear that only a few years into the life of this community patterns of institutionality have already become established and are emerging in increasing diversity. The traditions upon which Paul founded the community have become part of that institutionality, and they exist to inculcate the religious and moral behaviour of the community.

Conclusions

In many ways what is most fascinating about this Corinthian material is that it shows a community which has developed so much in such a short period of time. It shows how connections and allegiance, difference and diversity, direction and leadership and institutionality have clear outlines in the character and life of these Corinthian Christians. It is also clear that God is present in this community and that its rich diversity is validated as the activity of God. Unity in this community is a unity of connection and common allegiance to Christ. The leadership which is exercised, that is to say, the influence which helps the community to find direction, is also quite differentiated, and the patterns of institutionality which are already emerging in the Christian community are similarly differentiated as to their importance and significance.

At first blush one might say that this looks like an ecclesiology of chaos. But it is an ecclesiology born of a conviction that the community is in the process of being created by the very presence of God and that God's presence is manifested clearly and definitively in the Christ who is preached in the gospel. It is that connection and allegiance which holds the community together. It is similarly that connection and allegiance which creates the difference and diversity in the Corinthian community and enables the direction and leadership to emerge in a way which marks it out in terms of interdependence and diversity.

The English Reformation

We have had occasion already to note the constitutional importance of the English Reformation monuments for Anglicanism generally and Australian Anglicanism in particular. Part of the ambiguity in the relationship between Australian Anglicanism and the English Reformation is the difficulty that the English Reformation was cast in particular contexts and defined in particular terms which are no longer relevant to the Australian environment or indeed generally in the modern world. That disparity has long been part of the history of the interpretation of inherited English law in Australia. We have already seen how the English Reformation coincided with the legal establishment of an independent and separate national church. That revolution and the terms of the settlement owed a great deal to the political movements of the fifteenth and sixteenth centuries. The break with Rome was part of a significant political movement which can be observed throughout western Europe with the rise of the monarchies and, in the case of England, with the rise of the power of the house of Tudor. The English Reformation legislation took some trouble to claim that the English church had the resources within its own membership, institutions and traditions to maintain orthodox Christianity within the realm of England. We noticed in the previous chapter how that political agenda impacted upon the way in which authority in the English church was defined in Reformation legislation.

An assertion of independence was one thing. Given that it was a church organised on a national basis and given the imperial political framework, the next step was inevitably a uniformly ordered church. Nisbet and Hastings are right to draw attention to the sixteenth century as the high point of English nationalism. That nationalism was expressed in statutory form and shaped the way the English church was restructured. The church became a national organisation under the crown. The first among the bishops was the Archbishop of Canterbury, then the Archbishop of York, and then came the dioceses, whose bishops were effectively appointed by the crown and were often directly controlled and instructed by the crown. Then came clergy, who again were subject to the authority of the bishop.

There were national assemblies, mainly of bishops. In the thirteenth century the convocations consisted of bishops, abbots, deans and archdeacons, and two representatives of clergy from each diocese and one from each chapter body. However, this convocation, which had the capacity for some independent action, was effectively muzzled by the Reformation legislation. In 1532 Henry VIII obtained the submission of the clergy, which was embodied in an Act of Parliament in 1534. Eventually convocation was disbanded early in the eighteenth century and was not reconvened until the second half of the nineteenth century.

The dramatic changes in the organisation in the Church of England at the Reformation can only be appreciated against the wider political backdrop. Such a perspective also helps us see what significant differences had come to be implied by the organisational structure which had emerged in western Christianity from the sixth century onwards.

In earliest Christianity bishops were office holders of a community of Christian people—a local community of people.[171] They were, as a Cyprian pointed out in the

---

171 For a general review of these issues see Campenhausen, H v, *Ecclesiastical Authority and Spiritual Power in the Church of the First Three Centuries.*

second century, associated with the church in the local vicinity. In the fourth century, when the political authority of the Roman Empire came to support the church and thus the bishops, dramatic changes took place. In AD 380 the Emperor Gratian issued an edict which gave the Bishop of Rome jurisdictional, that is to say, coercive disciplinary power not only in Rome but also in Italy and Gaul, Spain, Africa and Britain. Now the bishop was not simply the bishop of a community of people but a person who had politically backed jurisdictional power over territories. In the eleventh century, Pope Gregory VIII issued a series of dictates which claimed jurisdictional authority over the whole of western Europe.

Of course, this particular political alliance eventually collapsed, though some of the imperial notions recurred from time to time, usually with other political alliances.[172] As the Roman empire began to decay in the West, particularly in Gaul and Spain, Roman influence remained mainly in the towns where Roman settlers had established themselves with administrative and even judicial arrangements. Bishops and clergy in the towns mostly ministered to Romans, who had become an expatriate social elite. Villagers were often thought of as pagans. Christianity was the religion of the governing classes. Following the Teutonic invasions of western Europe, this pattern still managed to maintain itself. The Germans preferred to dominate the countryside, and the towns were left somewhat to their former inhabitants. The Germans also allowed existing laws to continue. It was a time when bishops and communities in the towns increased their status, effectiveness and power. As the countryside became Christianised in subsequent times, it came under the influence of the bishop in the towns. Thus emerged the notion of the diocese and of the diocesan bishop going beyond the immediate community of which he was originally the officer.

In England the Romans were less numerous, and the Roman administration had less hold upon the population. There were bishops in England when the Romans left, but the diocesan organisation in England essentially originates with the reforms of Archbishop Theodore (602–690) in the seventh century, just as the diocesan system in Germany originated from the reforms of Boniface (680–754) in the eight century. Thus, in this development, bishops became officers of a territorial district rather than of a community of people.

---

172 See Hatch, E, *The Growth of Church Institutioins: The Organization of the Early Christian Churches.*

A similar transition can be seen in the way in which the notion of a parish has developed in the history of Christianity. By the fifth century the early church had broadly taken over the Roman administrative districts as its pattern of organisation. This pattern was retained in the East, but it fell away in the West. The reforms of Theodore in England and of Boniface in the Frankish empire more or less restored the eastern pattern. The new system was established by cooperation between church and state, though it was a slow process. Under Boniface's reforms the bishop was to visit the presbyter's church once a year to preach, to confirm and to exercise discipline in the community. In this role he was, in fact, acting as a commissioner for the government. Besides this, the presbyter was to report to the bishop once a year. Under the reforms of Theodore in the seventh century, a parish came to be an area or unit where the bishop had the opportunity to appoint a clergyman. However, often the clergyman was appointed by a patron, and there was conflict between the rights of the patron, the rights of the bishop and the rights of the clergyman. In the end, a system prevailed which gave the right of institution to the bishop, though the patron retained the right to nominate and to present. The incumbent retained his position against the bishop by means of an agreed freehold, which effectively amounted to lifelong tenure.

In England the parish districts were also often districts used for other local administrative purposes. Indeed, the coextensive character of the ecclesiastical parish and the administrative parish established at the Reformation became one of the points of real conflict during the eighteenth and nineteenth centuries, as people sought relief from ecclesiastical control in these administrative areas.

Prior to the Reformation a great deal of the pastoral care of people in England was provided by religious orders. The monasteries scattered throughout England provided a network of care and ministry which was extremely significant. That ministry was lost to the populace when the monasteries were dissolved at the time of the Reformation. The effect of this was to narrow the organisational arrangements for the pastoral care of the people down to the parochial system alone. These institutional changes at the Reformation made the Church of England a national and single organisational conception. It was a national faith with a national church structure.

The impact of that political environment can be seen in the homilies authorised by Elizabeth in 1562. The homily on obedience begins its scriptural exposition in the following political terms:

Let us consider the Scriptures of the Holy Ghost, which persuade and command us all obediently to be subject, first and chiefly to the Queen's Majesty, supreme governor over all, and next to her honourable counsel, and to all other noblemen, magistrates, and officers, which by God's goodness be placed and ordered. For almighty God is the only author and provider of this aforenamed state and order.[173]

The tenor of the homily against wilful rebellion is extreme. After describing Lucifer and his rebellion in heaven, the homily says, 'Here you may see the first author and founder of rebellion and the reward thereof'.[174]

The two longest homilies deal with idolatry, and disobedience and wilful rebellion. Of course, it may properly be said that this was an appropriate concern with contemporary questions. But the reality in terms of the contents of these homilies is that they were deeply affected not just by the problems of the day but by the concerns of the rulers.

Similarly, Article 37 draws very appropriate distinctions between the things allowed in sixteenth-century England to the crown in terms of power and authority on the one hand and the rights and privileges of ministering God's word or sacraments on the other. Nonetheless, the assertions of the supremacy of the crown in this article clearly reflect the legal circumstances and political ideology which shaped the Tudor revolution.

What the sixteenth century created for England was a national church, separate and independent from churches in other territories and specifically from the bishop of Rome. It was a nationally organised church emanating from the crown and the Royal Supremacy and ruled in a very singular fashion without interposing qualifiers such as religious orders. It expressed a national faith and a national religion, and, of course, it had to express a singular and national way of worshipping.

The idea that every parish in every diocese throughout the length and breadth of the land should use exactly the same liturgical words enforced by law would have

---

173 Griffiths, J, *Certain Sermons or Homilies Appointed to Be Read in Churches in the Time of Queen Elizabeth of Famous Memory*, p 110f.
174 Griffiths, J, *Certain Sermons or Homilies Appointed to Be Read in Churches in the Time of Queen Elizabeth of Famous Memory*, p 588.

struck someone in England before the sixteenth century as odd, and five hundred years before it would have been incredible. Liturgical worship took on regular patterns as a result of local churches developing regular patterns of praying. Service books often differed from one another, and often different service books could be used side by side in the same church. A movement began during the twelfth and thirteenth centuries to regularise this diversity at the diocesan level. Naturally enough, these corresponded with the increasing significance given to the diocese and the diocesan bishop in this period. So in the thirteenth century, service books developed which were guided by the sanction of the bishop and which began to give expression to a diocesan 'use'. The diocesan liturgical use contained within itself significant diversity. Similarity was created as a result of influence, often influence from the practice of the cathedral church, but influence nonetheless. In the fifteenth century it was thought that the proper thing to do was to follow a provincial pattern or use, but this was by no means the case for the whole of England. Diocesan bishops retained significant authority in regard to liturgical use. That changed at the time of the Reformation.

Whatever common law tradition supported the bishop's authority in this matter was excluded by sixteenth-century legislation. The Acts of Uniformity in this period brought into existence two very important changes. First, liturgy would be the subject of statute law rather than custom and common law and, second, liturgical use would be uniform throughout the whole nation. It is in this context that we are to understand the Preface in the Book of Common Prayer, which, from the vantage point of a centralised political interest, deprecates all of this diversity which had served the church in England for a thousand years. Some have suggested that the Book of Common Prayer eliminated corruptions which had found their way into some church practices. This point of view is reflected in the document *Concerning the Service of the Church*. No doubt that reflects the theological commitments of Cranmer and colleagues. But the enduring fact remains that in the sixteenth century the liturgical perspective was made subject to the requirements of a national ideology and a legislative conception of the ordering of church affairs.

What was happening in England was not isolated from elsewhere in western Europe. The struggles which had been taking place at the Council of Constance (1414–18) and the Council of Basel, (1431–49) reflect similar struggles about the nature of the church and the ordering of its life. The attempts on the part of the papacy to establish a more extensive and a more comprehensive jurisdiction in western Christianity were not achieved easily and, in many ways, reflected the same kinds of processes which are evident in the general political life of western Europe. Gallican Christianity expressed similar kinds of independence as can be found in England. Western Christianity at the dawn of the Reformation was quite variegated. Throughout the previous five hundred years, Christianity had developed in different ways in different places throughout western Europe. Of course, there was connection. Of course, there was some common notion of orthodoxy, and, of course, it is possible to make generalisations about western Christianity. But it is nonetheless the case that there was widespread diversity. There were what Peter Brown (Brown, 1996) has called micro Christendoms cast around the western perimeter of Europe.[175]

At the end of the twentieth century we can be tempted to view the distant past through the lens of the more recent past. So we can easily be tempted to picture the fifteenth-century papacy in terms of the notion of infallibility claimed for the pope in the nineteenth century. During the fifteenth century the bishop of Rome did not represent the highly centralised papacy that has subsequently emerged. Similarly, we can easily imagine that the Reformation formularies were simply the expression of the religious tradition of renewed English Christianity. In fact, the Reformation legislation was cast in terms and categories of sixteenth-century political thought and practice.

The way in which the Reformation changes were effected had a dramatic impact on the way in which the church as a community of people was described. We may be tempted to think that these things belong to the essential character of the renewal of faith which happened in England in the sixteenth century. The reformers asserted theological principles about prayer, faith and authority which, in the end, may be able to tolerate the kind of political ideology which is expressed in the formulations of the sixteenth century but are not themselves inevitably committed to those terms. Indeed, as we saw with Richard Hooker's understanding of the Royal Supremacy, such a theological approach had the capacity to be, in the long term, subversive of the legislative institutional formulations which came to expression in England at that time.

175 Brown, P, *The Rise of Western Christendom: Triumph and Diversity AD 200–1000*, ch 13.

Not only so, but the legislated pattern proved to be unsustainable politically. Claire Cross has drawn attention to the fact that, even as the 1662 Act was being passed, it was clear that it did not represent a viable political option, despite the vehement Anglican episcopal response to the Restoration. The revolution of 1688 not only precipitated a crisis in thinking for Anglicans on church and state but also introduced the obverse of the tradition of power in the church to what had come in 1662.[176] The subsequent history of the position of the Church of England demonstrates the political futility of the Reformation settlements in this kind of society.

Conclusions

It is difficult to get away from the fact that the English Reformation has had a profound impact on the form and dispositions of modern Anglicanism. What is less often noticed is the clothing with which that Reformation tradition has been received. It is my contention that the political and legal form of the Reformation settlements have been carried forward into the ongoing institutional and attitudinal tradition of Anglicanism. For sustaining the idea of the church as community, particularly an interdependent and diverse community, those English Reformation monuments, with their centralist and conformist political assumptions, have had a mainly malign influence.

We have already seen in a previous chapter that the theological interpretation of the Royal Supremacy, the key concept in this legislative program, was subject to such significant qualification as to be acceptable in only a very limited sense. I argued that Hooker affirmed the Elizabethan settlement in order to secure acceptance for the best that could be achieved at that time. At one level he was concerned to respond to the Puritan revolution and to Roman ecclesiastical imperialism. However, under the surface, in the grain of his argument, he was also concerned to secure the best that he could in the context of the powerful political ideology of his day. In some ways this political ideology was more of a problem to him than the Puritans or Romans, even though all three were cast in broadly the same categories of power. The underlying theological position from which Hooker developed his position, makes it impossible to think that he really

---

176 Watson, W, 'Rethinking the Late Suart Church: The Extent of Liberal Anglicanism 1688–1715'.

believed in the Royal Supremacy, even though he found it a tolerable possibility. He was therefore engaged in a piece of occasional rhetoric. One needs to read carefully the underlying argument to see the colouration of that rhetoric and distinguish it from the more enduring values of the substance of the argument. It is precisely this interplay that produces a form of argument which stamps his genius and has prompted some to regard Hooker as the creator of Anglicanism. I would prefer to say that Hooker brought to expression in theological argument the tacit lineaments which had been forming in British Christianity over the previous thousand years. That he was able to do this is not only a measure of his gift but is also a measure of the crisis with which he was dealing.

In relation to the four presenting questions this chapter has been concerned with, namely difference, connection, direction and institutions, the English Reformation monuments have had a powerful and generally malign influence.

Difference and diversity within the church community was significantly discounted by the Reformation legislation in two respects. Firstly, it occurred in regard to uniformity of worship through the operation of a single compulsory liturgy. This represented a liturgical revolution in the history of English Christianity, but, more than that, the way in which it was enforced dramatically changed the character of the categories by which worship was understood in English Christianity. In this respect the Act of Uniformity was an act of political ideology.

A similar thing can be said about the way in which organisational structures were changed by the Reformation legislation. We have seen that the church structure was narrowed not only in a national direction but also in a diocesan and parochial direction. These changes were driven by political concerns and expressed a Tudor political and national ideology. These influences in the surviving Reformation monuments ought to be recognised for what they are and discounted as of any real theological significance in the pedigree of Anglicanism.

The basis upon which Anglicans were connected with each other was also reshaped in the English Reformation legislation. They were connected on the basis that they were citizens of a Christian king. Diversity and dissent, such as might be expressed in the practice of 'prophesying', were sternly repressed. So, once again the issue of connection within the framework of community was narrowed and distorted by the Reformation legislation.

The pattern of direction and leadership in this Reformation community was also influenced by this political ideology. Leadership was given by the power of the crown and often by the personal power of the monarch. Obedience to the power of the crown and its derived structures thus became the mechanism by which this community found direction. Of course, there were other forces and groups at work at the time, but the power of the crown was overwhelming, a point nicely illustrated on numerous occasions in MacCulloch's biography of Thomas Cranmer, particularly in relation to Cranmer's erastianism.

In relation to the institutions of the church community, two things from the English Reformation monuments stand out. The first was the establishment of new institutions by statute law. Traditional ways and the common-law traditions were set aside, particularly in regard to worship. Secondly, the institution of the state was a national entity supreme in all things.

Richard Hooker made an extraordinary attempt to demonstrate how a defence for these things might be established. His defence is very persuasive and has historically carried a great deal of weight. What has less often been recognised is that many of the elements which I have described are not central to Hooker's theological position or embodied in the terms of his argument. Rather, he embodies issues of difference and diversity, concepts of connection which are wider than simple citizenship, and ways of effecting influence within the Christian community which go beyond mere political power. His whole discussion of law reveals a foundation different from any narrow commitment to the single structure of statute law. However, because these things stand on the surface of the English Reformation laws and the legal monuments which have been embedded in the constitutions of many Anglican churches around the world, especially in Australia, they have often been regarded as of enduring significance and therefore in need of constant defence and legitimation. In the Australian environment, if one simply looks candidly at this aspect of the Reformation monuments, then one is bound to say that almost none of it is of any relevance or significance, and the categories of community implied in this legislative material are in fact quite harmful to the formation of an appropriate Anglican community.

Our appreciation of the significance of the English Reformation monuments for Anglicanism needs to go more profoundly and more deeply into the theological, religious and spiritual issues raised by the English Reformation which are reflected in the analysis of people like Richard Hooker and his antecedents in the tradition of British Christianity.

Theological tradition

The twentieth century has been described by many people in theological circles as the century of the church. This has gained some popularity because of the emergence of the ecumenical movement and the way in which national churches have come into closer contact with other national churches through unprecedented levels of population migration. The process of decolonisation in the middle of the century has also brought into prominence the task of relating the church groups brought by colonial missionaries to the local population with the emerging local social and political institutions. That process has particularly affected Anglicans. The century has also seen two horrendous wars fought in Europe between nominally Christian countries. It is also a century marked by the Roman Catholic Second Vatican Council, in which major changes were initiated in Roman Catholic ecclesiology. For Orthodox communions in the eastern tradition, the fall of the east European communist regimes marked a similar traumatic watershed in the twentieth-century experience. Large-scale and traumatic social and political changes have therefore raised questions about the nature of Christian community and our understanding of the Christian church in its various manifestations.

Roman Catholic thinking on the church began to move in the middle of the century during the 1940s and 50s, largely as a result of theological work in France.[177] There theologians sustained a serious study of the early church fathers and focused their work on the notion of the church as the mystical body of Christ. One of the leading theologians in this group, Yves Congar, worked in close contact with a number of Protestant theologians in developing a more historical perspective on images and concepts of the church. Congar focused on the difference that he saw between the first millennium and the second millennium. In the first millennium the church, he said, did not have such massive power and did not dominate. In the first millennium he saw a more spiritual, praying understanding of the church. He perceived that the second millennium was more

---

177 For a convenient summary see Dulles, A, 'A Half Century of Ecclesiology'.

preoccupied with organisational structures and the exercise of power. The terms by which he drew this contrast point to his preference for an understanding of church for the third millennium. He sought to describe the church as a community in the Spirit.

Congar also gave a more prominent role to lay people in the church. Lay people were active participants in the life of the church rather than passive recipients. They were also called to an apostolic mission by their baptism. The Worker Priest Movement in France gave some expression to this, and it is a theme which has been most recently taken up by Pope John Paul II in his encyclical on the vocation of the laity. There the pope takes up many of the French themes, giving to the laity a special place in their vocation in the social structures of society.[178]

The Second Vatican Council gave prominence in the Roman Catholic Church to the notion of the church as a community of people. The key document of the council, *Lumen Gentium*, appeared to move the Roman Catholic Church from a static institutional vision of the church to one which was much more open and dynamic. This notion of the church as communion has become very significant beyond Roman Catholicism, in large measure through the bilateral conversations between Roman Catholics and other churches, as well as through the use of this motif in the World Council of Churches discussions and more recently in some Anglican documents.

In its introduction, the Anglican–Roman Catholic International Commission's (ARCIC) final report said that the underlying ecclesiology of all the agreed statements included in the final report had been based upon the notion of *koinonia*, that is to say, communion. This motif has been taken up in Roman Catholic dialogue in the United States and particularly with Orthodox churches. ARCIC II treats extensively the idea of church as communion. This report, published in 1991, led to an open letter from the Roman Catholic Congregation for Doctrine of the Faith dealing with the question of the church as communion. This open letter to the bishops sought in some way to highlight some of the questions as well as the possibilities associated with this way of approaching church and church unity discussions.

---

178 See Kaye, B, 'Signposting the Future: Why the idea of lay vocation in society has become a bad idea for Australian Anglicans'. See also John Paul II, *The Vocation and the Mission of the Lay Faithful in the Church and in the World*.

At the World Council of Churches assembly in Canberra in 1993 a document entitled *The Unity of the Church as Koinonia: Gift and Calling* was adopted by the assembly. The statement began by saying:

> The purpose of God according to holy Scripture is to gather the whole creation under the lordship of Christ in whom, by the power of the Holy Spirit, all are brought into Communion with God (Ephesians 1). The church is the foretaste of this Communion with God and with one another.[179]

The statement then goes on to talk about the difference between this gift, which is God's in Christ to humanity, and the calling of the church to give full expression to this gift. The document speaks somewhat complacently of the way in which 'in the ecumenical movement the churches walk together in mutual understanding, theological convergences, common suffering and common prayer, shared witness and service, and they draw close to one another'. The document then goes on to say that 'nevertheless the churches have failed to draw the consequences for their life and from the degree of Communion that they already experience and the agreements already achieved. They have remained satisfied to co-exist in division.'

This document raises most of the questions involved in understanding church in terms of a notion of *koinonia*. How, in fact, are unity and diversity to be blended? What in actual concrete terms does unity mean? In the theological discussions of *koinonia*, or communion, it is simply not a matter of fellowship, being together, but a matter of common possession by Christ.

It seems to me that this notion of the church as communion draws attention to some very important aspects of the Christian tradition which are particularly significant in the modern world. It draws attention to the connectedness that is given in Christ between every Christian. It draws attention to the fact that this common belonging to Christ and being united with Christ creates a bond of communion with all other Christians which transcends any other consideration. In that sense the notion of communion in God highlights a priority for the church's life. That priority is to participate in the divine through Christ and to do that for the sake of the mission which is God's in the world. In one sense communion is a very abstract idea. That is part of its rhetorical strength and, of

---

179 The text is printed in the official report, Kinnamon, M E, *Signs of the Spirit: Official Report Seventh Assembly. Canberra, Australia.*

course, part of its weakness as well. To assert the communion which exists in Christ between Christians, and to concentrate simply upon that point, may mean that other real but not ultimate differences will be glossed over or sidelined.

This notion of communion also provides the possibility of a better sense of diversity within the church, even among the churches, because it does not focus upon the necessity for organisational correlation or identity of arrangement but on common belonging to Christ. In that sense communion can be a very important way of opening up relations between different churches as well as relations between Christians within particular churches.

Yet, in conversations between churches issues such as the place to be given to particular forms of the ordained ministry remain significant stumbling blocks to agreement. There is widespread agreement in ecumenical conversations that apostolic succession, that is to say, the connection between the present contemporary church and the apostolic church, is secured not by some kind of continuity of order of bishops or priests but rather by a continuity of faith in the community of the church, a point made precisely by Irenaeus is his argument with the separatist Gnostics in the second century and in the World Ccouncil of Churches document of 1982 from Lima. Nonetheless, when it comes down to it, that point does not appear to remove the difficulties for some by their commitment to a particular interpretation of the significance of episcopacy. This is especially true in Anglican conversations. The ECUSA agreement with the Evangelical Lutheran Church of America suspended the strict insistence on episcopal ordination for a transitional period, but that step has been strongly criticised by some other Anglicans as a betrayal of principle, that is, of an absolute principle.

The notion of communion in understanding the church does have the great advantage of focusing on people and personal relationships, both to God and to others, rather than on the more contingent issues of institutions. This emphasis also enables Christians to recognise Christ in others, and for churches to recognise genuine real ecclesial validity in other churches with whom they differ, either in terms of their doctrinal emphases or their institutional arrangements.

There is another aspect of the use of this idea of communion in recent theological writing and discussion that forces itself upon anyone looking at this literature. The idea of *koinonia* is widely used in ecumenical discussions and bilateral conversations between churches, but within each particular church it is often used in quite different ways. That does not mean that *koinonia* is really some sort of rhetorical chameleon. Rather, I think it means that the idea that we belong to Christ and to each other raises different questions within different traditions.

In the Roman Catholic Church the idea was used both before, during and after the Second Vatican Council as a way of emphasising collegiality and connection of a kind which transcended the in-built hierarchical emphasis in that church's life and tradition. Indeed, it would be fair to say that after the Second Vatican Council the tensions seen by some within the Roman Catholic Church between a democratic church and a hierarchical church are questions of tension between the idea of the church as communion on the one hand and the church conceived of in its institutional arrangements on the other.[180] In the Roman Catholic Church *koinonia* has been used to modify the centralising impulses of the hierarchical structure which are such a crucial part of the Roman tradition. The impulse therefore operates in a diffusing and centrifugal direction.

In the Orthodox tradition there is a strong claim that the whole truth is contained in Orthodoxy and also that the tradition is itself unified. *Koinonia* functions in this context to facilitate a creative handling of some growing diversity among the autocephalous families of the Orthodox tradition. In this sense, in the Orthodox tradition the notion of *koinonia* or communion seems to me to operate at several levels at the same time, at once asserting unity and justifying diversity.[181]

In the Anglican tradition, *koinonia* is used in a way somewhat similar to its use in the Canberra World Council of Churches assembly debate. *Koinonia* is mainly used in discussion about the relationships between the independent provinces of the Anglican Communion and the Anglican Communion itself. Anglicanism has never claimed to be a worldwide church in the same sense in which Roman Catholicism makes that claim. In Roman Catholicism the universal church takes priority over the local church in conceptual understanding and in priority of organisation and significance. The opposite is the case in Anglicanism. It is not

---

180 Bianchi, E and Ruether, R E, *A Democratic Church: The reconstruction of Roman Catholicism.* Hans Küng has returned to this theme on a number of occasions. His exposition of lay participation can be found in Küng, H, *Structures of the Church,* especially chapter V.

181 See Zizioulas, J, *Being as Communion,* and Tillard, J, 'The Church of God Is a Communion: The Ecclesiological Perspective of Vatican II', and the comparative study Volf, M, *After Our Likeness: The Church as the Image of the Trinity.*

surprising therefore that *koinonia* functions in Anglicanism in a centripetal direction. So, in the recent Virginia Report there is talk about moving towards the greatest degree of communion possible. That argument was used to support the idea of stronger and more powerful sets of things which were called 'instruments of Communion', which turned out to be a select number of mainly episcopal organisational arrangements.

It is not surprising, therefore, in ecumenical dialogue to find the notion of communion being used in different ways in different bilateral conversations. This difficulty is compounded by the fact that these major traditions, Orthodox, Roman Catholic, Lutheran, Reformed and Anglican, can all reasonably claim an integrity and a legitimacy from the origins of Christianity in the person and teaching of Jesus and the teaching of the apostles. Despite the imperial rhetoric that all of these traditions have engaged in from time to time, the truth is that there is a great deal to be said for each of them.

That fact draws attention to something significant about the nature of Christianity and the nature of the unity which Christianity can and cannot bring. Christianity cannot bring sameness. Indeed, it brings division and it brings diversity. We have seen this in the New Testament tradition, both within the local church and between different local churches. We have also seen in Tudor England at the height of English nationalism that diversity within the Church of England was threatened and attacked in the name of uniformity and orthodoxy over against Rome, but in the end the imperial attack of uniformity, in the name of Reformation orthodoxy, could not be sustained. Not only could it not be sustained, it proved impossible to sustain an unqualified theological defence of it in principle within the Anglican tradition of Christianity.

The development and use of the notion of the church as communion, especially in the last twenty years, has a great deal to offer in terms of understanding how a church community can think of itself. If one asks the question, what is the Anglican Church of Australia, and begins with this catalytic concept of communion or *koinonia*, then one will more directly and immediately see that the Anglican Church of Australia is a community of people scattered across this land. It then becomes easier to see that the institutional arrangements of ministry, dioceses, parishes, church order and all of those structural things are second-order issues that exist to serve that community of people. In fact, that is what the constitution of the Anglican Church of Australia implies and the ordinals all say. The catalytic concept of the church as communion helps us more easily and more immediately to express the point.

But seeing that point is only the beginning of the task, for it only raises more sharply the four presenting questions which we identified at the beginning of this chapter. How, in such a dispersed community, can one sensibly speak about and effectively and realistically experience connection and belonging? How, in such a dispersed community, can diversity and plurality be fostered and encouraged in a way which is creative and constructive for the life, faith and mission of the community? How, in such a scattered community, can direction be discerned and leadership exercised? How, in such a dispersed community, can institutions be seen as vehicles for sustaining the beliefs and practices to which the community is committed? Clearly, such questions can only be answered in relation to a variety of levels and locations within that community. In the history of Australian Anglicanism, the institutionalisation in the independent dioceses of significant theological and cultural differences has been a significant challenge to effective connection and belonging—not just connection and belonging between institutions in some organisational sense, but connection and belonging between the individual Christians who are located in different dioceses. The problem is often affected by the capacity of dioceses to isolate their members from those in other dioceses.

One of the astonishing achievements of the National Anglican Conference in 1997 in Canberra was that it brought such people into contact with each other in a way which they had hitherto not experienced. It was discovered across the distances, both geographical and perceptual, that there was a commonality, a connection and a belonging in Christ which they had not previously realised. That discovery proved to be a liberating and energising experience for most people present. In one sense that experience was both a terrible judgment and a sign of hope for the reinventing of this church community in terms of interdependent diversity.

Interdependent diversity

This review in a critical vein of some elements in the tradition of Anglicanism in relation to community has shown very different strands in the tradition. The presenting questions—difference, connection, direction and institutionality—are touched on in the elements of each aspect of the tradition which we have examined. Again, at key points the New Testament shows a high level of relevance, even though the example of the Corinthian church is a small local congregation set within a regional context.

The English Reformation tradition has again been shown to be most ambiguous. At one level the theological interpretation of the Reformation in England shows an openness to change, an awareness of diversity and clear notions of connection. However, in the actual formulation of the tradition in its institutional expression, principally in the legislation and governmental activity, there are continuing and residual elements which are resistant to any kind of recovery of a scriptural or broadly Anglican sense of community.

We have seen in previous chapters that while it was possible for Richard Hooker to offer a justification of the Elizabethan settlement with its strong national centralised uniformity, he did so in a way which makes it plain that ultimately he did not believe that this Royal Supremacy pattern was of ultimate value. His argument, and the qualifications which he placed upon it, his emphasis upon participatory church life and the way in which he analysed the significance of the sacraments and the institutional framework, make it clear that those aspects of Tudor political theory and Tudor political action which provide the clothing for this religious settlement were not only contingent, of passing significance, but were also in themselves inadequate. Despite these qualifications, Hooker could still accept these political settlements. While that conclusion might be possible for Richard Hooker in the sixteenth century, it is entirely unsupportable in the twenty-first century. The critical appropriation of the Reformation tradition forces us to look beyond the clothing to the religious and theological substance, which in this analysis has been epitomised by the work of Richard Hooker, though it could be found in others.

In the theological tradition, the twentieth century renaissance of the idea of the church as communion provides many opportunities for the development of a sense of connection which directly addresses the four presenting questions with which we began. It is to those presenting questions that we now turn as the first step in outlining a model of community which can be characterised in terms of interdependent diversity.

Interdependent diversity draws attention to two tensions in the nature of

Christian community which will have to be a mark of any reinvented Anglicanism. Within the community two principles will need to operate creatively together. On the one hand there is the principle of interdependence. The Anglican faith of each is dependent on the contribution of the other. That is true of individuals as much as it is true of sub-groups within the community. The other side of this is the recognition and, indeed, glad acceptance and embracing of diversity.

Of course, there are questions about the extent of diversity and the quality of diversity which is tolerable within a community. That, however, is best decided by working out what that diversity is and by looking back upon what has been accepted, achieved and made possible. Diversity in combination with interdependence can be creative; indeed, for the community to be creative this combination must necessarily be present.

These two principles operating together embody something fundamental about the nature of the God whom Christians worship. In recent literature much has been made about the importance of the doctrine of the Trinity for an understanding of ecclesiology. People have rediscovered what the Cappadocian fathers discovered when they were trying to bring the three persons of the Trinity into some kind of creative relationship. Beginning from the point of the threeness of the persons rather than from the singleness or unity of the Godhead, the Cappadocian fathers developed a notion of *perichoresis*. This notion of mutual interchange has been rediscovered in recent writing and has been made use of in some attempts to explain the nature of the church as a community of interdependent people.

It is a valuable insight and tells us as much about the circumstances in which we live as it does about the nature of God. David Nicholls has drawn attention to the way in which our conception of God is often a reflection of the circumstances in which we live.[182] This important insight draws attention to the symbiotic relationship between doctrine and living circumstances. Nonetheless, our conception of God affects the kind of community values which we seek to bring into existence in our immediate circumstances. The rediscovery in the second half

182 Nicholls, D, *Deity and Domination: Images of God and the State in the Nineteenth and Twentieth Centuries.*

of the twentieth century of the significance of a doctrine of the Trinity is not unrelated to the renewed interest in ecclesiology. Some uses of the doctrine of the Trinity in relation to particular patterns of ecclesiology seem to use the doctrine as a talisman for an ecclesiology already formed. However, the point which I wish to underline from this observation is that any reinventing and renewal of the church must be enterprised in terms of the dependence of that church on God who is the creator of that community.

The community which is the church is a community being brought into existence by the activity of God. Christian people are brought to God by the movement of the Spirit and by a variety of agents provided with the gifts that are necessary to achieve this mission of God. So an interdependent community of diversity must also necessarily be a community of interdependence with God. In Paul's terms, we are fellow workers with God. That means, among other things, that the first and most important task of the Christian community is to attend to God. The quality of listening and waiting upon God in activity and inactivity, in silence and in speaking, in resting and in doing will be a mark of the degree to which that Christian community is susceptible of re-creation and reinvention.

As is the case in much of western civilisation, and particularly so in Australia, we live in a noisy society, a society which is prone to speak rather than listen. It's a society in which the group dynamics which operate are often marked by a waiting to speak rather than a waiting to hear. Hugh Mackay makes an astonishingly good point in his book *Why Don't People Listen?*. He points out that listening is an exercise of entering into another person's world, so that in order to speak in order to be heard one must listen. It is not an easy thing in a noisy non-listening culture. But any church which is to be on a pilgrimage of reinvention must attend to the God who is re-creating. That church must be a listening church.

So the community to which I want to draw attention is not simply a sociological phenomenon. It is not an interdependent community of diversity in sociological contrast to some kind of absolute community, or some authoritarian community, though at a certain level it is that. This is a community which is being brought into existence by God, as people are caught up into the divine life through the gospel which it is the mission of the church to express. Such a community has all sorts of other qualities to it as well. It is a community which is built upon forgiveness, because it is a community pockmarked by failure and sin. It is a community marked by patience, because it is a community made up of frail human beings. It is a community marked by all of the virtues which are embodied in the Christian tradition. It is, in Stanley Hauerwas's felicitous phrase, a community of character.[183] However, in its re-createdness it is first and foremost an interdependent community of diversity.

At the beginning of this chapter I identified four questions about community which present as issues in the modern world and in particular in Australia. They were questions about difference, connection, direction and institutionality, and it is to those question to which I now turn in the light of the tradition which is the Anglican heritage.

Difference, diversity and pluralism

Of course, it is a fact that Australian Anglicanism is diverse and is marked by differences of various kinds. That is the fact. But it is not always the fact that such diversity has been marked by interdependence. It has sometimes been seen to be a church marked not so much by difference and diversity as by division or even schism. It is often said, when some serious debate comes up, that it will collapse and splinter and break up. In this context I want first and foremost to assert that diversity in the Christian community is the result of the activity of God. The creation itself is marked by diversity. We have noticed Paul's astonishing tour de force that enabled him to see that the differences in the Corinthian church were actually differences given by God. However, the very characterisation of differences of this kind as being from God and designating them as gifts marks the community out as something more than just a diverse gathering. It marks them out as a community that is being created by God. It marks them out as a community which belongs to God. It marks them out as a community which can also be characterised as the body of Christ.

Of course, as in Corinth, diversity can easily slide into division and then to dissension. There are at least two kinds of differences in the church. There are the different kinds of contributions which are made. Paul gives a Corinthian list in 1 Corinthians 12: apostles, prophets, teachers, deeds of power, healing, assistance, leadership, tongues. However, there is also diversity born of different perceptions and visions. This is the diversity which, when married to communion in the

183 Hauerwas, S, *A Community of Character: Toward a Constructive Christian Social Ethic.*

church, creates argument. That argument is a consequence not just of the inadequacy of our vision but also of our individual and common commitment to the God who is the subject of these visions. Argument out of diversity and difference is part of the activity of God. It is only when we turn our back on each other that difference turns into division.

One of the very important backgrounds for understanding the English Reformation, and particularly the thought of Richard Hooker and Thomas Cranmer, is the conciliar movement of the fifteenth century, particularly as it came to expression in the Council of Constance and to a certain extent in the later Council of Basel. At the Council of Constance the problem of a divided papacy was an immediate question. But also a more enduring question was the issue of continuity in the life of the church and the character of the life of the church as a whole. The document of Session IV of the council, *Haec Sancta*, was one of the most debated and important documents of the council.[184] It sets out a notion of the church as a community of diversity, but a community which is responsible as a whole for its life over against a centralised and absolutist conception of church office.

At the beginning of this century the Anglican historian John Neville Figgis delivered a series of lectures called *The Fellowship of the Mystery*. He drew upon this conciliar tradition in order to develop a notion of a federal participatory church. He said that 'all alike share it, all in some ways submit to it, and all contribute to it'.[185] Figgis argued that the two principle bulwarks against an absolutist ecclesiastical tyranny were devolution of power and the operation of individual conscience within the church. Clearly, these are important considerations and necessary in any conception of the church for its decision-making purposes if it is to be marked by interdependent diversity. However, when it comes to groups which are larger than immediately local, and even in local groups such as parishes, I believe that a third principle needs to be introduced and one which was developed in the conciliar movement, namely that of representativeness.[186] Being a representative involves not just participating with other representatives. It means bringing those who are represented to the table and bringing that table exchange to those represented. There must also be some sense in which the

---

184 For the documents see Tanner, N, *Decrees of the Ecumenical Councils.*
185 Figgis, J N, *The Fellowship of the Mystery,* p 189.
186 See Tierney, B, *Church Law and Constitutional Thought in the Middle Ages.*

decision-making bodies of the church community are genuinely representative of the totality of that community. It is one of the distinctive marks of the Australian Anglican tradition that the church as a whole is responsible for the life of the church as a whole. That was how synods emerged in Australia in the mid-nineteenth century.[187] Such corporate ownership can only take place within a community in which difference and diversity are nurtured and encouraged. The extent to which that tradition is not alive and well in Australian Anglicanism is a measure of the extent to which the church needs to be reinvented.

Connection and allegiance

We have already noted that at the time of the Reformation people were held together by common membership of both nation and church. They were all bound by the same law under the same sovereignty. The primary point which constituted their connection was their citizenship under the law. At the end of the twentieth century in Australia, and in most parts of the Anglican communion, such a conception is simply impossible. More than that, any attempt to sustain such a notion even in covert or tacit form will in the end be destructive of real ecclesial life. The kind of connection which will enable an interdependent diverse community to emerge is a connection which brings people personally into contact with each other, primarily by physical proximity. It is at this point that the recovery of the notion of the church in terms of communion (*koinonia*) makes such a helpful contribution to the Anglican scene. In a society where law and organisation increasingly define social connections, and where individuality is increasingly conceived of in terms of units in a mass society, such a notion as *koinonia* can make a vital contribution.

The recovered sense of the church in terms of *koinonia* is both rhetoric to bring itself to birth and also a reality in terms of the givenness in hope that the church is the creation of God. The connection which makes a church community creative is the connection of each to Christ and thus to each other. If connection and allegiance to the community are not first and foremost conceived of in terms of personal connections, in terms *koinonia*, then the temptation would be to think that the church is actually the organisation. That would be a fatal capitulation to the spirit of the age.

---

187 Kaye, B, *The 1850 Bishops Conference and the Strange Birth of Australian Synods.*

Direction and leadership

It is increasingly recognised, particularly in the study of corporations in the modern world, that direction and vision are crucial for the vitality of any enduring institution. I want to argue here for a notion of leadership which is about the articulation of vision. It is about the capacity to listen and to persuade about that vision, about serving the community and the theological values of the community in that persuading and in that listening. Therefore, in that sense, the direction which a community is able to take is a corporate conspiracy together to move in a given direction, and leadership is the catalyst that enables that to happen. In that sense, leadership is part of the interdependence of the community as it moves on its pilgrimage through time. For the church, such leadership is not simply listening to the voices of the people who make up the community, though it is certainly that. It is also a listening to the voice of the God who is at work in that community creating it.

Institutions

I have already tried to elaborate my understanding that institutions are continuing patterns of relationship between people and/or things and that these relationships, when sustained over time, teach us habits which are moral and theological in character.

The history of Christianity has seen the emergence of such institutions. In the modern period we have become less clear about the institutionality of our arrangements and their theological significance. Some time ago in New Testament scholarship it was fashionable to regard some of the later documents of the New Testament as in some sense representing 'early Catholicism', as if there were a secondary development from the pure Pauline Christianity of the so-called main epistles of the apostle. One of the distinguishing marks of this 'early Catholicism' was the emergence of institutional patterns, of church order. However, the truth, as we have seen even from our very brief excursion into the situation in Corinth, was that from the very beginning there was of necessity an element of Christian institutionality which Paul instilled in his congregations.

In the process of time in the early church three main institutional arrangements came to have leading significance, namely the idea of having a recognised collection of writings from the apostolic age, the regular use of rites of admission (baptism) and a fellowship meal (which came to be called the Lord's supper), and a recognition of an ordered ministry. These three practices did not emerge uniformly in all places nor immediately. They usually emerged in response to a series of developments both within and external to the Christian community.[188]

The origins of the idea of having a canon of Scripture has been a subject of much discussion among scholars. Some have suggested that it was a response to the acceptance in the second century of a collection of sacred writings by Judaism. Some other scholars suggest that it was a reaction to the teaching of Marcion, who wanted to select and edit the apostolic writings which were beginning to circulate.

My own view is that the idea of having a canon which emerged in the second century was in large measure a natural institutional instinct to provide a point of reference, which was necessary in the emerging and growing Christian church for two reasons. On the one hand it was necessary to provide some point of common reference, and in the second place it was important to provide some basis for a continuing sense of connection with the origins of the faith in Jesus' death and resurrection and the teaching of the apostles. There being no temple, or law, or sense of sacred land or place as in the case of Judaism, Christianity required some cohering institutional point of reference.

The idea of a canon of apostolic writings was an obvious and natural institutional arrangement which could satisfy the needs of the growing Christian community. It indicated that the faith of this generation must be related to that of apostolic Christianity as reflected in all its variety in these documents. The identification of this list or canon and of the idea of having such a list clearly emerged as a matter of community habit rather than some general decision making. The success of the rites of baptism and of what came to be called a Lord's supper was the result of a variety of historical circumstances, and they were traced back to Jesus' own example and teaching. The emergence of an institution of an ordered ministry is much more ambiguous and can be less easily identified than the first institutional pillars of the emerging Christian community. The idea of a canon of apostolic writings carried a crucial role in maintaining a point of reference for the increasingly scattered and far-flung Christian communities. Because of this

---

188 See the general discussion in Kaye, B N, *Web of Meaning: The Role of Origins in Christian Faith*.

apostolic role, it obtained a priority in the logic of the institutional arrangements within Christianity in relation to both sacraments and ordered ministry. It was at once more foundational and therefore also more determining.

These three institutions have come to be key pillars in the identity structure of the Christian community. These institutions have two important qualifications. First, they exist to serve the religious and moral values which brought them into existence and, second, they are themselves contingent on those truths and the activity of God in this community and the creation. Hence the precise form of the institutions and their actual operation may probably change through time and differ from place to place. History shows how much they have changed.

Of course, within Anglicanism there are many other institutions, as there have been down through the history of Christianity. We have seen that these different institutions—synodical arrangements, the idea of having canons, rules, ordered ministries, ways of deploying ministers, along with other institutional organisational arrangements such as independent Anglican societies or agencies—all exist to serve the community of Christian people. Anglicanism has a multiplicity of different kinds of institutions which serve the different kinds of needs that exist for that community, both in terms of sustaining its identity and of fostering its mission.

Each of these institutional arrangements have implicit theological values, or 'goods', in them which at once provide their justification, their use and the terms upon which they might properly be reformed. These institutions relate to such things as clergy deployment, synods, parish councils, the way in which groups of Christians make decisions, parishes, dioceses, the idea of a national church, the idea of belonging to the Anglican Communion, welfare agencies, church schools and a multiplicity of others. Each has its own historical background. Each embodies and fosters particular values deemed to have been significant and continuing to serve some value for the life of the community. These institutions often become so important, and often so powerful, that the theological values which they were formed to foster, protect and express are sometimes lost sight of. The way in which institutions in this community might properly be reformed is to recall them to the theological values they serve and to identify whether their manner of operation truly represents the values which are appropriate for the community in its present circumstances.

One very interesting example of this exercise can be seen in relation to clergy deployment. The way in which clergy are deployed in the Anglican church has a long history. Basically, Anglicans have inherited a tradition which goes back to changes which were made in the eighth century under the reforms of Boniface. For a variety of reasons a pattern emerged which saw clergy appointed by land-holding patrons. Their livelihood was sustained in much the same way as other people who were appointed by such patrons, that is to say, they were given land from which to gain their livelihood. The land was given on the basis of a tenancy. So the provision of the support for clergy seen in more recent centuries in the provision of glebe land attached to a parish goes back a long way and to a particular historical situation. It was where clergy were appointed to serve as chaplains in feudal estates. However, sometimes clergy were dismissed by the patron, and their capacity to fulfil their ministry with any kind of independence was significantly at risk. Also at risk was the capacity of the bishop to support the clergy in these kinds of circumstances. As a consequence, a trade-off was established between patron and bishop and clergy which enabled clergy to have some independence in the name of being able to preach the gospel freely and also at the same time have some protection of their livelihood. An area of responsibility between temporalities and spiritualities was established between the patron and the bishop. Bishops were given the opportunity to visit, and a requirement was made for the clergy to visit their bishop at least once a year. On the other hand, the tenancy of the clergy was established for their lifetime.

Such protection of independence in order to carry out the proper functions of the priest without undue pressure or insecurity of livelihood has analogies in more recent times in the case of judges and academics. The independence of the judiciary or of academics provides an analogy. The very nature of the professional activity requires a degree of independence, yet, at the same time, for livelihood, professors and judges are dependent upon the institutions within which they are located. Indeed, during the nineteenth century it was the professionalisation of the clergy that drew the parallel between these professions and clergy much closer together. Each, of course, clergy, professor and judge, claim certain distinctive qualities in their vocation which require, for the good of society, a level of independence not enjoyed by others who work in that society.

In the modern situation, the judges have a vocation which is still manifestly public and serving the common good at large. Because in Australia universities are in large measure public institutions, and because professors have continued to sustain a belief in the public utility of their role, they have to some degree been able to sustain an argument in favour of tenure. The degree to which either of these elements is diminished is the degree to which this tenure is at risk. However, the clergy have not been able to sustain a claim about their public role and have had to maintain the claim to tenure and independence within the narrower framework of the church community. In the Australian context that strategy has succeeded largely by controlling the decision-making processes of diocesan synods.

The changed social institutional arrangements within which the church operates have made the position of the clergy particularly ambiguous in regard to a number of legal frameworks within Australia. One of the vexing legal questions is whether they are employees and, if so, of whom? Moreover, in the urban environment, where most clergy are deployed, the definition of their tenure in relation to property is increasingly less relevant. These are the patterns in Australia, and, with some variations, the issues reflected here can be found in many parts of the Anglican Communion.

The patrons in the medieval system are in large measure now replaced by the parishioners, who contribute by their donations to the parish finances. The thought that they pay but have no influence as to the terms of the appointment or the conduct or the performance of the clergyperson strikes many such parishioners as odd and incongruous. Similarly, if the licence of the clergy to a parish cannot have a time limit, then that clergyperson enjoys a situation entirely separate from the working environment in which the parishioners find themselves. In Australia some dioceses have now introduced fixed terms for such licences for both the clergy and the diocesan bishop.

Having said all of that, it nonetheless remains a fact of our human condition that institutional arrangements cannot solve every problem. Indeed, the present ambiguous, clumsy and significantly irrelevant arrangements that currently exist can actually be made to work if there is a large amount of goodwill and acceptance on all sides. The difficulty is that institutional arrangements only come to bear on this question when that goodwill has been evaporated by the dissatisfaction of one or other of the parties concerned.

In the modern situation, particularly in the last fifty years, there have been interesting developments in the legitimating rhetoric for the present arrangements. Church documents and many people now begin to speak of clergy, and particularly parish clergy, as necessarily the leaders in the parish. A short glance beyond the beginning of the nineteenth century in Anglicanism makes it clear that this is a quite novel idea. This claim to focus leadership with the clergy in the parish environment is in reality little more than an understandable reflex to defend a position in a situation where their role has been socially marginalised. In a way it is a rhetorical claim to power. The same can be said of many of the demands that clergy submit to professional development assessments. By and large clergy throughout the Anglican Church of Australia have been resistant to the notion of professional assessment because they see it for what it often is, an attempt to re-construe the power relationships between themselves, the parish and/or the bishop. The same sort of rhetorical dialogue takes place when clergy are described as staff.

These indulgences in legitimating rhetoric do not advance the question very much, nor, indeed, it must be said, does the failure to resolve the problems which exist in the present arrangements. Neither the rhetoric nor the problems assist in the development of a community of interdependent diversity in the church. In such a situation it is more helpful to ask, what values do we want in arrangements for an ordained ministry, both in its terms of authorisation and in terms of its deployment? I believe that there are only two broad theological values which ministerial deployment should express in its different circumstances. The first is that the ministry is for the whole church. That is to say, it must be a ministry which is open and public. It must serve the whole of the community and be authorised for the whole of the community. The authorisation of a ministry is not just a matter of the assertion of the individually powerful but rather a way of recognising that those ministries which will be authorised in the church community on a broad basis are ministries which are accepted by and acceptable to the whole church. It is in that sense, I believe, that the ordinal is correct when it envisages that the authorisation of ordination is an authorisation in the whole church. But it is an authorisation, as well, by and for the whole church. In this respect the bishop acts on behalf of the community. While there is a sense in which bishops and priests are ordained into an order by the members of that order, they are still doing so on behalf of the church.

Recently there has been a good deal of discussion in theological literature about the nature of ordination, and in particular episcopal ordination, in relation to apostolic succession or the apostolicity of the faith which this ministry serves. In ecumenical discussions there has been an emerging consensus whereby apostolic succession is thought of in terms of the succession of faith in the whole community in its various dimensions, local, regional, national and international. Thus, authorisation is not an individual matter but a representative matter, and it is representative of the apostolic succession of the faith which resides in the community. So the first theological value that I would look for in an ordered ministry is that the ordered ministry should be from and for the whole church.

Second, that ministry fundamentally exists to serve, to facilitate, to sustain the apostolicity of the faith and life of the community. The ministry, however authorised, cannot guarantee the apostolicity of this faith. It cannot guarantee that the particular exemplification of the gospel in this community, local, regional or otherwise, is in fact a genuine exemplification of the apostolic faith. All that the ordered ministry can do is to seek to serve, to sustain, and to facilitate that apostolic faith. There is thus both a historic and a contemporary dimension to this ministry. The ministry exists as an instrument by which the faith of this present community is able to sustain an effective and creative connection with the tradition of the faith, a tradition reaching back to Jesus himself. This institution of the ministry is one way in which that apostolic connection with the historical incarnation is maintained in the present life and experience of the Christian community.

The ministry fulfils this apostolic role not simply by being there but by the apostolic character of its activity. In other words, this ministry is, in a certain sense, an interpretative exercise of the faith of the apostles for the present circumstances in which the community being served is called upon to live out that faith. There is thus a historical dimension to the value of sustaining the apostolicity of the faith, and also there is a contemporary or present dimension. Christianity is not simply the recitation of a past set of insights from the first century. Rather, it is a claim that God uniquely and distinctively revealed himself in the historical person of Jesus of Nazareth, but not exclusively so. The risen Christ, the power and exhortation of the Holy Spirit abide continually after the death and resurrection of Jesus in the life and mission of this Christian community. The uniqueness of Christ is effected not by being isolated but by being the touchstone by which all other claims are tested.

That kind of past–present continuity and discontinuity is one of the things being preserved in the doctrine of the Trinity. In that doctrine is preserved a conviction about the reality of the incarnation in a particular time and place, and also the reality of the presence of God throughout time and space. Scripture and the sacraments are the focal points of reference in this ministry of the ordered life of the community in its role of mission, mission which embraces the vocation of Christians to be godly citizens and also the vocation of Christians together to be a godly community.

These two fundamental values, that the ministry is for the whole church and that it exists to facilitate and serve the apostolicity of the faith, are the key things which hold together and justify a notion of ordered ministry in Anglican Christianity. Other things, I believe, are attempts to legitimate less significant and often less worthy matters.

Aside from these two fundamental values, there are also other considerations which arise out of the institutionality of having an ordered ministry of the kind which exists in Anglicanism. The range of skills and qualities required in the ministry will not necessarily be preserved in all ordained individuals. The profiles of those skills and qualities will differ from person to person, as will the profile of the needs of local communities. In that context, what is at issue here is not so much the ordaining of an individual but the ordering of a ministry in the church that is effective for the church as a whole, at least in its broader regional or national horizon. In the Anglican tradition it has been an important responsibility of oversight, or *episcope*, that the ordered ministry for the whole church is effective through the operation of the particular ministries of particular individuals.

As with individuals so with communities and institutions, repentance, forgiveness and reformation are ever-present claims upon our spiritual courage. The institutions in Anglicanism are no exception, and they need to be regularly scrutinised in terms of the theological values which they have in the religious tradition of the faith rather than in terms of some of the popular rhetoric, much of which is drawn from contemporary social models. So the synod as an assembly for discovering God's will has, in the conciliar character of the Anglican tradition, a more profoundly religious and divine dimension than the imagery of the parliament can suggest. While it is understandable that synods have imagined themselves to be like parliaments, that imagery is secondary and, in the present circumstances, almost always unhelpful. Any idea of the parish, the diocese, the national church or the Anglican Communion similarly needs to be criticised and appraised in relation to the theological values in the tradition which embodies and carries forward the faith for Anglicans. At this point to do that would take more space than is available, but each of the institutional arrangements will only be kept faithful if the values which they exist to exemplify and sustain are themselves regularly re-identified and claimed.

CHAPTER FIVE

ENGAGEMENT—RESPECTFUL VISIONARIES

We come in this chapter to the third of the foundational issues which provide the basis for the core argument of this book. It might be helpful to recap where we are. I have tried to set out the lineaments of the crisis facing worldwide Anglicanism. It is a crisis of identity and thus of interpretation of the meaning for today of the journey so far of this tradition of Christian faith. I have taken Australia as an example of these interpretative issues, because, for a range of historical reasons, the questions are well represented here, and, in any case, the Australian story is the one to which I belong. I have tried to show that in the last thirty years Australia has been going through a period of rapid social change. This has affected not only institutional arrangements and organisational patterns of life but has also had an impact upon expectations and ideas of social right and wrong. Therefore it is not surprising, in this context, that the issue of personal and community identity has flowed beneath the surface of social activity as a current of ambiguity and uncertainty in the last thirty years for Australians.

These changes have had a particular effect for Australian Anglicans, because they have drawn attention to significant longer-term shifts in the position of Anglicans in Australia. When Europeans came to Australia in the late-eighteenth century, Anglicanism came as the religion of the colonising power. Not only that, it came as the religion of the governors and chaplains of the jail which was the colony. Even when the colony expanded beyond being a jail for transported convicts, Anglicanism remained in a dominant social institutional and religious position. However, by a series of steps, mainly in the second half of the nineteenth century, that dominant position was eroded and has now been eclipsed. For the first sixty years of the twentieth century the underground tectonic shifts in the position of Anglicans in Australia were disguised by the social conservatism that was sustained during that period.

The last thirty years of the twentieth century, however, brought to light those underlying changes for Anglicans and, as a result, they find themselves at the beginning of the twenty-first century in a deeply ambiguous and uncertain position in Australia. This uncertainty affects their social role, their institutional relations and their own community identity within a modern plural Australia. Australian Anglicans face an urgent challenge fundamentally to reinvent or rediscover the church which is theirs. In that reinvention or rediscovery there are three foundational questions.

1. What is the basis and the character and the confidence which they have as Australian Anglicans to be participants in the life of this country?

2. What are the marks and characteristics which hold them together as a community of people? What kind of a community are they?

3 How does that community with its particular characteristics actually engage with others who are not part of that community?

I am approaching each of these three foundational questions—confidence, community and engagement—with what I have described as a tradition critical approach. What I mean is that the clue to understanding how Australian Anglicans might reinvent themselves is to be found in the qualities that are embedded in their own tradition. However, the tradition cannot simply be re-pristinated, it cannot be simply repeated. The circumstances require a much more critical appraisal. In particular, some aspects of the tradition have been continued from the past without sufficient reinterpretation for the situation in Australia. Anglicans are influenced by three important issues. There are, of course, other things which influence Anglicans, but these three are important:

- the scriptural material, particularly the New Testament
- the monumental declarations that remain from the English Reformation which are embedded in the church constitution
- the theological tradition which has been part of Anglicanism and more broadly of western Christianity for the last two centuries.

We need a critical reappraisal which focuses upon these three elements in order to reformulate or reconfigure the understanding framework in the new and changed situation in which Anglicans in Australia find themselves. Such a foundation can then be the basis of a revisioning exploration.

It is in that sense that we now come to the question of engagement. The thesis which I want to argue is that the model for engagement for Australian Anglicans can be characterised as that of 'respectful visionaries'. They ought to be people who respect the position of their fellow Australians as being different from their own in important respects. Yet, at the same time, they ought to be people who can provide a vision for what a human condition shaped by Anglican Christian beliefs might look like in the Australian environment. Even more than that, it is what that Australian environment, in its best human characteristics, might also look like. Let me be very clear about this. I am not suggesting that Anglicans should develop a blueprint for Australia, even as a utopian dream, though I do think that utopian language can be used as a rhetorical device to comment on the present. That is precisely what Thomas More was doing in his *Utopia*. Rather, what I am talking about here is a capacity to uncover the realities of the human condition which lie behind the presentation of the particular details of social activity which we see every day of our lives. By vision here I mean an explication of this reality which is shaped by an Anglican experience of the God of Jesus Christ in the context of living in and with the present.

Nature of engagement

In 1947 the Jewish philosopher Martin Buber wrote an important and very influential book called *I and Thou*.[189] In that book he made a distinction between

189 Buber, M, *I and Thou*, New York, Scribner, 1937.

the kinds of relationships which exist between me and an object. My relationship in this context is that of 'I to an it'. This is a relationship in which there is not a lot of interaction. It is the relationship of an observer or a user. This is in some contrast, said Buber, to a relationship with another person. That is a relationship of 'I and thou'. It is a relationship of personal interaction, of personal address, of personal involvement. It is a relationship which establishes some kind of connection, engagement, community. Sometimes our human relationships have the characteristics of an 'I and it' relationship rather than an 'I and thou' relationship. Buber, of course, deplores this. Writing after the Second World War, Buber was particularly concerned that the war showed that human beings could treat others as if they were mere things. In so far as that happened, both parties were fundamentally dehumanised.

Buber was powerfully drawing attention to the interactive character of human relationships. The qualities of those relationships differ in different combinations. The 'I and thou' qualities which exist in a relationship between a husband and a wife are quite different from those that exist between a police officer and a jaywalking pedestrian. It is different from the kinds of relationships that exist between institutional representatives. Nonetheless, these human relationships are, and must remain fundamentally, 'I and thou' relationships. Buber went on to draw an analogy between these relationships and the relationship between the individual and God. Writing out of his Jewish perspective, he saw God as the personal one who addresses us and calls us into an 'I and thou' relationship.

Such relationships are not always straightforward, and we often have a great deal of difficulty with them. Particularly is that so where our expectations are not as clear-cut as they might once have been or in circumstances where we are uncertain about those to whom we are relating. Hugh Mackay's 1994 book called *Why Don't People Listen? Solving the Communication Problem* began with the declaration that 'communication is probably one of your favourite subjects—and so it should be. After all, we humans are "herd animals". We belong in communities. We thrive on relationships. We need to communicate. But communication has had a tough time during the 1970s and 1980s.'[190] He attributes these tough times to the changes which have taken place in society. The form of the book's title illustrates

---

190 Mackay, H, *Why Don't People Listen? Solving the Communication Problem*, p vii.

the key issue for him in this matter: *Why don't people listen?*.

Hugh Mackay argues that listening is really the clue to communication, and communication is really a 'sharing of meaning'. He draws attention to what he calls the power of the cage. This is the cage of assumptions, meanings, connotations, associations, images and values in which we all live. The problem and the power of that cage is that it very often does not enable communication to take place between two people who are in two different kinds of cages. A sharing of meaning is when communication takes place, not just the passing of information. He talks about the 'injection theory', as if you could pass information to someone and they received it in the same sense and with the same meaning as it had for the person delivering the message. Nothing, he says, could be further from the truth. We each receive what we hear in the light of the dynamics of our own cage.

Mackay distils his argument into two tablets of a decalogue at the end of his book, ten laws of human communication. Those laws are:

1. It's not what our message does to the listener, but what the listener does with our message, that determines our success.

2. Listeners generally interpret messages in ways which make them feel comfortable and secure.

3. When people's attitudes are attacked head-on, they are likely to defend those attitudes and, in the process, to reinforce them.

4. People pay most attention to messages which are relevant to their own circumstances and point of view.

5. People who feel insecure in relationship are unlikely to be good listeners.

6. People are more likely to listen to us if we also listen to them.

7. People are more likely to change in response to a combination of new experience and communication than in response to communication alone.

8. People are more likely to support a change which affects them if they are consulted before the change is made.

9. The message in what is said will be interpreted in the light of how, when, where and by whom it is said.

10. Lack of self-knowledge and an unwillingness to resolve our own internal conflicts make it harder for us to communicate with other people.

All of these laws reflect a particular picture of the human condition and of interpersonal engagement. They portray a picture of each of us living, in a certain sense, in our own world, and that world will affect the way in which we receive as well as the way in which we give messages of whatever kind. Our capacity to understand each other is directly related to the level, quality and character of the relationship that exists between us, and our capacity to communicate with others depends on us engaging with them in a way which resonates with the circumstances and realities of their lives.

Furthermore, we tend to be conservative. We will generally reinforce where we are with what we hear. We will generally reinforce things which underline our own security. Insecurity will inhibit our capacity to listen to other people, because we will be preoccupied with our own concerns and will be unable to enter imaginatively into the circumstances and the world of the person with whom we are speaking.

It is for that reason that Hugh Mackay makes a sharp distinction between hearing and listening:

> When I hear, I simply receive a message which I may or may not think about. When I listen, I am involved in the transaction: I am not just hearing what you say, but I am attending, understanding and interpreting ...[191]

In a totally different literary tradition and context, the eighteenth-century philosopher Adam Smith sought to establish in his *Theory of Moral Sentiments* the possibility of society on the basis of our capacity as human beings to exercise creative imagination which would enable us to enter into the circumstances and situation of another human being.[192] It is creative because it involves a leap out of the known of the single person, and it is a matter of imagination because it has to be somehow an entering into where the other person is. The Swiss philosopher Jean Jacques Rousseau also spoke of 'sentiment', or compassion, as being the basis for human society. He appealed to an account of the individual who sees another

---

191 Mackay, H, *Why Don't People Listen? Solving the Communication Problem*, p 143.
192 Raphael, D and Macfie, A, *Adam Smith: The Theory of Moral Sentiments*, eg pp 116 and 317.

human being suffering, and, because of a welling up of sentiment and feeling for the other person, a bond is established which provides for the foundation of human society.[193] Each of these writers points to an enduring truth in the human condition.

These images, however, speak only of engagement in terms of personal relationships. In the process of time, engagement involves not only individuals, or individuals and groups, but also relationships between groups, including groups which exist through time. These relationships are clearly much more complex, and their dynamics are often very different and usually are contained within institutions. Nonetheless, the people who inhabit institutions and seek institutional relationships defined in terms of engagement and community are compelled to come back to the kinds of issues which we have just looked at.

Institutional relationships involve important issues of representation which can be seen in some recent debates in Australia about church involvement in government contracts. In 1998 the coalition government established a pattern of contracting out a variety of social services previously provided by government agencies. The provision of labour-market services was one contentious example. A tendering process was established and a variety of different organisations were successful in gaining tenders. However, at the end of 1999 church-based and Christian-inspired organisations tendered very successfully in the second round. In the early part of 2000 this caused considerable public debate as to whether or not it was appropriate for these church bodies to be involved in this government tendering process.

Two aspects of the matter emerged. Some church people questioned whether church agencies should be involved in this work, on the grounds that it was not part of the mission of the church. Some who accepted the appropriateness of the church providing job-search services argued that the tendering process entangled the church agencies in government policy in a way which compromised Christian values. On the other side of the question, it was argued that church agencies compromised the non-discriminatory policies of the government.

---

193 Cole, C, Brumfitt, J and Hall, J, *Jean-Jacques Rousseau: The Social Contract and Discourses*. See the section in the 'Discourse on the Origin of Inequality', p 61.

This is not a new question in Australia. It was widely debated in the education arena at the end of the nineteenth century and again in the 1970s. Roman Catholics emphasised the independent coherence of their identity and claimed that this implies a 'total' approach to educational theory which made it imperative to establish a parochial school system. Anglicans took a more open approach which allowed for participation in a state system of education. These approaches to involvement and representations reflect different theological understandings about truth and engagement with others.

On the state side, the Australian framework has its own very considerable particularities. For example, they are quite different from those that exist in the United States of America. There the development of a strict separation between church and state has also led to a judicial doctrine of 'non-entanglement'. That is to say, the state should not become entangled in any church matters, and church institutions should not become entangled in the arrangements and provision of government services. Thus the exclusion, indeed forbidding, of prayers in state schools is a natural expression of that particular doctrine. Such a doctrine does not exist in the Australian environment. On the contrary, section 116 of the Constitution of Australia, and indeed the history of the Australian government and institutional life during the nineteenth century, has produced a tradition of positive entanglement on the basis of equity between the churches and religious bodies. This has an important bearing upon how Australians view church–state relations and how churches within the Australian environment may respond to institutional relationships and engagements with the state. That is a theme to which we must return later in this chapter.

First of all, however, we need to ask how a critical appreciation of the tradition might inform Anglicans to be respectful visionaries in a place like Australia at the dawn of the twenty-first century.

With these points in mind we now turn to the tradition, particularly that of the New Testament, the English Reformation, and the theological tradition, to try and draw out some pointers as to how Australian Anglicans might engage more effectively with those around them as respectful visionaries.

The tradition revisited—Corinth

In an earlier chapter I have tried to set out the broad social circumstances in Corinth and the particular difficulties that the church faced. Corinth was a very busy cosmopolitan city of some seventy thousand people when Paul was there. It had a seamy side to it and not a few self-advertising newly rich citizens. It was a Roman city and was the principal city of the area, where the Isthmian Games were held. It was a busy port, with lots of different religious and social points of view represented in its population. It was in one sense quite easy for a new religion like Christianity to be establishing itself, because there were so many religions and a high level of tolerance. However, while most of the other religions were tolerant of each other, Christianity, like the Judaism which was also represented in Corinth, claimed an absolute commitment, which made it stand out from other religious groups in Corinth. The total commitment called for by the Christian gospel in this city produced considerable pressures and strains as the Corinthians sought to maintain their connections with their fellow Corinthians and at the same time also sought to work out what kind of a Christian community they were.

How, then, did these Corinthians participate in public and social life? How did they engage with their fellow citizens and with the institutions of the city? How did they cope with conflict, both within their own group and between themselves and others?

We can gain a perspective on these issues by looking at the practices of hospitality and the social institutions of the law, marriage and slavery.

Hospitality

Corinth was a city where there was a lot of hospitality. Wealthy patrons would extend hospitality to those who were in a client relationship with them or simply their social friends and peers. They would have houses large enough to entertain people. However, public places were also used for hospitality, not least temples, or rooms associated with temples. Many of the poorer members of the community did not have housing which would enable them even to cook and dine at home let alone entertain. As a consequence, there was a good deal of eating out, though in very modest establishments.

In 1 Corinthians 5:9–11 Paul sets out some general principles about relationships with outsiders, that is to say, non-Christians. He had apparently written earlier to the Corinthians and told them not to associate with immoral people. It seems as if the Corinthians may have misunderstood this to mean they should not associate with any immoral people. Paul had in mind Christians who were behaving in an immoral way. To correct this misunderstanding he says:

> Not at all meaning the immoral of this world, or the greedy and robbers, or idolaters, since you would then need to go out of the world. But now I am writing to you not to associate with anyone who bears the name of brother or sister who is sexually immoral or greedy or an idolater, reviler, drunkard or robber. Do not even eat with such a one. (1 Corinthians 5:9–11)

Such a misconception is very understandable in a city where the moral habits and standards were different from those of the Christian gospel. But Paul's rhetorical proposal, 'You will then have to go out of the world', is a final point in his argument. He does not elaborate it or question it, he simply assumes it is not possible. He comes back to the point two verses later when he says that it is not his place to judge those outside; God will judge those outside.

The tacit assumptions reflected here are that continuing social interaction and engagement were part and parcel of Paul's 'world' or 'cage'. There was no question of a separatist community. The Corinthians would continue to associate with, have contact with, and engage with the immoral, robbers, idolaters, revilers or drunkards who were their Corinthian neighbours. There is no sense here of the Christians being involved in any kind of guilt by association or being contaminated by such contact. It is simply assumed that the contact will continue.

However, that very set of assumptions inevitably must lead, and indeed did lead, to quite difficult problems. Two of these questions are illustrated in Paul's letter to the Corinthians. In 1 Corinthians 8:8 Paul addresses the question, which has obviously been raised to him, about eating food offered to idols. Such food could come either from the marketplace or from a meal which was held in the precincts of a temple. Paul's starting point is that any food is good, because it has been given by God, and there is only one God from whom are all things and for whom we exist.

However, he acknowledges that not everyone shares those convictions. Some, indeed, do believe that the idols really have some kind of sacred significance and therefore that the food offered to them shares in that sacredness. Nonetheless, for the Christian such food is a matter of indifference. It will not bring us nearer to God nor move us further away. What is really important is the character of the engagement with our fellows and the possibility that the freedom arising from our knowledge of God may create some kind of stumbling block for the weak, who presumably believe that these idols have a real divinity. That preliminary exposition of issues brings Paul to the particular point in 1 Corinthians 8:10.

> For if others see you, who possess knowledge, eating in the temple of an idol, might they not, since their conscience is weak, be encouraged to the point of eating food sacrificed to idols?

Because meat is of no great significance to Paul, he will not eat meat if it causes that kind of offence or cause some person with a weak conscience to stumble. There is no sense here that Paul concedes that these people who have this view are anything other than 'weak'. That is to say, his theological point of view that the meat is nothing, sacrificed to idols or not, is not brought into question. At issue is the personal engagement with the other person.

This story carries the fascinating implication that it would be entirely understandable for a Corinthian Christian to be present in the temple of an idol dining with his fellow Corinthians. That possibility is not challenged by Paul. It is entirely consistent with what he had said earlier in Chapter 5, and here it is described as actually taking place.

A similar situation is envisaged in 1 Corinthians 10:27. Here it is a question of accepting an invitation to a meal from an unbeliever. Basically the same kinds of issues are raised, and Paul's response is similar.

Hospitality was an important part of the social scene in Corinth, particularly among the better-off members of the community. That it was an issue and that it can be illustrated in the way in which Paul does in this letter, suggests that in the Corinthian Christian community there were a number of such better-off people. Perhaps the differences in socioeconomic background among the Corinthian Christians is illustrated in the difficulties that they had with their common meal, which Paul discusses in 1 Corinthians 11. However, it is clear that Paul does not challenge continuing hospitable engagement by the Corinthian Christians, even in a pagan temple. It is assumed to be part and parcel of what the Corinthian Christians will do.

Paul's view on this matter is distinctive and dangerous. It is understandable that the Corinthians might have felt that it would be better to withdraw from such people because of the moral challenge they might face or the difficulties in relationships and conflicts which might be uncovered by such continuing social contact. Paul's point, however, is quite clear. That kind of social contact should continue. Indeed, from what he says elsewhere, it is part of the continuing expression of the mission of the Christian gospel to embody a presence in all aspects of the life of the believer.

Legal processes

From elsewhere we know that Paul was a Roman citizen, and he accepted the protection of being a Roman citizen on a number of occasions. There is an account in the Acts of the Apostles of his appearance before the proconsul Gallio in Corinth, but the case was dismissed. Here in Paul's letters to the Corinthians there is a notorious passage where the attitude of Paul towards the use of the legal processes of the day is discussed. In 1 Corinthians 6 Paul speaks about litigation between Christians. It is a very precise and circumscribed example: 'When one of you has a grievance against another . . .' This is not a case of someone else bringing a Christian before the magistrate. Nor is it a case of a Christian initiating litigation with an unbeliever before the magistrate. The issue here is simply, and quite narrowly, litigation between Christians.

It is almost certainly the case that the law and its processes in Corinth at this time would probably have favoured the rich or the social and political elites. Such people in Corinth might feel that it was better to use the courts, where they might be confident of getting a better hearing if their opponent was less privileged. If that context is relevant to this discussion, then it adds considerable point to the argument which Paul makes. It would be quite improper for a wealthy Corinthian Christian to take advantage of a favoured and privileged position before the magistrate in relation to a poorer disadvantaged Corinthian Christian. However, that point is not made explicit in this passage.

In broad terms there were three stages to civil cases. First, the plaintive would appear before a magistrate requesting that a case be laid. It might be agreed that there were grounds for a suit, and only then, if there was a prima-facie case, would the plaintiff be summoned to court. At that stage the questions of evidence and fact would be argued before the magistrate and an agreed statement of the facts would be concluded. That would lead to a second stage, when the magistrate would assign a judge or a mediator who was agreeable to both parties and would pass on to him the statement of fact from the first part of the process. That judge would then hear the case and would pass whatever sentence or judgment was appropriate. It was then the plaintiff's responsibility to see that the judgment was carried out.

It is, in effect, a mediation process with the power of enforcing a judgment, though the enforcement is not directly carried out by the court itself. Paul's argument is that the Corinthian Christians should find someone within their own community to make the judgment. In other words, what he is saying is that the processes that are used in the magistrates court and the agreement on an arbitrator or judge should be done within the confines of the Christian community. He does not suggest at any point that the public system would produce unjust results, though other historical evidence does suggest there was bias in the courts.

Of course, Paul thinks that such disputes ought not to happen at all, and, where they do, it is a matter of shame that the Christian community cannot resolve them within their own membership. His objection is expressed in rhetorical questions designed to shame the Corinthian Christians. The force of his argument arises from the world view implied in the rhetorical questions. The unrighteous will be judged by the saints, who also will judge the world. We are to judge angels, and therefore can we not judge in ordinary matters? Why would you look for a judge outside the community of faith? Are there not enough wise people within the church? Is that lack not a shame on the Christian community? In any case, to allow disputes to reach such a point is a disgrace and a shame for those involved, and where that happens it is a further shame that the Christian community cannot handle them within their own membership.

There is no issue here about criminality. There is no issue here about breaking the law. There is no issue here about Christians using the legal processes in relation to those outside the Christian community or defending themselves.

So, as far as this particular case of litigation between believers is concerned, Paul does not provide any criticism of the legal system in itself. Rather, he wants to underline the distinct moral identity of the Christian group and to assert, on the basis of its destiny, a community role for itself in settling conflict within the Christian group. The presenting problem may be about engagement with the legal system, but Paul's response is driven by a conception of the church in Corinth as a self-sustaining moral community.

Marriage

There is a good deal in the Corinthian correspondence about marriage and relations between the sexes, especially in 1 Corinthians 7. It is important to put Paul's remarks in the context of the Roman pattern of marriage as an institution. In general, marriages were arranged and were concerned primarily with property. They were clearly unequal relationships. The man was in a superior and more powerful position than the woman. There was no sharp public–private demarcation involved in this understanding of marriage. Education took place in the home, and slave ownership was widespread across the society. The home was a place of work and business, and, as a consequence, social pleasure was more frequently to be found outside the home. In general, there were no marriage ceremonies and a woman could be simply sent away. Cohabiting was the basic establishing step in confirming the marriage contract.

Paul's reactions to the various questions referred to him by the Corinthians need to be set in this context. The general pattern of the marriage relationship which Paul envisages is set out in 1 Corinthians 7:1–7. It is in striking contrast with the Roman pattern. There is to be reciprocity in conjugal relationships, an almost inconceivable idea in the Roman pattern. When Paul says that the wife has authority over the husband's body, he utters an entirely counter-cultural idea. There is a strong emphasis in this passage on the sexual relationships, and they are only to be broken for the purposes of prayer. There is a background assumption that sexual desire for males and females should be channelled into the marriage relationship. Paul says that he himself is single, and he prefers that status, but he concedes each has their own particular gift from God.

It is easy to make anachronistic assumptions and not to recognise the strikingly different picture of marriage that is presented in this passage by Paul. It is a relationship of mutuality. It is a relationship of personal engagement. It is also a gift from God.

The description of marriage as a gift enables Paul to regard it as something which not everyone will experience. In the later part of chapter 7 he returns to this terminology in relation to the unmarried and the widows, though he underlines that the married should stay married, indeed even those who are married to unbelievers.

What Paul seems to be doing here is identifying a particular picture of marriage and then trying to work within the possibilities that are available to the different positions in which Corinthian Christians find themselves and, as far as possible, to give expression to the picture of marriage that he has laid out at the beginning of this section. That is not dissimilar from what generally happens in the New Testament in relation to the marriage institution. Various passages in the New Testament refer to relationships between members of the family. In 1 Peter the situation is where a wife is married to an unbeliever. In Corinth a variety of circumstances are alluded to. In Colossians it appears to be in a mixed environment, and in Ephesians it appears that both parties are Christians. These differences reflect a pragmatic approach which takes advantage of the capacity that the social environment provides within the family structure of the day for Christians to develop a particular way of being married.[194]

Once again, with this particular social institution we see pragmatic opportunism put in combination with a pattern of relationships within marriage which might more properly express the mutuality and interdependence which Paul sees as the characteristically Christian pattern of marriage relationship.

Slavery

Slavery is referred to on a number of occasions in the New Testament. Slaves were part and parcel of the scenery from which many of Jesus' stories were drawn, just as they were part of the social scenery within the apostolic communities around the Mediterranean Sea.

Here in 1 Corinthians Paul refers to slaves in chapter 7, where he is considering the question of the social and personal circumstances which the Corinthians were in when they were called to be Christians. He turns to those who were slaves: 'Were you a slave when called?' (1 Corinthians 7:21). Slavery was a reasonably important part of economic and commercial life in Rome. It was a growing enterprise, and Corinth was a significant centre for buying and selling slaves. At that time in the Roman Empire slaves were literally 'living property'. They fulfilled a wide range of responsibilities, and many could buy themselves out of slavery, though some chose not to. The patron–client system of social

---

194 See Kaye, B N, *Web of Meaning: The Role of Origins in Christian Faith.*

relationships provided coherence within the framework of a very stratified social structure. Slavery often overlapped with those client relationships. Corinth would have had different kinds of slaves among its inhabitants: mercantile slaves, household slaves and some civil servants. Paul must have been aware that in the Roman culture slaves were unprotected at law and that the system was widely accepted. This was in some contrast to Jewish traditions, where slaves were protected and, indeed, under the law of the Jubilee Year should be released. It is hard to know exactly, but recent estimates suggest that nearly a third of the population of Corinth would have been slaves at the time when Paul was there.

Paul's reaction here in 1 Corinthians is, do not worry about it. There are much more fundamental criteria for identifying who you are. Were you a slave when called? Do not be concerned about it. Of course, if you can gain your freedom, then do so. The real freedom that is important is the freedom which is given by the Lord, and to this relationship Paul applies the imagery of slavery: you were bought with a price, therefore you should remain in that relationship. For that reason it would be inappropriate to sell yourself into slavery.

Again, Paul's critical strategy is to take advantage opportunistically of the institution where he can but not to take an absolute view about it. That is because it is an entirely contingent matter. What is absolute is the belonging to Christ. There is a freedom which is beyond any kind of human slavery. That is the freedom which comes because the Corinthian Christians were purchased with the price of Christ's death. Paul is providing a basis to enable the Corinthian Christians to live with this social institution and to express their vocation to be Christians within the terms of that social institution.

Paul's responses to the problems in Corinth are particularly significant because of the sharp contrast which existed between the commitments, standards and beliefs of the Christians as compared with their fellow Corinthians. Despite this great contrast, Paul clearly does not envisage any diminution of engagement with their unbelieving fellow Corinthians. Nor does he envisage any kind of significant or substantial withdrawal from the institutions of the city of Corinth. He wants to transform marriage where he has the opportunity, and he has a vision of what a Christian marriage might look like. Slavery is not to be entered into, but it is not a fundamental problem if you are a slave, as indeed one third of the Corinthian Christians probably were. Hospitality was to be persisted with. The legal institution should not be used for matters which can be handled within the Christian community.

All these engagements were to be the occasions for Christian witness. On the other hand, the Christian community should be developing their gifts, skills, capacities and values to be able to sustain its own community of character. It ought to be able to deal with conflict within its own ranks. By this process it ought to be manifesting itself as a community of reconciliation.

The Reformation

When we turn to the English Reformation and its impact upon Australian Anglicanism, this general theme of engagement leads us into quite different territory. At the very beginning we are faced quite starkly with the question of what actually happened in the sixteenth century in England much more precisely when we ask about engagement and interaction. The issue here is made more acute by the historical research of the last thirty years on early modern English history. Out of that research has grown a lively debate about the nature of the English Reformation. The so-called revisionist account of the English Reformation directly affects the issue of engagement because of the way in which it confronts the question of what changes actually took place.

This new line of interpretation has arisen partly because of the investigation of new and different kinds of sources at local levels in society and an attempt to revisit the question of what actually happened in the sixteenth century on the ground. Patrick Collinson says that 'historians of the English Reformation describe it as a double process, part official, part unofficial. Reformation from above and below.'[195]

He then immediately goes on to say that, even though the distinction breaks down, it is nonetheless quite a helpful polarity to use. On the one hand, there is what one might call the legislative and imperial picture of the Reformation expressed in the legislative instruments of Henry, Edward and Elizabeth, and, on the other hand, the activity of preachers and others in towns, villages, and in London seeking to change the hearts and minds of people.

195 Collinson, P, 'The Elizabethan Church and the New Religion', p 177.

Christopher Haig suggests that there are two matrixes to understand the Reformation and his reconstruction of it, which are not quite the analytical matrixes suggested by Patrick Collinson. They are the question of how quickly religious change took place, and the character of the motive force behind the progress of Protestantism in England. For Christopher Haig the Reformation is a very broad label in which to embrace a collection of things which include the break with Roman obedience, secular control of the church, the suppression of Catholic institutions, prohibition of Catholic worship, and the Protestantisation of services, clergy and laity. Already the terminology reveals the interpretation from which it is developed.

Christopher Haig identifies four types of interpretations in terms of his two matrixes:

- a reformation which takes place rapidly as a result of imposition
- a rapid reformation from below, which has religious rather than political roots. This reformation he criticises as depending upon two assumptions, namely that the English Catholic Church did not command support in the fifteenth and sixteenth century, and that Protestantism proved to be very attractive to the population at large. He questions both those assumptions.
- the imposed reformation changed but with slow impact on the localities
- a slow reformation from below.

Christopher Haig also suggests that there were three political reformations:

- a Henrician political reformation between 1530–38 (significantly reversed between 1538–46)
- an Edwardian political reformation 1547–53 (almost completely reversed 15053–58 under Mary)
- an Elizabethan political reformation 1559–63.

Alongside these political reformations was what he calls an evangelical reformation of preachers spreading out from London, Cambridge and Oxford from about 1520. Thus he concludes, 'England had blundering reformations, which most did not understand, which few wanted, and which no one knew had come to stay'.[196]

---

196 Haigh, C, *English Reformations: Religion, Politics, and Society under the Tudors*, p 14.

His principal conclusion as to the reason for the change is compulsion. 'For it is likely that most of those who lived in Tudor England experienced reformation as obedience rather than conversion; they obeyed a monarch's new laws rather than swallowed a preachers new message.'[197]

While it is not possible to go into all of the intricacies of this reinterpretation of the English Reformation, it is important to draw attention to the implications of this recent historical interpretation for the purposes of understanding what the Reformation might tell us about the nature of Christian engagement with others.

It seems to me to be clear that the Reformation is a good deal more complicated than simply imagining that when the Acts of Henry, Edward and Elizabeth were passed everything changed. It also seems to me to be far too simple to imagine that Richard Hooker, as the principal interpreter of the sixteenth century, was unaware of these complications. The nuances and character of his rhetoric and polemic of the argument indicate that he was quite well aware of these kinds of differences, but we shall come back to that shortly.

Elements of engagement

It is quite clear, of course, that while Sir Henry Powicke was right to say that the English Reformation was an 'act of state', it was not just that. Nonetheless, one aspect of it was an act of state, and many in England experienced the Reformation in terms of obedience to those legal and institutional changes. In that sense it was a matter of conformity, and also in that sense the result was a 'constrained union'.[198] The Acts of Uniformity of 1552 and 1559 secured attendance at church by force and sanction of law. The close relationship between the role of clergy and the magistracy was part of that process. Whereas in Germany religious symbols in churches were destroyed by zealous reformers, in England they were dismantled by the church wardens on instructions from commissioners from London. All of that was clear, well known, and well rehearsed in the popular tradition of the history of the Reformation. That pattern of reformation inevitably meant conformity, either willing or reluctant. In the end, however, a good deal of internalisation of these institutional and legal changes took place, and the impact of the changes upon the population cannot entirely be discounted. Furthermore,

197 Haigh, C, *English Reformations: Religion, Politics, and Society under the Tudors*, p 21.
198 Collinson, P, 'The Elizabethan Church and the New Religion', p 173.

that particular way of effecting change influenced the framework and pattern of possible interactions within the society by individuals or groups.

When we turn to the question of how engagement took place in terms of persuasion to adopt different religious points of view, what Christopher Haig has called the evangelical reformation, it is quite clear that this took place in a variety of contexts and in different ways. One can observe it taking place within the locations of nation, town and family.

The sixteenth century has been described by Adrian Hastings as the high point of nationalism in Europe and in England. Furthermore, he argues that it is in this period that the concept of a nation and nationalism gains its most emphatic statement and in no small measure is influenced by the imagery of Israel in relation to England. It is true that there are many images of England drawn from the Bible. John Speed speaks of 'this very Eden of Europe'.[199] Many preachers and writers of the period compared England to Israel. Indeed, the front piece of Henry VIII's Royal Supremacy legislation is cast in exactly those resonant terms. On the other hand, the papacy was increasingly characterised as the antichrist. This, of course, was not new, although during the period of the Reformation the deployment of this imagery was certainly intensified. But this 'very Eden of Europe' was not perfect, as Protestant preachers denounced the sins of England and Englishmen, just as the prophets in the Old Testament had denounced the sins of Israel.

While John Fox, among others, had spoken of Englishmen being as it were 'in one ship together',[200] it was nonetheless still the case that there was much division and dissension. The very character of the official homilies that dealt with disobedience and dissension points to concern on the part of authorities. Engagement between Englishmen was coloured by the sense that they were part of an English nation, perhaps not as intensely conceived as Adrian Hastings suggested, but nonetheless an English nation with a destiny drawn somehow from the hand of God.

However, the popular preaching which spoke of England in terms of Israel of the Old Testament was popular preaching which spread out from the towns of

---

199 Collinson, P, *The Birthpangs of Protestant England: Religious and Cultural Change in the Sixteenth and Seventeenth Centuries*, p 6.
200 Collinson, P, *The Birthpangs of Protestant England: Religious and Cultural Change in the Sixteenth and Seventeenth Centuries*, p 25.

England. Other images were also used, London, thought of in terms of Jerusalem, for example. Compared with Germany, England was at this time essentially a country of towns and villages; there were no large cities. Indeed, the only city of comparable size to those in Germany was London. It was from the towns that preachers went forward into the countryside to evangelise and to preach. London undoubtedly was a centre and an originating source, as were Cambridge and Oxford, but so were other towns throughout the land. In this context change naturally came with the arrival of the reformer of influence, someone who was either an effective preacher or who could make provision for preachers. At this much more immediate level it is not surprising that this kind of reformation brought to the towns and villages of England not a little division. The nature of the engagement between people in such a circumstance became an issue of considerable debate and importance in the life of the town.

The same can be said for the social institution of the family. The family in the sixteenth century was not the arena of privacy which it has become in the modern world, but it was still a discrete area of influence. It is not easy to identify exactly what happened in families in terms of the evangelical reformation and the changes to people's lives, habits and dispositions. Such sermons as we have, the many conduct books which were published during the sixteenth century, records of ecclesiastical courts, and the literary and dramatic sources as well as popular ballads all point in the direction of a balance between social prescription and practice. While there were certain kinds of expectations about the arrangement of marriages, it was still the case that many understood that they had the opportunity to choose their partner. While, of course, the position of women was not the same as that of men and there was a deal of patriarchy, it was also the case that the history of the Reformation looks a little like the history of the emancipation of women. Clearly the institution of family had a continuity from previous centuries, but the Reformation does appear to have made the family somewhat more contained, and there was even, one might say, perhaps a certain privatisation.

In the context of town and family, social relationships had a profound impact on the character of people and on personal dispositions and habits. Also powerful in this context was the growing effect of preachers and teaching and lecturing.

The government did not make much provision for preaching in England in the sixteenth century. Rather, the existing arrangements in the church were presumed to be adequate to the purpose. Growth and innovation were largely the result of private patronage. In 1650 parliament did provide resources for the establishment of preaching in Wales, but that was a somewhat unusual step on the part of the parliament.

The plain reading of Scripture became a much more common practice in the sixteenth century. Richard Baxter's father is said to have been converted by the simple reading of Scripture. Many so-called two-penny 'books' were published on religious topics in the sixteenth century, and there were many catechisms of popular style available in the marketplace. All of this provided possibilities for religious discussion and engagement. 'Godly company', as in the context of the family, provided a powerful impulse and opportunity for engagement on 'religious matters and religious change'. Puritans in this period emphasised preaching as being more valuable than 'bare reading' of Scripture, which was not enough. The Second Admonition to Parliament in 1572 declared that it was better to read the Bible than to read homilies, but, nonetheless, 'the ministry of faith is the preaching of the same out of the Word of God by them that are sent of God'.[201]

The preacher in this conception was the messenger of God. Elizabeth's Royal Injunctions of 1559 required four sermons in each year and also a sermon every month, in somewhat oddly contradictory terms. An appropriate pulpit was required in every church, according to these admonitions. The canons of 1604 set down topics for different times of the year, and these were to be preached by 'licensed preachers'. However, there were at this time some staffing problems in terms of having graduates in parishes who might be such licensed preachers in order to preach these sermons. Archbishop Whitgift calculated in 1584 that only seven per cent (ie about 600 out of 9000) parishes yielded an income adequate to attract a graduate licensed preacher.

Patrick Collinson suggests that there were four stages in the development of the evangelical preaching pattern in the sixteenth century. First, there was an itinerant ministry, such as that exercised by Thomas Bilney in East Anglia, often supported by benefactors.

Second, there was the development of a concentration of preaching in a number

---

201 Collinson, P, 'The Elizabethan Church and the New Religion', p 183.

of centres, and at this stage the development of 'prophesying'. Prophesying was preaching to a voluntary assembly. The preaching which went on in the parish church had a captive audience by the terms of the Acts of Uniformity. Prophesying was for those who chose to come. Prophesying was in one sense part of clergy training. It was not ecstatic utterance, as the term might suggest, but rather the gathering of a number of clergy together to hear sermons from different members of the group on the same text.

In 1557 Elizabeth acted against Grindal for not suppressing this prophesying. The effect of this action by the queen simply meant that the term 'prophesying' was in large measure dropped as a title for what went on, which, with some modifications, simply continued. 'No episode did more to dramatise the distance between Elizabeth's attitude to religion and that of the growing and ebullient Protestant and Puritan movement.'[202]

The third stage was when effective preaching ministries were established in the market towns of England. In this phase people went to hear sermons from different preachers in nearby market towns. This 'gadding' to sermons was not so much an indication that there was an absence of adequate preaching but rather a desire on the part of such people for variety in the diet of the preaching which they heard.

The fourth and final stage, according to Collinson, was reached when it was possible to say in England that sermons were commonly heard throughout the whole realm. Such preaching clearly re-configured relationships and the pattern of engagement between individuals and between groups within society.

Significance of the Reformation for engagement in Australia

All of this has very important consequences for the way in which the Reformation tradition inherited in Australian Anglicanism is understood. The constitutional and statutory expressions of the Reformation embedded in the constitution of the Anglican Church of Australia, and the protection of the Book of Common Prayer together with the relationship between English canon law and Australian canon law mean that the formal terms of the constitutional environment for Australian Anglicans are directly influenced by the Reformation monuments. Uniformity of

202 Collinson, P, 'The Elizabethan Church and the New Religion', p 191.

religion by law, the central authority of the Royal Supremacy, the single conception of the commonwealth politically and religiously, and authority are by law and coercive. These constitutional arrangements were cast within a set of strongly territorial categories. Not only was England an empire, it was an empire set within a territory. Not only so, that territory was divided into regions and localities within which these authority categories operated. Jurisdiction defined within dioceses and parishes represented at different levels the centralising and exclusive conceptions of the national model.

These elements are embedded in the constitutional documents and the inherited instruments of Anglicanism in Australia. This is particularly so in the territorial definition of jurisdiction. They are in one sense the top-down aspect of the sixteenth-century Reformation in England. Along with that, there are doctrinal commitments embedded in these monuments which are part of the inheritance from the Reformation that have valence in Australian Anglicanism. These include an emphasis upon the doctrine of justification, the priority of faith as an exercise of the individual, and the authority of Scripture as having priority—indeed, in the terms of the constitution, supremacy among other authorities. These are the terms of the statutory monuments which have come down into Australian Anglicanism.

However, recent historical research on the Reformation has shown that the ways in which engagement was conceptualised at the time were quite different. Clearly there was division in the Christian commonwealth. One does not have to accept all that Christopher Haig says to recognise that the picture of uniformity suggested by the Acts of Uniformity of 1552, 1559 and 1662 do not actually come to expression on the ground.

Furthermore, it is quite clear that the theological or the religious demographics of sixteenth-century England were quite different from the theory of Tudor politics and the central singular authority of the Royal Supremacy. In that respect, it is interesting to note that Hooker's argument with Presbyterianism is essentially an argument about epistemology. Hooker's position sits much more comfortably with the reality on the ground as revealed by the recent historical research. Hooker's more open, porous conception of authority and the qualifications already noted in regard to the Royal Supremacy resonate more with the social reality. His opposition to the almost monistic notion of authority in Presbyterianism proved a more realistic representation of the sixteenth century and a more continuingly useful defence of a conception of Anglicanism drawn out of that context.

The Australian realities, socially and politically, are dramatically different from those portrayed in the Reformation monuments, and even significantly different in degree from the realities of what was happening in England in the sixteenth century. Australia is federal in politics and in social authority. It is a society marked by social and religious pluralities. The Christian state imagined by Henry, modified slightly by Elizabeth, and re-pristinated in the 1662 Act of Uniformity is totally different from the Australian example. There is not quite the church–state separation of the United States but, nonetheless, a secular state where all religious groups are treated in the same way equitably under the constitution. The terms upon which engagement therefore takes place within this society could hardly be more different from those which are implied in the Reformation monuments, and, in any case, as we have seen, those monuments did not come to full expression in the England of the sixteenth and seventeenth century.

The consequence is that an appropriate understanding of the terms of social engagement for Australian Anglicans is positively harmed and inhibited by this aspect of the Reformation monuments in the inherited traditions of Australian Anglicanism. Clearly the new revisionist account of the Reformation helps us to see a fuller context in England itself and thus have a better appreciation of the significance of the Reformation monuments even in the sixteenth century. The fact remains, however, that those monuments, as they are embedded in the institutionality of Australian Anglicanism, need to be radically reinterpreted, and reconceptualised. Even the interpretation offered by Richard Hooker, which has more contact with the realities on the ground in the sixteenth century, and which is more alert to the diversity, differences and qualifications that are appropriate in any evaluation of the Reformation settlements, is still addressed to a situation in which church and state are united in one commonwealth.

It is a curious thing that the English Reformation monuments have no conception of inter-faith mission. They have a conception of Christian edification and Christian growth and Christian behaviour, but because they are cast within a set of presumptions about the nature of a Christian society complete unto itself, there is no sense in which they develop any awareness of engagement with others who either have a different faith or no faith at all. In this respect it is striking that the Reformation monuments have little or no sense of evangelism or mission. Any sense of challenge for Christians to live out their vocation to be Christian in a hostile or unbelieving context is quite absent. It is a tribute to the power of these monuments in subsequent Anglican history that Anglican instincts have been strong on pastoral care and teaching but not on evangelism.

Theological tradition

'The foundation of all religion must be laid in the belief of an over ruling Providence.' Thus William Grant Broughton, newly appointed archdeacon in the Colony of New South Wales, began his sermon on 12 November 1829 in St James Church, Sydney. The service was held on a day which the governor had appointed 'for a general thanksgiving to Almighty God, in acknowledgment of his mercy in putting an end to the late severe drought and in averting his threatened judgments from this colony'.[203]

How are we to engage with others? That question depends on how the inner relationships of the created order are characterised, because humans are part of that created order. In the history of Christian theology, various categories have been used to describe this relationship. There is a strong tradition, particularly in Roman Catholicism, of natural law. Another category which is used in this area is that of the providence of God. The providence of God is useful for our purposes because it has a reasonably variegated history, and that very fact points to some of the issues we confront in this matter of engagement.

Throughout the biblical material there is an underlying concern with the question of theodicy. Does the presence of evil in the created order speak against the goodness which is said to belong to that created order because of the creative activity of God? In many respects the projection of the resolution of such a theodicy into an eschatological domain arises from the tensions created by the covenant with David and the commitment to the particular social institution in Israel of the Davidic throne. Of course, the calling of Israel as a special people already itself raised that question, but the Davidic covenant sharpened the issue considerably, particularly when it appeared that the line of David was lost in the exile.

203 Broughton, W G, *The Counsel and Pleasure of God in the Vicissitudes of States and Communities*, p 7.

In the New Testament, Jesus clearly breaks any necessary connection between evil and sin. Thus those who suffer are not necessarily those who are the greatest sinners. This step raises significant questions against any simple identification of suffering with evil and, in the process, reshapes the nature of any defence of the idea of the sovereignty of God and the goodness of God in relation to suffering and the presence of evil. That issue has preoccupied Christian theology throughout its whole history.

However, the idea of providence has been shaped by the kind of mental universe in which the theologian works. Thomas Aquinas underlined the great scope of a notion of providence by deploying the idea of secondary causes which mediate divine activity. In the early Reformation, Luther focused the idea of providence more particularly on the practical experience of the Christian believer. Belief in providence was a matter of trust in God's ultimate goodness. In that sense the idea of giving some theoretical answer to the problem of evil moved into second place in favour of the awareness of the presence of God in the experience of the believer as a way of gaining some assurance. That way of handling the question became much more common from the eighteenth century onwards.

In 1687 Isaac Newton completed his *Principia Mathematica*. In that vast book of 550 pages he brought together a theoretical explanation which united previous theories into a mathematically and experimentally supported picture. It was this coherent picture expressed at the theoretical level in relation to causes and effects that provided the basis for the Industrial Revolution. However, at the same time it had the dramatic effect of offering an explanation of the phenomena of the world which did not require anything other than an understanding of the laws and forces at work within the natural order. At this point God became, if not unnecessary, then certainly an inoperative idea. It is not surprising that in this context the notion of God as present in the natural order became difficult to sustain, and the notion of God's transcendence took on a quite different configuration.[204] It took it out of the realm of the created order. That intellectual context, while modified to some extent by twentieth-century physics, still affects the understanding of divine providence.

204 Placher, W, *The Domestication of Transcendence.*

This mental framework was certainly the context within which Bishop William Broughton spoke in 1829 as he tried to address the problem of a disastrous drought in the Colony of New South Wales. Archdeacon Broughton had just arrived to find the colony suffering from the most horrendous sustained drought. Soon after he arrived the drought was broken with plentiful rain, and the governor ordered a service of thanksgiving. Broughton preached and declared that 'the foundation of all religion must be laid in the belief of an over ruling Providence'.

Broughton went on to argue that, while there was that sense of an overruling providence fixed in the heart of the individual, an inlet was open for the admission of devout impressions and for the sanctifying influence of God's grace to operate on individuals.

The idea of the providence of God directly affects not only how we conceive of our capacity to engage with others but also how we might enterprise that engagement. It also affects how Christians might relate to those who do not share their Christian perceptions and how Christian institutions might conceive of their relationship to other institutions. It has to do with the way in which we conceive of God as active in the world, how we see ourselves as free yet constrained, how we conceive of natural law and whether we think there is such a thing as creationism. It has to do with the role of chance in our perceptions of the ordering of events and the way in which we might characterise the accidental circumstances which place us in our own particular time and place and the degree to which we recognise the contingency of our own circumstances. In trying to understand how we might appropriately engage with others, the conception of the providence of God will sharply raise issues of continuity and discontinuity, whether the world is evil and the church is good, whether the Christian is right in all things and the non-Christian wrong. Clearly such dualism is a stark and strong expression of a particular conception of the providence and presence of God.

In this argument I want to propose that the appropriate theme is to sustain an idea of the living action of God in his creation in terms of a balance of continuity and discontinuity. These are traditional and classical issues in Christian theology, but they relate quite importantly to the way in which we characterise our engagement with others. I want to argue that in this arena the characteristically Anglican approach has been to underline and to use a doctrine of God's providence on the basis that it enables more flexibility in dealing with the issue of engagement. Of course some construals of God's providence look very much like attempts to justify the status quo. Given the resilience of some Anglican institutions, one might think that was precisely what was intended by the use of the doctrine of providence, though that is less clear in the case of the actual theological arguments used by Anglicans.

I want to take three examples in order to illustrate how this principle might work and to see what can be learned from the theological tradition in order to shape, or assist, in the formulation of an Anglican theological notion of engagement. In order to do that I will take two Anglican works for illustration purposes and contrast them with the notion of witness as developed by Stanley Hauerwas.

E H Burgmann

Earnest Burgmann was born in 1885 and, after a somewhat disrupted education, was ordained and later became warden of St John's College, which he developed as a centre for theological and social comment.[205] He was widely regarded as a significant speaker on social affairs and was notorious in the Anglican Church of Australia for his support of communist union organisers and as president of the Australian Soviet Friendship League during World War II. However, Burgmann was widely influential and tried to establish some genuinely Anglican and Australian way of looking at social issues. He was deeply influenced by the development of psychology as a discipline, and this is brought out particularly in his booklet *God in Human History*, published in 1931. Burgmann declares in the preface that he hopes that the booklet may be

> found useful by those who desire to explore more fully the great and difficult themes of over ruling providence and divine judgment in history. No religion is adequate unless all history can be interpreted in the light of it and unless life today in all of its complexity can be lived in the power of it. A faith that only concerns a department of life is a withered flower.[206]

While this booklet is taken up with the question of Russia and communism, Burgmann's approach to these questions is shaped by a notion of humanity as

205 Hempenstall, P, *The Meddlesome Priest: A Life of Ernest Burgman.*
206 Burgmann, E H, *God in Human History*, p 2.

created by God. He traces that notion back to the Old Testament prophets and applies it to his analysis of the international situation in 1931 and, in particular, to what he describes as Russia's challenge. There is only one answer to this challenge, he says:

> By greater energy, wisdom, and devotion, we must order a world that will give deeper and truer satisfaction to the human soul than the Russian scheme of things can do.[207]

In this booklet he underlines a theme which had become fundamental to this thinking about all social questions, namely that a truly Christian conception of humanity must envisage a connection between individuals, that true personality is a personality which is at once representative as well as individual.

> We are one family. The solidarity of the human race must be more definitely and vividly recognised. It is the key note of truly catholic religion. Together, as a family of God, we can make a wondrously beautiful thing of life on this earth.[208]

This booklet puts into the arena of providence the arguments which he had developed a year before in another booklet entitled *Religion in the Life of the Nation*. This booklet begins with an exposition of what he sees to be the Christian conception of personality. He argues that such a conception originates with the prophets. He says, 'In thus discovering the individual in himself, Jeremiah did not merely find an isolated unit, rather he found a represented person'.[209]

Burgmann claims that this same kind of theme can be found in Ezekiel and Isaiah and is radicalised by Jesus. He describes this by using the terminology of personality.

> Personality is a relative term; it measures our representativeness and our sense of relationship to our fellows ... In personality, then, the problem of the one and the many finds concrete solution.[210]

Burgmann argues such a conception provides the basis for a unity in God towards which the whole of humanity might move.

207 Burgmann, E H, *God in Human Histor*, p 30.
208 Burgmann, E H, *God in Human History*, p 46.
209 Burgmann, E H, *Religion in the Life of the Nation: Four Lectures*, p 7.
210 Burgmann, E H, *Religion in the Life of the Nation: Four Lectures*, p 13.

> It gives us the whole human race for the scope of our love, gives us all creation as a field to explore in order that we might see and know the heart and mind of God himself.[211]

Such a person, Burgmann argues, is necessarily connected to his fellows. Sensitive to their emotions and with an intuitive understanding of their thoughts, such a person is the citizen of a nation for which the national institutions exist. He claims parliament is the ultimate national institution, and institutions which derive from it, or are related to it, must be seen in the context in this conception of the citizen as a human person. He criticises the developments in the 1930s, particularly writing in the context of the Depression and of a divorce between religion and politics. Such a divorce he traces back to the writings of Machiavelli.

> If we spread abroad Christ's view of man we shall in due time give the world new ideas and ideals by which to live, new conceptions of life will become enshrined in our national institutions, we shall move away from our sentimental materialism towards that view of man which sees in every human being a son or daughter of the eternal God. And in these living and immortal persons we shall find at last the true foundation of a life, not merely national, but human—as wide as the world and reaching out beyond all time.[212]

Burgmann goes on to apply these conceptions to what he sees to be the important economic and industrial challenges of the Depression years in Australia. He is preoccupied with the conflict between communism and capitalism.

The underlying question which Burgmann struggled with was, how could a Christian conceive of the human condition in such a way that it provided a basis for a coherent and organic human life? The conception that he used was a notion of the human personality as both individual and representative, and the concept that all are in some sense brothers and sons of God. Here the point of connection derived directly out of his foundational notion of providence, that it is the providence of God in the created order and in history that enables such a conception of the human person naturally and necessarily to be connected in a familial way with the whole of humanity. That does not mean that Burgmann was

---

211 Burgmann, E H, *Religion in the Life of the Nation: Four Lectures,* p 15.
212 Burgmann, E H, *Religion in the Life of the Nation: Four Lectures,* p 24.

not a social critic, quite the contrary. However, it does mean that the basis upon which he felt confident in making his social criticism was that he worked from an assumed continuity between the values of the Christian gospel and the rest of humanity. He developed notions of freedom, of respect, of service and servanthood out of the New Testament, which provided him with a basis for a criticism of both capitalism and communism, and certainly of the way in which capitalism in Australia in the 1930s seemed to be operating. The legitimation of the institutions of society was directly to be derived from their capacity to serve the conception of the human person, which he developed under the heading of personality.

Undoubtedly, Burgmann's thinking on this point is affected by his attraction to the emerging discipline of psychology. However, the underlying theological presuppositions about the providence of God provided him with the intellectual basis upon which he could develop his social criticism.

Oliver O'Donnovan

A similar presumption exists for Oliver O'Donnovan. O'Donnovan has been concerned with issues of natural law, politics, ethics and social comment for many years. His recent book, *The Desire of Nations*, develops a particular conception of what he calls 'political theology', which brings to expression and to more precise articulation his previous work. The issue of continuity and discontinuity between the divine and nature, between theology and politics is critical in O'Donovan's analysis. At the beginning of his book he clarifies that political theology

> does not suppose a literal synonymy between the political vocabulary of salvation and the secular use of the same political terms. It postulates an analogy—not a rhetorical metaphor only, or a poetic image, but an analogy grounded in reality, between the acts of God and human acts, both of them taking place within the public history which is the theatre of God's saving purposes and mankind's social undertakings.[213]

The alternative towards which his critique is clearly addressed is a theology which seeks to keep the two types of discourse distinct, 'so that one does not contaminate the other'.[214]

---

213 O'Donovan, O, *The Desire of the Nations*, p 2.
214 O'Donovan, O, *The Desire of the Nations*, p 2.

O'Donnovan sees his projects as a revisiting and recovery of the longer tradition of political theology which reached its high point in the twelfth to seventeenth centuries. He contrasts his exercise with that of the political theology of Latin America as a recovery which arises not so much out of the exigencies of the present circumstances but out of a revisiting of the tradition. O'Donnovan wants to place political history within the history of God's reign. In doing that, he believes that three important elements are added which are particularly important in the modern context where historicism has tended to fragment a sense of continuity in history.

First, if politics is seen in the light of the divine rule, that is to say the kingdom of God, it is 'to be assured of its world affirming and humane character'.[215]

Second, it will give priority to the political act as the divinely authorised act rather than to the institutional preoccupations of western thought. 'It is not its goal to describe an ideal set of political institutions; for political institutions are anyway too fluid to assume an ideal form, since they are the work of Providence in the changing affairs of succeeding generations.'[216]

Third, 'the Kingdom of God will, by this strategy be presented as a revealed history, which takes its form quite particularly as the history of Israel'.[217]

That history, of course, is brought to final effect in the death and resurrection of Jesus. On the basis of this proposal, O'Donnovan suggests that the interpretative principle governing the way in which the Bible might be read is 'the kingly rule of God, expressed in Israel's corporate existence and brought to final effect in the life, death and resurrection of Jesus'.[218]

It is on the basis of that approach that O'Donnovan then enters upon an exposition of the history of Israel and of the emergence of the church in the New Testament. What God gives Israel is victory, judgment and possession. That enables O'Donnovan to develop two theorems and a corollary.

1. Political authority arises where power, the execution of right, and the perpetuation of tradition are assured together in one coordinated agency.

---

215 O'Donovan, O, *The Desire of the Nations*, p 19.
216 O'Donovan, O, *The Desire of the Nations*, p 20.
217 O'Donovan, O, *The Desire of the Nations*, p 21.
218 O'Donovan, O, *The Desire of the Nations*, p 27.

2. That any regime should actually come to hold authority, and should continue to hold it, is a work of divine providence in history, not a mere accomplishment of the human task of political service.

3. In acknowledging political authority, society proves its political identity.

One should not imagine that this means that the institutions and the status quo are necessarily to be accepted as the result of divine activity and thus be regarded as of permanent significance. Richard Hooker struggled with precisely this question in his attempt to defend the status quo. He found himself unable to sustain the argument and was left with a defence for the status quo which itself implied its own contingency. O'Donnovan makes this clear when he talks about the church as a political society. By political society he means a community which is ruled by Christ. 'That rule, that is to say its essential nature which is under authority, is to be discerned by faith, as the ascended Christ who governs it.'[219]

Interestingly, he draws attention to the highly ambiguous consequences of the reforms of Pope Gregory VII, because they introduce a judicial element into the way in which the church thought about authority. He says that was a mistake. The mistake was not that there should be an order of ministry as such, or that the church's structures might be in some rivalry with those of secular authority. Rather, 'the mistake is quite simply to posit an order of ministry of whatever sort, and to deduce the identity of the church from it, as though *that* were the rule of Christ, and what it encompassed were the true form of Christ's bride!'[220] This is a point, it seems to me, precisely in line with Hooker's argument.

In relation to the church's political character, O'Donnovan insists that one formal principle must be respected, namely the church's catholicity on the one hand and its order on the other.

Throughout this argument, O'Donnovan constantly returns in different ways to the theme which he had identified at the beginning of the book, namely the way in which one thinks about the relationship between politics and the kingdom of God. His way of thinking about that underlines and affirms deep continuity between politics and the kingdom of God. The politics is understood as an

219 O'Donovan, O, *The Desire of the Nations*, p 166.
220 O'Donovan, O, *The Desire of the Nations*, p 168.

expression of the kingdom of God. The analogy between the two ways of speaking is an analogy embedded in reality. He asserts that,

> if the Christian community has as its eternal goal, the goal of its pilgrimage, the disclosure of the church as city, it has as its 'intermediate' goal, the goal of its mission, the discovery of the city's secret destiny through the prism of the church.[221]

He makes it clear that so far, in his view, 'the architecture of a Christian doctrine of society has yet to be established' even though many aspects of it have been discussed. He conceives of this task as distinguishing 'the various types of communication which frame communities: locality, economic intercourse, education, family affection. Each of these has its proper claim on the political order, and requires its own measure of deference; otherwise the governing authorities will be drained of their legitimacy. Yet none of them is autonomous, none dictates terms to the others or to governments.'[222]

This is a highly complex and deliberative exposition. It clearly is concerned with the question of continuity and discontinuity, between grace and nature. O'Donnovan's conception, as far as I can understand it, embraces nature with grace, that is to say there is an assumption, by the assertion of the importance of the kingdom of God, the divine rule, that the rule extends beyond the totality of created order, and therefore that Jesus Christ can rightly, in the terms of the title of his book, be described as the desire of the nations. His commitment to Israel as an expression of the kingdom of God for the purposes of understanding what political theology might look like and what its basic theorems might be is also a strongly underlined version of continuity between Old Testament and New Testament. Or, to put it another way, it reflects a diminished account of the differences that are implied in the idea that Christ fulfilled the law and the prophets.

There have been different variations of that in the history of Christianity. O'Donnovan is not asserting that the political institutions of Israel are in some sense paradigmatic. Rather, he is saying that the history of the politics of Israel provides an interpretive key for the totality of Scripture and for the subsequent

---

221 O'Donovan, O, *The Desire of the Nations*, p 286.
222 O'Donovan, O, *The Desire of the Nations*, p 286.

history of the church. He recognises the role of institutions but sees politics as affected by action and event. There seems to be quite considerable fluidity and flexibility in the way in which O'Donnovan is thinking about how Christian people exist in the world of politics, that is to say in the world of human society. Yet he does this on the basis of a significant assumption about continuity, both extensively and through history.

Stanley Hauerwas

What one misses in this analysis is some sense of the evil powers that threaten Christians in their pilgrimage and challenge the church in its mission. That element is not missing in the exposition of Stanley Hauerwas, particularly when he speaks about 'witness' as being the key role of the church as a community cast within the world.[223] The theme of witness runs through many of the writings of Stanley Hauerwas, but it comes in a very sharp form in an essay entitled 'The non violent terrorist: in defence of Christian fanaticism', which is published as part of his book *Sanctify Them in the Truth: Holiness Exemplified.*

Hauerwas seeks to discuss the ethics of terrorism in relation to just war theory in order to show that there is no significant discontinuity between terrorism and war. That whole argument is designed to raise radically the question about the nature of conflict. It is designed to provide a context in order to deal with those who have criticised his position as marginalising Christians from the social domain. Here he returns, as he has done on a number of occasions, to defend himself from the charge of being sectarian and detached from the social order. So he anticipates the charge that the kind of Christocentric ethics that he is trying to develop has the effect of preventing Christians from acting 'constructively in a world already far too divided. In such a divided world what is needed, it is argued, is a universal ethic capable of resolving conflict.'[224]

Hauerwas establishes this context with a critique of the distinction which is made between combatants and non-combatants in just war theory, and the claim in that theory that there is a continuity between the police function of the state and war. He criticises the idea that a universal ethic is the way in which such conflict and disunity is to be addressed by using Alasdair MacIntyre's account of the way in

---

223 A significant collection of Hauerwas's writings is now conveniently available in Berkman, J and Cartwright, M, *The Hauerwas Reader.*
224 Hauerwas, S, *Santify Them in the Truth: Holiness Exemplified,* p 178.

which epistemological crises are resolved. MacIntyre believes in a rationality which is tradition based, that is to say it is a rationality that belongs in and makes sense within a particular tradition. However, the way in which different traditions may relate to each other is in some sense capable of being addressed in the same way in which traditions deal with difficulties or conflicts that arise within the experience of that tradition. So when circumstances change and a tradition finds that its way of thinking or its approach to a particular question, its 'conclusions', no longer make sense or work, then it has to come to terms with some kind of change which will enable the tradition out of its own resources to respond to the crisis which is created by the changed circumstances.

Therefore, tradition might be regarded as being perfectly able to encounter rival traditions and be in the position of overcoming them or not, depending on the way in which those traditions interact with each other. Thus, in MacIntyre's analysis, 'a new narrative is required for the resolution of an epistemological crisis'.[225]

What Hauerwas makes of that is that Christians who face an engagement with contemporary society fail to recognise the integrity and validity of their own tradition if they do not in some sense also recognise that their tradition may well stand in conflict with other traditions that exist in the broader society with which they have to come to terms, or at least which they have to encounter or engage with. 'Our problem is not that Christians come into conflict with the world in which we live, but that we do not.'[226]

So Hauerwas says that MacIntyre's account of how epistemological crises are resolved is an important way of avoiding the dilemma of an appeal to universal principles which is unrealistic or to war. Hauerwas's analysis thus comes to the question of engagement in terms of difference and discontinuity, and in that sense it is somehow like theological terrorism. It is about engaging with alternative traditions, seeking for effective resolution of that conflict in terms of the tradition out of which the Christian comes.

That Christians are called to be witnesses 'by necessity creates epistemological

---

225 Hauerwas, S, *Santify Them in the Truth: Holiness Exemplified*, p 186.
226 Hauerwas, S, *Santify Them in the Truth: Holiness Exemplified*, p 187.

crises for those who do not worship the God of Jesus Christ'.[227] Such witness as the Christian conducts in this environment is an expression of hope rather than a conviction that some assured result might come, even some assured result which might not be seen from the beginning. Witness is a way of speaking about the contact that can take place, and must inevitably take place, between historically constituted traditions. As a consequence, 'no one tradition is in possession of *the* truth'.[228]

Witness thus is the way in which otherwise unconnected people are brought together. It certainly does not involve the absence of argument. 'Christian witness is an alternative to war just to the extent Christian witness establishes connections with those who have no reason to be connected'.[229]

Even this brief account of these three voices shows that the theological tradition is clearly very preoccupied with the issue of engagement under a variety of headings. Providence is clearly an important window into the discussion that is taking place in Christian theology on this theme. The three examples we have looked at approach the question quite differently, and all in their different ways are affected by the environment and context in which they are being argued. On the other hand, all of them interact with the broader theological tradition. Burgmann is much influenced by the impact of the Depression and the consequences of the First World War. O'Donnovan writes from the northern hemisphere in relation to the northern or western tradition of theology. Hauerwas writes out of the American environment.

However, for all of these theologians the issue is not simply a matter of how to conduct a conversation but rather how we are to understand that God is present in the church and with us in the created order in our everyday lives. All underline the contingency of the particular arrangements which exist in the church, and indeed in the broader society, whether they do that in terms of political theology, as in the case of O'Donnovan and his critique of juridical conceptions in the church, or, as in the case of Hauerwas, in terms of the emphasis upon the conversation which is a community tradition out of which Christians experience and understand the gospel.

227 Hauerwas, S, *Santify Them in the Truth: Holiness Exemplified,* p 187.
228 Hauerwas, S, *Santify Them in the Truth: Holiness Exemplified,* p 188.
229 Hauerwas, S, *Santify Them in the Truth: Holiness Exemplified,* p 189.

Two continuities drive O'Donnovan's analysis: on the one hand the continuity between Israel and the church, and on the other the continuity between secular political discourse and the vocabulary of salvation. Thus the church can be a prism for the identification of the destiny of the city. But more than this, the continuity is based on an analogy grounded in reality. This is a real 'analogy of being' (*analogia entis*) which Karl Barth so decisively rejected. That rejection led Barth to see the situation of the Christian and the church in terms of 'radical contingency'. It is not surprising that O'Donnovan's argument, while allowing for contingency, nonetheless overwhelms that principle with continuity diachronic and synchronic. Hauerwas, on the other hand, underlines the synchronic discontinuities and highlights diachronic continuities in terms of a tradition which itself is an amplification of the radical contingency of the Christian's existence.

There are two principal dimensions for Christians. On the one hand there is faithfulness to their faith tradition. For Anglicans that tradition gives supreme place to Scripture as testimony to apostolic Christianity and recognises the engaged and contingent character of each and every element in the historical tradition. On the other hand, there is faithfulness to the continuing presence of God in the created order and the lives of the Christian community. That is a particularly acute question if, as I have argued, the vocation of Christians is primarily to be located in the circumstances of their everyday lives rather than in their ecclesiastical activities.

This brief excursion into an aspect of the theology of providence shows that the question of God's presence and action in the world is a well-rehearsed theological theme. It also underlines commitment to the principle of engagement for Christians, and the Christian community, with the societies and environments in which God has placed them to fulfil their vocation to be Christian. That is where they are to work out their salvation. That necessarily involves them in connections with existing institutions as well as the formulation of church institutions to enable that engagement to be facilitated. In this context the point of connection between belief and unbelief is related to the common human experience, which we saw in Burgmann and in the capacity for intra-traditional conversation in MacIntyre and Hauerwas. It is that latter point, that Christ is the subject of this engagement in the various contexts of everyday life, that comes through so strongly in Stanley Hauerwas.

Conclusions from the tradition

This brief excursion into the tradition has highlighted important aspects of the issue of engagement for Anglicans. At the beginning of this chapter I argued that such an engagement involves elements of interaction, attending to the other and being engaged with their world. It does not only involve some vision as to how we understand our own cosmic canopy of our own view of the way the world is, and of God's presence, but also some vision of what might be possible for the circumstances of those among whom we live. Also in that sense, engagement implies openness to, and the possibility of, change.

We saw elements of these questions in Paul's dealings with the Corinthians, and indeed it is there in the New Testament generally. There were differences of standards between the Christians in Corinth and their neighbours, but there was no withdrawal. On the contrary, there was a persistent engagement, with a deliberate attempt to seek to transform not just relationships of an occasional character but also institutional relationships. The most immediate example of that in the New Testament was in relation to marriage, which, given the circumstances of the first century, was the institution most readily susceptible to change. The transformation came from within when the principals in a marriage became Christians.

The Christian community developed its own habits and practices, its own character and standards and was called by Paul in Corinth to develop the skills to deal with problems within its own life.

The Reformation brought different issues to bear, and the recent research in analysing the social realities on the ground as to what was going on in the sixteenth century in England enable us to see how the evangelical persuasive reformation took place in a variety of contexts. It took place in family, town and nation, and by a variety of methods, through preaching and classes of one kind and another as well as contacts in social groupings such as guilds. The significance of the Reformation for our purposes today, however, is that the constitutional monuments which have come down from the legislative reformation moved in different categories and do not envisage a form of change by persuasion but rather insist on change by legal coercion. They presume complete conformity of all citizens to Christian doctrine and practice, as prescribed in that legislation. They envisage a church community whose ordered life is the subject of the statute law of the state. Those categories in the plural environment in Australia are clearly not only unhelpful, they are positively harmful. These monuments also contain no serious attempt to address the question of inter-faith conversation, witness or evangelism and mission.

So we have observed that the elements of engagement are well-rehearsed matters through the history which has been inherited by Australian Anglicans, that there is a clear commitment to engagement of a personal and institutional kind, and that the point of connection is often the common human experience of Christians and their neighbours. But underlying that is a continuing commitment, a conviction about the divine presence in the created order and thus in the lives of other people and believers. Engagement therefore is conducted on the basis of witness into an environment which is not only hostile but is also an environment where God is at work, seeking to call people to faith.

What, then, do we make of these issues for Australian Anglicans wishing to engage appropriately in terms of their inherited tradition with their fellow Australians?

Respectful visionaries

Here I want to argue that a way of thinking about the kind of engagement which Australian Anglicans might adopt can be summed up in the phrase 'respectful visionaries'. I will return to that more fully shortly, but first of all I want to highlight the way in which the context of Australian Anglicans has significantly changed as compared with the context in which their inherited traditions have been formed. This change requires a reinventing of the categories which are important for their engagement. The New Testament clearly portrays the Christians as a minority within society. Their religious commitments were configured differently from those of their neighbours. Their discipleship to Christ was exclusive and complete. The values which derived from that discipleship were similarly all-demanding. Those very values drove them to the task of engaging with their fellow citizens and to relate to the institutions of their day so that they used their opportunities to transform what they could.

The Reformation monuments are cast in a totally different context. The institutional models are drawn from Tudor imperial theory and political practice. Within that context there is an assumption that all citizens are Christians and that institutions should therefore express this particular kind of Christianity. It is in that sense a presumption about conformist religious practice. Despite this, there was none the less dissent and argument in the sixteenth century which was worked out in various contexts such as households, relationships within the town and an understanding of the nation, and other social institutions such as guilds. This dissent and argument was a persuasive matter. It was opportunistically taken up and, in the end, shaped a political environment which eventually became more open and pluralist than the Tudor theory allowed.

The context within which a doctrine of God's providence has been developed has varied dramatically throughout history. Sometimes the providence of God has been used as a doctrine to defend the status quo where the church has been in an elite and established position. Sometimes it has been used to justify passivity and to explain God where the current cosmic understanding seems to have driven the possibility of God off the agenda. One sees this last point most particularly in the eighteenth century, arising out of the mathematical and scientific reconceptualising of the world brought to such fruitful exposition by Isaac Newton. Of course, that has not been the only framework out of which a doctrine of providence has been developed, and in the present context of the twenty-first century the matter would necessarily have to be very differently configured.

The issue before us at this point is not so much the reconfiguring of the context within which the doctrine of providence might be elaborated but rather the way in which Australian Anglicans might approach the question of engaging with their fellow Australians in a way which is faithful to their tradition and at the same time being effectively engaged with the circumstances in which they now find themselves. In this respect the Reformation formulations which provide such a strong formal element in the heritage of Australian Anglicanism are positively distracting. However, what underlines that Reformation experience of Anglicanism and its theological interpretation by a variety of writers, including, of course, Richard Hooker, is certainly germane to the task in hand.

Such a theological tradition as we have just been looking at underlines that the most fundamental engagement that the Christian is called upon to be part of is an engagement with the living God. Engagement, therefore, in a plural society, such as the one which Australia now is, is nonetheless still essentially an engagement with the activity of God in that society, including in the life of the Christian community.

The reinvention of that church community and the conception of engagement that goes with such a reinvention will work out according to this fundamental truth about the character of God: God is present and a part of the life of humanity. By his word it is sustained and held together. The presence of this God, exemplified in the calling of the Christian community, makes a difference, and that difference is always radically histological. The difference is the difference which Christ makes. That difference is worked out in the contingent character of the life which every individual person and group occupies. The Christian community in its arrangements, habits and institutions is constantly called to recognise the shape of its life as conditioned by radical contingency. We are where we are by the providence of God. We are not ideal, nor an exemplification of an ideal, but we are the very particular which God has created, and, in that particularity, we are called by God to manifest the character of Christ.

It is those theological dimensions which, when located in the reality of the mission situation of the church in Australia, establish the basis, character and direction of the engagement of the Christian community with their everyday life circumstances. It is according to these key truths that the issues which go to make up engagement are to be re-construed and understood. Those common elements are: commonality, attending, life as conversation, change and risk, and vision. When brought together, these elements will go to make up a foundation for Australian Christians to be respectful visionaries in their own land and in their own time. Furthermore, it is these elements which will foster the kind of 'I thou' relationship which Martin Buber called for. These elements will also be marked by the struggle to converse across the distance between the 'cages' in which we come to our conversations with others.

Commonality

Commonality with my neighbour must inevitably be set in the context of living with that neighbour. Living with others means that the commonalties which exist between us are invariably tacit in the habits of our lives. Those commonalties only become a question when difficulties are encountered. When difficulties of understanding, cooperation and conversation arise, then the character of the commonalties is brought to attention. Such conflict may produce a withdrawal and contact may be broken off. But it may also lead to a better understanding and reshaping of relationships.

What is needed is not that we all agree or even that we share the same values. Such an ambition is impossible and in the end an ambition for some kind of hell on earth. Rather, what is called for is enough commonality to sustain a conversation when time is taken for that conversation. Jesus was more often misunderstood than understood. His occasional listeners very rarely understood him. His disciples had to hear what he had to say often and regularly in different contexts. It was not because what he said was complex, technical, theoretical or in a strange language. It was rather that he spoke out of a differently construed reality than that of his hearers. He was speaking out of a different 'cage' and into the 'cage' of his hearers, seeking to open that 'cage' to the kingdom of God, which was his cage of understanding.

There was enough commonality for his hearers to understand something, and where a conversation was continued, then the commonalties provided a basis for a deeper unity. That was the experience of the disciples, and that was the difference between the disciples and the occasional hearer.

Attending

Any serious conversation requires that we attend to the other person, to what they are saying and who they are. Listening means listening not only to the words but to the world out of which the words come, not just to what is said but to the experience which is shared and the actions which are displayed. In any serious conversation with another we have to attend seriously to them and to the world and being out of which they speak. There is a further listening which the Christian must engage in, namely the listening to God in that conversation with the other.

The history of the doctrine of the providence of God shows us that, while it has been differently construed at different times, it is about God's presence in his creation. It is constantly about how God is present. So we listen to God out of our tradition, reaching back to Jesus, and out of our experience of the Spirit of God. In other words, we listen according to the orthodox truth about the character of God and the revelation of the word of God in the person of Jesus Christ, who was crucified and is continually present with his people.

At the same time, we listen to God, who is providentially present in his creation and in the other person with whom we converse. This is not an attempt to assert that God is different and everyone's God is God. Rather, it is to assert that the God and Father of our Lord Jesus Christ is not absent from the lives and circumstances of those with whom we converse. That voice for which we listen is an echo of that presence of God, and that echo is shaped by and identified from that word of God which is Jesus Christ. Any real engagement requires not just a workable level of commonality but also active attending to the other and to the presence of God.

Conversation

It is in that context that serious conversation can take place. Such a conversation is a speaking out of faith, and it is a speaking about faith on the basis of the commonalties and in the context of our attending to the other. Such a conversation is out of faith for faith, and it occurs in the common place. Parker Palmer pointed out some years ago that as Christians we have lost the capacity to enjoy and converse in the company of strangers.[230] Our fellow human beings have become alienated from us. But a conversation which attends to the presence of God in the other, and speaks out of our own tradition and faith without embarrassment, has the possibility of re-establishing a presence in the company of strangers. The conversation therefore occurs in a common place. Such a place may be physical or imagined. But very often such common places are located within institutions in our society, since institutions shape and make up the fabric and dimensions of our existence in modern society.

Yet this conversation inevitably has within it the difference which is Christ. The undoubted truth of the presence of God in his created order cannot displace the truth embedded in the doctrine of the fall and of the sinfulness of humankind. That difference inevitably raises conflict, and therefore in that sense Stanley Hauerwas is right to speak as if this witnessing can be likened to a form of terrorism. But such conflict can be at least managed or resolved in some way, and where it is resolved appropriately it will uncover the real issues of difference. Therefore the Christian is called to be a conflict resolver, not just to bring peace but to bring to light the fundamental difference between belief and unbelief.

The conversation is also words which are embedded in actions, actions which take

230 Palmer, P, 'The Company of Strangers: Christians and the Renewal of America's Public Life'.

place in the common public experience. This was the point that Irenaeus made about the orthodox against the Gnostics. Orthodox Christians, in Irenaeus's exposition, belong to a faith which has a public tradition, and he set that position over against the Gnostics, who claimed an esoteric and secret knowledge. The conversation of the Christian is not only words but actions, and it occurs in the common place of everyday life and brings to birth in that everyday life the reality and difference which is Christ.

That, of course, does not mean that somehow or another every conversation will lead to some exposition of a theory of the atonement or of a histological formula. Indeed, what it means is that the reality of true humanity which the redeemed are called to exemplify will find its particular expression in the particularities of our contingent existence.

Change and risk

When we live in this way, speaking out of our own faith tradition to other traditions, and when we engage in the kind of conversation which arises out of the tacit commonalties of our human existence as Australians together and of our attending to the other, listening for the presence of God, we will face change and risk. This conversation inevitably leaves us and our conversationalists open to change and therefore to risk. Openness in such a conversation is a risk strategy. There are no absolute guarantees for the Christian in such a conversation. There are claims that may be made upon the living God, but there are no guarantees, just as Paul's commitment to such engagement for his Corinthian converts in a hostile environment left them in a position of risk and uncertainty.

Any kind of conversation which is both word and action in such a plural society like modern Australia inevitably involves matters of judgment by the Christian and by the Christian community. Those judgments will not always prove to be enduring or, in hindsight, correct. That also means that we are called upon to make some accommodation or compromise. We are seeking tentatively and partially to find practices which are appropriate for us to live in an environment which enables us to be different as Christians and as a Christian community. In this context compromise is not just inevitable but is a virtue. The conversation which creates that situation implies not only the possibility of change and of risk but also respect for the other and therefore the terms upon which the other might be invited to be persuaded.

Vision

Vision, which the Christian holds to, is always the vision of Christ. It is the histological vision of God's rule. It finds its definition in the announcement of that kingdom by Jesus and the exemplification of it in his life, death and resurrection. It raises its eyes to the future hope in the resurrection and the last days when that vision will be fulfilled and the city of Jerusalem will come down from heaven like the clouds. Such a vision is personal, communal and identity marked. It is a vision of the city of God, and it is an ultimate vision. It is a vision bursting for expression in the present.

What I will call a penultimate vision is an exemplification of the vision of Christ which is appropriate to the contingent and present circumstances of the Christian believer. Such a vision arises out of questions as to what kind of society in the present circumstances is more suitable, one in which Christians can believe and practise their faith. This, of course, is not a Christian society. When Constantine was converted and the Roman Empire became Christian, it had a dramatic effect upon the way in which the ultimate vision of Christ seemed somehow to have coalesced with the penultimate vision of what a society with all its particularities might look like. The Constantinisation of the church radically changed its character, its vision, its eschatology and its conception of how the conversation between belief and unbelief might take place.

Such a radical and revolutionary reordering of Christian faith meant that the penultimate became ultimate. The invisible became visible. It is not surprising that Christianity as a whole could not accommodate itself to such a radical change. Even the Reformation, with its early promise of systematically addressing that Constantinian revolution, failed in the end to do much more than simply rearrange the Constantinisation of the church and its faith.

One of the great virtues of Richard Hooker as a theologian is that, while he was so enmeshed in such a Constantinian conception, he nevertheless saw beyond it. He recognised that the God whom he worshipped and sought to explain could not be contained by the Royal Supremacy and the church settlement which he sought to defend as penultimate. This penultimate vision is about care of the other and about forgiveness. It is about the echo of God's presence in the modern world. It is about a true humanity in Christ, and it is always cast in the context of sin and pride, the overweening pride which Augustine rightly saw was so hard to overcome.

Respectful visionaries

Such engagement is a conversation built upon tacit commonalties that are assumed in the everyday and continuing contact with others. It is marked by attending to the presence of God and is conducted as a conversation whose subject matter is Christ, entertaining the possibility of change in the light of a vision of the character of Christ. Such a conversation calls Anglicans in Australia and elsewhere to be respectful visionaries in their land. They are to be respectful, firstly, of the gospel and of Christ, by whose compelling claim they are constrained. They are to be respectful of others with whom they converse in the daily trivia of their everyday lives. They are to be respectful of the difference, which in part has been created by the God whose providential presence is a basis for Christian confidence.

However, they are to be not only respectful but also visionaries, whose lives, habits, practices and conversation are orientated to the vision which is Christ and who are committed to the creative exploration of a penultimate vision for their fellow citizens which will be a mark on the way to, an enabling and a facilitating of, the understanding and dawning of that ultimate vision which is Christ.

Such respectful visionaries will often find themselves in conflict with those among the Gentiles who seek to lord it over them. But in their conversation these disciples of Christ are not to be like those Gentiles; rather, they are there to serve and give their life for others.

Therefore any reinventing of the Anglican Christian community in the Australian environment—so different from that of the legal monuments of the sixteenth century in England which have shaped much of the institutional heritage of Anglican life and practice—needs to yield to the present realities of the everyday life of Anglican Christians and attend to the presence of God in those circumstances. It will mean a radical re-configuring of the church, so that we Anglican Christians are nurtured as visionaries who therefore may be respectful dissenters. Such a church will need to be marked by habits and practices that nurture such respectful visionaries but yet are open and susceptible of receiving creativity. If Anglican Christianity in Australia and elsewhere is to reinvent itself, then it will need to address in fundamental and radical ways the character of its own institutionality. In the process it will need to address with the utmost seriousness the contingent and unsatisfactory character of the institutional formulations it has received from the English Reformation in the sixteenth century.

CHAPTER SIX

IMAGINATION AND CHANGE

We should pause at this point to review the path of the argument so far. I have argued that worldwide Anglicanism has been facing a major transition for at least the last fifty years. Of course, the religion of the Church of England was transplanted from England to other countries and cultures long before in the early colonial period. However, in the last fifty years of the twentieth century the demographics of Anglicanism worldwide have dramatically changed. Now the majority of active church attenders are to be found in the southern hemisphere. The cultural differences between the churches and provinces which make up the Anglican Communion are greater now than they have ever been. All of these churches look in some sense to the historical tradition of English Christianity as part of their claim to be part of the one holy catholic church. This connection with the Church of England compounds the issues created by the great change in the demographics of worldwide Anglicanism and highlights the critical transition which Anglicanism faces in the world today.

The transition is heightened by the fact that the tradition of Christianity represented in Anglicanism has an instinct for social engagement and cultural enmeshment. The commitment can be seen in the relationship over the centuries between English Christianity and English society. This principle of enmeshment complicates and heightens the problems of coherence in global Anglicanism, since the separate churches of the Anglican Communion are committed to local cultural and social enmeshment.

Anglicanism faces a number of issues in this transition. There are, of course, those general issues which Christianity has always faced of continuity and creativity, of change and constancy. These are perennial issues in any tradition, but they are especially pointed in Christianity which is committed to the defining importance of its historical origins in first-century Palestine and also to the continual enlightenment of the Holy Spirit in the subsequent experience of individual Christians and of the Christian community.

The particular issues which Anglicanism faces have to do with the English pedigree of this form of Christian faith and the increasing diversity of the localities in which the particular tradition is expressed. Anglicanism also faces the tension seen in other aspects of the human condition of the increasing diversity of localities set in conjunction with a globalisation of many aspects of modern life, sometimes referred to as the tension between globalisation and tribalism.

Anglicanism also faces the challenge of the particularities of the sixteenth-century Reformation documents, which continue to play an important constitutional role in most Anglican churches around the world. Those documents have that role in some degree because of a perception that the identity of Anglicanism was critically focused in the Reformation. However, we cannot avoid the fact that these documents also play a powerful role because they were caught up in the processes of colonial imperialism at the time these church constitutions were established. The question canvassed in the first chapter of this book is critically important, namely, what is the historical horizon against which the Anglican pedigree is to the characterised. Did Anglicanism begin in the sixteenth century with the English Reformation or is its tradition to be construed differently and over a longer historical perspective? The view taken in this book is that the tradition begins in the earliest days of English Christianity, though the foundational importance of Bede is recognised.

Australia has been chosen as a case study in this book because it provides a good example in which to set the discussion of this transition and the reinvention of

Anglicanism which the transition demands. An interpretation of the position of Australian Anglicanism was offered earlier, in chapter 2. Australia was chosen as a good example of the problem because of the continuing and continuous connection of Australian social, political and institutional traditions with those of the United Kingdom. It is also a good example because the Anglican Church of Australia gives particular prominence in its constitution to the sixteenth-century Reformation documents. At the same time, the relationship between Australian Anglicans on the one hand and the social institutions of Australia on the other have been sharply brought to clarity in the past thirty years. Up until the third quarter of the twentieth century it was possible for Anglicans still to imagine themselves to be in some kind of informal establishment position. However, the radical institutional changes which have occurred in the last thirty years in Australia have made it quite clear that such a perception is no longer possible, and what has for many years been in fact the case is now manifestly clear. The issue, therefore, of transition is quite acute in the Australian context and provides a useful framework for a discussion of the general questions affecting Anglicanism.

The key questions for Anglicans in this transition process have to do with the degree to which they are confident, or may be confident, about their religious tradition, the truth which they hold in conversation among themselves and with those who differ from them, particularly their fellow citizens who may not share any kind of Christian convictions. One might talk about this in terms of authority. By what authority should Anglicans commend their faith to their fellow citizens, formulate their decisions about what is good in their own personal lives and the lives of their families, or contribute to the formation of social life and the shaping of social and political institutions and policies? Alternatively, one may think of this in terms of knowledge. What kind of knowledge is appropriate for these kinds of Christians located in this kind of society so that it is both faithful to the religious tradition and at the same time enables realistic engagement with the world in which they live? I have construed this question in terms of confidence, because it seems to me that what is at stake is not so much a precise epistemology, though that is extremely important, nor a precise definition of authority though that is not unimportant. The question most acutely before Anglicans concerns the basis upon which they may contribute, the basis upon which they may converse with each other and with their neighbours, the basis upon which they may make reasonable decisions about the direction of their life of faith. For the purposes of living, deciding and engaging, what is required is a sufficient level of appropriate or due confidence.

The second key question in this transition concerns the nature of the community to which Anglicans belong. Of course, this is a question of ecclesiology. However, while it does not involve all of ecclesiology, it is essential to ecclesiology and essential to the social exemplification of the religious tradition to which Anglicans belong. The third question concerns the basis upon which these Anglicans might engage with their fellow citizens and the social institutions which they themselves inhabit. What ought to be the character, the shape and the understanding of that engagement?

It is these three issues which have taken up the central chapters of this book, and they have been examined in a tradition critical fashion, focusing particularly on an example drawn from the New Testament, the sixteenth-century Reformation settlements and aspects of the contemporary theological tradition. In this tradition critical analysis an argument has been developed as to the nature of the transition facing Anglicans and the character of the reinvention which is necessary in order to sustain both faithfulness and the vitality of Anglicanism in the modern world.

There have been three general themes which have been argued in this book throughout the consideration of the three central areas of confidence, community and engagement. First, it has been argued that Anglicanism is best understood as a tradition in the sense of a continuing conversation and community life over a long period of time. Furthermore, this tradition goes back at least to Bede and has tributaries before that time. Clearly this is a reasonably contentious point of view and is related in part to an interpretation of western Christianity in the formative period of the first six hundred years of the second millennium.

Second, I have argued that Christianity in England developed with certain broad theological and rationality characteristics which distinguished it within western Christianity. In this respect it has some similarities with the cross-channel tradition of Gallicanism. If Anglicanism is set in this longer context, it becomes apparent that the sixteenth century must be understood in the more local and particular context of the nationalist political characteristics which mark that century in western Europe.

Thus, third, I have argued throughout this book that the sixteenth-century Reformation legislative monuments have been shaped by the contemporary political concerns of those who formulated the legislation and the categories of Tudor imperialism. In the Reformation legislation these conceptions are expressed in terms of the Royal Supremacy. They are encapsulated in a telling incident in 1604 at the Hampton Court conference when the Puritans sought to establish freedom for their 'prophesying' from James II. James quickly realised that these gatherings provided the opportunity for an alternative source of authority to his own singular rule. Thus he turned to the bishops and said, 'No bishop no king'. It was not so much that James required the political support of the bishops to sustain his crown. Rather, it was that episcopacy had the potential to work with a singular monarchical conception of authority, whereas recognition of the 'prophesying' would have institutionalised a form of legitimate dissent in the authority structure of society. The king's instincts were political, and he was enrolling the bishops and thus episcopacy into that political conceptuality. Such political conceptions have shaped the clothing of the Reformation monuments and have not always been effectively distinguished from the theology and religious significance of the Reformation movement itself.

Approaching Anglicanism as a tradition with identifiable characteristics reaching back at least to Bede, and noting the exceptional character of the political categories of the sixteenth-century Reformation monuments has provided the context for the three key issues of confidence, community and engagement.

Imagination and change

Before turning to these three issues, we should pause and give our attention to the matter of how the reinventing of Anglicanism might actually take place. It is not the proposal of this book that there is a clear blueprint into which Anglicanism can be turned. Rather, what is suggested here is that there are certain guidelines which can be identified from within the tradition as to the religious and theological character of Anglicanism. At the same time, it is clear that the form in which the tradition is now received presents some real problems for Anglicans. The tradition critical approach of this book is not simply a critique of the past but rather a critical participation in the tradition. It is the sort of work which arises from a respect for the tradition and at the same time is open to the contingent character of the experience of that tradition at any given point in time.

Being thus open means also openness to the possibility, indeed the necessity, of change in the tradition.

Such change does not take place entirely in a vacuum or all at once. It occurs in steps which, taken together, amount to change in direction. Such steps can, of course, be taken because of immediate circumstances, or they may be forced upon people by external considerations, either practical or conceptual.[231] If we are to seek to remain faithful to the inner dynamics of the tradition and to the present experience of God in this community, then we will need to have some more proactive or intentional approach to change and the means of achieving it. But before such change can take place in any directed sense, we need to be able to imagine, at least in part, what the future might look like. For that reason we turn to what such imagining might mean in the context of this Christian tradition.

In 1981 Edward de Bono published a powerful little book, *Lateral Thinking*, whose title has now passed into common use in the language. The book suggested that important creative endeavours require us to think outside the normal parameters or boxes within which we habitually think. Thus we need to be lateral, to cut across the normal grain of customary thinking. Such lateral thinking became a vogue for business enterprises and a host of others who wished to make changes in their own lives and in the institutions in which they worked. Edward de Bono has published a stream of books since then elaborating his initial proposal, all directed to trying to break through the logjam of localised habits of thinking.[232]

Hugh Mackay, in his book *The Good Listener*, makes a similar point when he speaks of the need to try to enter into the world of the other person in any communication. It is only as we are able to get out of our habitual ways of thought that we will be able to emerge with any kind of engagement or communication which in turn will make genuine change and relationship possible. Such creative listening requires an exercise in imagination, precisely that same kind of leap of sympathetic imagination to which Adam Smith drew attention in the eighteenth century. Smith was trying to provide the basis for some kind of social values and,

231 See Lansbury, R, 'Managing Change in a Challenging Environment', Senge, P, Kleiner, A, Roberts, C, Ross, R, Roth, R and Smith, B, *The Dance of Change: The Challenges of Sustaining Momentum in Learning Organizations*, and Kaye, B N, *Web of Meaning: The Role of Origins in Christian Faith*, especially chs 4 and 5.
232 See his later development of this idea in De Bono, E, *Lateral Thinking for Management: A handbook of creativity*.

like Rousseau, he formulated that in terms of the connection that is created between humans on the basis of their imaginative shared sentiments. In Smith's case the sympathetic imaginative leap enabled the individual both to understand and to feel the inner constraints which directed the moral behaviour of the other. In Rousseau's case it was the capacity of a stranger to enter into the sufferings of another that created the bond which could be the foundation of human connection and thus of human community.

Rousseau quickly understood that this sympathetic imagination was not the whole story, for humans were born into civil society, and that society had institutions and habits of thought which meant that the individual was not free and that society was an agonising balance of community and alienating externalities. That presents one of the most profound dilemmas for anyone thinking about change in any discrete community. The habits of feeling and thinking which are the result of having internalised the values and tacit assumptions of the institutional framework within which we live are very powerful. In a religious context the institutions which convey these tacit assumptions are inordinately powerful, because they bear images of divine legitimation. It easily and readily becomes the case that the members of a religious tradition have the greatest difficulty in imagining some different expression of their faith, even though the religious tradition itself professes the importance of the continuing contemporary inspiration of the Holy Spirit. This dilemma is rooted deep in the history of Christianity and has its own particular form in the various Christian traditions.

In the biblical history, imagination of this kind came through the prophets and was often set in contrast with and over against the knowledge of the priest (the representative figure of institutional religion) and the king (the representative figure of institutional political power). In the Old Testament, Moses was the archetypical prophet, and he was looked to as *the* prophet. Moses had the classical marks of a prophet as they later appear in Israelite history. He had a personal call from God. The story in Exodus 3 and 4 of Moses' encounter with God through the form of the burning bush shows how Moses was identified as God's servant for a particular task. He declines God's call, on various grounds of unworthiness, but he was brought into the counsel of God and given a message which he was to deliver to Israel and to Pharaoh. That message opened with the rubric, 'Thus says the Lord'. This declaration in the courts of Pharaoh shows not only that the word of the Lord comes to Israel but that it comes in the realities of the historical arena.

Like his successors as prophets, Moses found himself in a dissenting position in the courts of contemporary power, and, also like the later prophets, his message for Israel had a strong ethical character. The prophets were God's servants, men of God. They were people who came from the presence of God to declare in various ways the word of the Lord. The prophets were the instruments by which God exercised his theocratic rule in Israel. It was to defend precisely this theocratic rule that Samuel objected when the Israelites came to him and asked for a king like the nations around about (1Samuel 7). The first two kings, Saul and David, were indeed described as prophets, but none of the kings after them. Similarly, the proposal by David to build a temple was seen by the prophets as a declension from the temporary visible artefacts of worship (2 Samuel 7). It is not surprising that the prophets in Israel often found themselves in conflict with the king and the priests as the two centres of institutional power. The external intervention of God in the life of Israel was at times to contradict the internalised instincts and habits of thought and action framed by the instutionalities of power, religious and regal, in the life of the nation.

Of course there were false prophets, and tests were used to tell false from genuine prophets. Those tests essentially marked whether or not what the prophet said was continuous with the prophetic tradition and, in particular, the law. Naturally, predictive failures by prophets brought their prophetic claim into doubt, while not necessarily verifying it.

In the New Testament, Jesus is seen to fulfil the role and function of priest, king and prophet in Israel. That is because he is seen as the fulfilling and complete expression of the presence of God in the human condition. Thus the writer to the Hebrews begins by asserting that the many and various ways in which God has hitherto revealed himself are now completed in the revelation through his Son.

The early Christians still had prophets among them. Some, such as Agabus, are named individuals who, among other things, tell of future events. The church at Antioch had teachers and prophets among their number, and Paul speaks of prophets who contribute to the life of the church in Corinth. The spirits of such prophets are subject to their own control, and what they say is to be attended to and tested, much as was the case in ancient Israel.

While these slight references in early Christianity reveal a continuation of prophets, their role is entirely shaped by the fulfilment sensed in the life and presence of Jesus Christ. The presence of such prophets in Christianity fades in time, because the testimony of the Christian community has become the prophetic statement of the creating and redeeming presence of Christ. The church community saw itself as a theocracy. The universal gospel which lies at the heart of Christianity meant that all God's people were prophets, since all had been brought into the presence of God. Similarly, they are described as a royal priesthood, a holy nation, God's own people. The overwhelming significance of this sense in apostolic Christianity meant that processes towards institutionalisation, inevitable as they were, were always inhibited and kept in check by the sense of the completeness of the revelation of the counsel of God in Jesus Christ and the complete accessibility of that fulfilment to all people without distinction. This makes all the more significant the challenge for the church community constantly to bring such institutions as it has developed over the years into question and to seek to listen to the counsel of God, to do what in other contexts not so theocratically conceived would be called the cultivation of imagination.

Of course, the evaluation of institutions in the development of the different Christian traditions varies somewhat on this very point. In Roman Catholicism the institution of the papacy and of episcopacy is given an ultimacy which it has not been accorded in Anglicanism. In this respect, early modern Anglicanism has been more influenced by a more immanent sense of the presence of God in the community, impulses which were later expressed in conciliarism and the ideas represented by the doctrine of the priesthood of all believers. That theological quality has been compromised on a number of occasions in history by the association of Anglican institutions with the political powers that be and the political ideas current at the time. This is precisely the nub of Hooker's critique of the Royal Supremacy. Lamentably, Anglicans have often uncritically internalised into the life of the church such notions of power and authority, so that the underlying religious tradition has been obscured. This is the more serious, because institutions have power to influence not only external conduct but also, by processes of internalisation, the habits of the heart. That power has considerable corrupting capacity. Furthermore, the fact that these issues have not always been spelled out and made part of the public debate about authority in Anglicanism has meant that the radical non-commitment to such institutionalities has often been lost. For Roman Catholics the theology of the absolute significance of papacy and episcopacy is an open issue in the life of the church, and this makes for a more robust and transparent debate in that church about the nature of the authority of these institutions. Anglicans often make changes or develop practices without sufficient theological reflection, in part because the issues are formed in the tradition in less publicly sharp-edged form.

For Anglicans, then, there is a very particular importance for them to attend to the 'word of the Lord', for them to foster the cultivation of imagination. For a church which sees access and authority as given to the whole church community, listening to the God who is lord of the church and whose rule in this theocracy is not limited to particular institutions or individuals is peculiarly important. It is in this context not surprising that the modern emergence of synods of the whole church community occurred in Anglicanism, since they represent an attempt to allow the whole church to listen to the word of the Lord. The challenge is thus to practise this kind of authority so that it is not authoritarian. Authority in the church does not arise because of some deficiency of direction or resource which needs to be overcome. Authority arises in the church because God gives gifts to people and those gifts are given to be exercised for the purpose of building up the community in faith and for mission. If Anglicans were able to exercise and accept this kind of authority, they would enable the cultivation of imagination and vision to shape the life of the church community. If they were able to do this, they would be well on the way towards the possibility of change and the reinventing of Anglicanism.

Given that Anglicans have a special reason to focus on these issues of imagination and listening, and given that the present external environment is filled with alternative institutional patterns of power and control, and given the present situation of the institutions Anglicans have inherited, particularly from their recent colonial past, it becomes a central issue in any intentional reinventing of Anglicanism to seek to listen and become engaged in a lateral imaginative discourse. With that in mind, we turn to the three areas which I have argued are crucial to any reinventing of Anglicanism, namely, confidence, community and engagement.

A confidence of persuasive resonance

In chapter three I used Richard Hooker's interpretation of the English Reformation to argue for the importance of a notion of the providence of God in interpreting the present and the application of the principle of utility in discerning the significance of the presence of God. I also used his contrast between the imperial and external authority of the Royal Supremacy with the inner and extensive authority of Christ, an authority marked by the moral character of the crucifixion. I also argued that Paul's appeal to tradition in his Corinthian letters pointed to the possibility of interpreting this presence in terms of the history of God's dealings with humanity. That appeal provided a backdrop for using the doctrine of the Trinity as a tool in the interpretation of the present.

These elements from the sixteenth century, the New Testament and the theological tradition point to a notion of confidence which is sufficient to engage in persuasive resonance with our neighbours and with society and its institutions. These themes highlight the fact that confidence is itself an act of faith which seeks to resonate with the presence of God in the individual, the community of Christian people and the creation as a whole. Because of the character of Christ's lordship and the exemplification of the sovereignty of God in the crucifixion, such resonance offers not only a point of contact but also the mode of operating of the authority of Christ. Thus we must speak not of coercion but of persuasion, because humility was the central mark of the revelation of God in the crucified Christ. We speak of persuasion because of the particular moral and religious character of the authority which is exemplified here, and of resonance because of the conviction that God is at work in his creation. That resonance does not mean simply or necessarily acceptance of the status quo. On the contrary, it may mean quite the opposite. But it does mean that whatever judgment is exercised by Anglican Christians, individually or with others, they have by this kind of authority and these beliefs a sufficient basis for confidence to engage with others.

Such a conclusion means that the external political language of sixteenth-century Tudor nationalism, repristinated and extended in 1662, is clearly unhelpful in this plural society as a way to construe authority both in society and in a discrete church community within that society. More than that, it fails to express in any fundamental sense the core dynamics of authority in this Anglican religious tradition.

If we take these themes and then try to ask how they might look in a reinvented Anglicanism, or at least what steps might be appropriate in order to foster this kind of authority of persuasive resonance, then two aspects of the question become immediately obvious. On the one hand, there is the issue of how we actually understand Christian faith and authority and how we interpret the assumptions of our contemporary culture. On the other hand, there is the question of what kinds of institutional arrangements would foster such a mode of authority.

In order to be able to exercise any kind of authority in a plural environment, Christians, both individually and as a community, need to be able to relate to and engage with the tacit assumptions of their neighbours and of contemporary culture. Theology therefore has a crucial role to play in seeking to enable the appropriate categories to be developed in the Christian community, in shaping the assumptions which might be used in any kind of engagement with the neighbour. Theology has a crucial role therefore in the development of dispositions, language, categories and concepts which will enable contemporary Christians to engage with the contemporary categories and questions among which they live and with which as Christians they need to deal.

In the present circumstances it is easy to see how we can be caught between a rock and a hard place. The rock might be the singular authority of imperial categories. Because these categories do not have particular valency in a plural environment, we internalise them and make the internal subjective authority of our own religious experience and sentiments the single authoritative element in our beliefs. One might internalise them within a community, so that the community becomes marked by a singular notion of authority transmitted either by a priest or a teacher which focuses either on a sacrament or a book as if that were the only authority and, because of this, can only operate in an imperial, determining fashion. On the other hand, one simply might give up such a notion and adopt the undifferentiated priority of multiple authorities, the consequence of which is the dissipation of any sense of truth or priority in understanding.

What we need, rather, is a moderated and community-supported theology which enables us to re-configure the way in which we actually conceptualise these questions, so that the alternatives that are before us are better seen because they arise from the underlying truths of the Anglican tradition and a sense of the presence of God in the created order and, at the same time, can resonate with the categories of modern culture. In this context, of course, we are in a classic situation of contextualisation and interpretation. The difficulty for Anglicans is that the recent practice of theology has not prepared us for such a style of theology or such a role for theology.

One of the most interesting examples taken from current corporate and institutional theory which points to how we might proceed with this agenda is to be found in the book by Peter Senge called *The Fifth Discipline: The Art and Practice of the Learning Organization*. Peter Senge is responding to the modern explosion in information technology and the reshaping of the institutions of corporate life in the western world. He draws attention to the way in which intellectual disciplines have tended to suggest that reality is made up of a series of separate, indeed individual, fragments of insight and understanding. The difficulty is to see the big picture. In this book he seeks to destroy 'the illusion that the world is created of separate, unrelated forces'. When we give up this illusion 'we can then build learning organizations', where people continually expand their capacity to create the results they truly desire, where new and expansive patterns of thinking are nurtured, where collective aspiration is set free, and where people are continually learning how to learn together.

Peter Senge says that there are five disciplines in the learning organisation. The first four are: personal mastery, which is the discipline of continually clarifying and deepening our personal vision; building shared vision; team learning; and mental models, which are the 'deeply ingrained assumptions, generalisations, or even pictures or images that influence how we understand the world and how we take action',[233] what in this book I have called the tacit assumptions. The fifth discipline is systems thinking, 'a conceptual framework, a body of knowledge and tools that have been developed over the past fifty years, to make full patterns clearer, and to help us to see how to change them effectively'.[234] It is this discipline that integrates all the others and enables them to be fused together in an overall conception.

Peter Senge, of course, is concerned with the activities of business corporations, and his analysis is shaped by that context. Anglicanism is a very diffuse and scattered community of people. It is a volunteer community. It is not a command structure. Even though many corporations recognise that the most effective

---

233 Senge, P, *The Fifth Discipline: The Art and Practice of the Learning Organisation*, p 8.
234 Senge, P, *The Fifth Discipline: The Art and Practice of the Learning Organisation*, p 7.

compliance is achieved by persuasive methods of various kinds, in the end the command element is always in the background. While once that might have been true of Anglicanism, when it was most fully established, for example, in the sixteenth century, it no longer is true. Given that qualification, what Peter Senge says about the fifth discipline of systems thinking is pertinent. First he says that today's problems are yesterday's solutions and that to replicate the solutions is only likely to replicate the problems. The harder you push, the harder the system will push back.[235] Short-term remedies might work in a local sense, but they will not affect the overall operation of the system. Easy solutions generally will lead you back to the problem that you started with, and some cures may turn out to be worse than the problem. In complex systems the cause and the effect are not usually closely related in time and space. While moving fast may be good in some circumstances, it is not always the way to make lasting changes.

These laws of Peter Senge point to the importance of having an approach to the reinvention of Anglicanism which addresses fundamental questions and looks to the long term, not to the immediate. Theology, as an attempt to understand in a systems way the nature and characteristics of Christian faith in the twenty-first century in its Anglican mode, is what we are about in the reinventing of Anglicanism. We are in the business of trying to re-configure the tradition as it has been handed down, especially in the way in which we see and use the sixteenth-century Reformation monuments. That means that the constitution of many of the provinces of the Anglican Communion, and in particular the constitution of the Anglican Church of Australia, needs to be taken in a significantly deconstructed way. The role of the synod as an imperial parliament needs to be entirely re-configured. The whole exercise needs to step aside from the political assumptions of the Reformation material and ask more fundamental questions about the nature of this community and the nature of the authority which will enable a conversation both within and outside the community to take place.

In that sense, therefore, the institutional priorities need to be significantly rearranged. For example, in many provinces in the Anglican Communion the official governance structures are synodical. In their present format they are increasingly irrelevant and inappropriate for the future of Anglican Christianity in the way they operate. Two problems are obvious. The first is the operation of

235 See Mead, L, *Five Challenges for the Once and Future Church.*

synods as cast in the image of a sovereign state. This carries with it the assumption that the synod has immediate coercive powers for its laws and decisions. National synods have different powers in different Anglican constitutions. In the Episcopal Church of the United States of America the canons of the General Convention apply automatically in all dioceses. In the Anglican Church of Australia the canons of the General Synod are permissive only, and, where they affect what happens in a diocese, they only have force in that diocese if the diocese chooses to adopt them. But, even given such differences, the assumption that such canons passed by synods national or diocesan have coercive power for the community is simply out of touch with reality and, in any case, inappropriate. They may influence the way a court rules on the use of church property and, by that means, gain some force. They can certainly influence the behaviour of bishops and clergy, but there is no power by canon to coerce the people of a voluntary church community. What is true at the diocesan and provincial level is dramatically much more true at the international level.

However, the second problem is whether synods should be trying to do this anyway. Such a conception of the authority of synods has more to do with the accidental imperialisms of some temporary episodes in the Anglican historical experience rather than with the underlying nature of the Anglican theological tradition. The point applies *a fortiori multa* to the activities of the three orders of ministry, particularly bishops and priests.

Those institutions which directly and necessarily interface with the values and assumptions of the surrounding societies will be at the centre of any future strategy for Anglicanism. Schools which are part of a state system, or welfare agencies which are part of a state or integrated system, as they are in Australia, would be good examples of institutions which are necessarily at the interface institutionally with the assumptions of the host society. Those institutions, therefore, necessarily must face all of the challenges involved in any reinvention of Anglicanism. In western societies the parish structure increasingly reflects the territorial expression of the social tribalisation of urban life. The situation is different in regional and rural areas, certainly in Australia. However, in the metropolitan areas the parish system tends to operate in ways that disintegrate the capacity of Anglican Christians to engage significantly with the host society in all of its diversity, yet it is in that society that they are called to live out their Christian vocation. Revolution will not help. That is a short-term mechanism. What will help is a re-evaluating of the priorities for Anglican Christians in terms of the way in which they give themselves to institutional activity. Setting church communities in necessary connection with a school is a striking example of a re-configuration which has great promise, even if it presumes a transient and sectional community. Doing the same with a welfare organisation would be another interesting example. So the instruments or institutions which facilitate the development of an external conversation with the contrasting assumptions of the wider society are the arenas within which reinventing impulses in Anglicanism are more likely to take place.

Institutions and activities which disperse activity and initiative rather than concentrating and narrowing it will help to cultivate a better sense of authority as persuasive resonance. We need something like the equivalent of the contribution made by religious orders prior to the sixteenth century in England. The tendencies in the Anglican community towards dispersion of initiative and activity inevitably run into opposition because of the understandable instinct to contract in an environment where there is a loss of confidence. The reality, however, that should be identified is that the God whom Anglicans are committed to is the God who is creator and redeemer and is continually present in the creation in order to create and to redeem. Tracing the echo of that presence and calling forth with confidence the resonance of that presence is the way in which Anglicanism will not only discover its roots but proceed to its own reinvention.

In the wider global context of the twenty-first century new imperialisms are not hard to find, and they are not just military or political imperialisms. Late capitalism has become the vehicle of some notable colonial imperialisms. One does not have to accept Fred Jameson's claim that late capitalism is a vehicle for American military power to recognise that multinational enterprises and financial institutions exercise vast power and colonise extensive areas of human activity. These are dangerous and tempting times for a religious tradition elementally dispersed and community shaped in its authority. The proposal that first there be a primates meeting, then that it should meet more often and 'be given more power', and then that it should develop a program of 'action', while the community representative body, the Anglican Consultative Council, appears to stagnate and be marginalised speaks volumes about the model of authority that such deliberate changes imply.

A community of interdependent diversity

Our consideration of the theme of community led to the identification of four key issues—difference, connection, direction and institutions—and once again the Reformation monuments proved to be inadequate. I argued that Paul points us in the direction of thinking of the church as a community being created by God. As such it is a community with God-given gifts and thus of diversity of contribution. It is a community of moral character which gains it direction from the divinely orchestrated contributions of the different gifts that have been given to the church. The recent attention given to *koinonia* provides a valuable key to understanding the church as a community in which the quality of connection is more significant than the particular institutional arrangements that might be in place.

I argued that these elements in the Anglican tradition pointed to church as a community of interdependent diversity, but it is an interdependent diversity set within a conception of the presence of God creating this community and actively creating both the interdependence and the diversity.

Modern institutional theory draws attention to the different ways in which organisations emerge in a globalised environment. David Limerick has developed a notion of the transition from the corporate culture of the late twentieth century to the postcorporate networked organisation of the twenty-first century.[236] He draws attention to the discontinuities that have emerged at the turn of the century and argues that, increasingly, the effective organisations in the corporate sector are not management focused but participation focused and that the organisations are made up of individuals who are networked for the purposes of particular tasks. Such networks are transitory in relation to projects, and the whole structural character of the enterprise is held together by the sustaining founding vision for which it was brought into being.

---

236 Limerick, D, 'The Shape of the New Organization: Implications for Human Resource Management' and Limerick, D, Cunnington, B and Crowther, F, *Managing the New Organisation: Collaboration and Sustainability in the Postcorporate World*, and in relation to the changing pattern of national organisation in the Episcopal Church of the USA see Douglas, I T, 'Whither the National Church? Reconsidering the Mission Structures of the Episcopal Church'.

The church, and particularly the Anglican Church, has shown these kinds of characteristics for a long time. Particularly during the nineteenth century, in a context of greater social freedom, the emergence of a strong central administrative quality to the Church of England was matched with the growth of societies and religious orders. The societies were in large measure the vehicles for the expansion of Anglicanism overseas during the colonial period. In any part of the Anglican Communion, the synodical governance structure by no means comprehends all of the activities that are conducted in the name of Anglicanism. There are all sorts of independent Anglican institutions—educational, welfare, publishing and advocacy—which exist as Anglican entities and serve the interests of the Anglican community but are not necessarily created or controlled by the synodical structure. Australian Anglicanism is particularly diocesan in its constitutional shape. The dioceses are where most of the resources are located, and the national constitution gives the General Synod essentially permissive authority. It guards the inherited faith. Most of the direct activity and resources are located in the diocese. But even here the reality is that within the diocese many networks of an informal kind sustain a wide range of activities. Networks exist, in association with the General Synod in Australia, which are concerned with youth, children, schools, welfare, catechumenate, cursillo and many others. There are missionary organisations and other entities which exist as Anglican but are independent of this synodical structure.

Let me suggest a mind game. Imagine that the organisational structures are not hierarchical in a top–down command sense but rather stand, as it were, alongside the church community and, as a consequence, the organisational image is turned ninety degrees on its side. In such a picture it is apparent that the synodical structure is one of a number of institutional arrangements which exist in order to serve the interests and promote the values of the Anglican Christian community. Furthermore, it shows that the different elements in the synod structure—national/diocesan/parish—serve the same people but do so on a different horizon or from a different perspective. Such an inversion of the mental diagram enables us more easily to see that the crucial question is not so much the character and shape of the organisational structure, as if this controls things, but rather the degree to which these institutional arrangements actually benefit Anglican Christians. Conceptualising the 'church' as a network, or at least a series of networks, is likely to be more productive of innovation and the cultivation of independent diversity.

There is a further problem with the operation of synods, at least in western countries. If synods are held over an extended period of time, then the people who are not employed by the church of by church organisations are at a very significant disadvantage. They must take annual leave to attend and, even then, may not be able to take such leave at the time of the synod. As a result, some kinds of people are excluded from participation simply because of the practical arrangements. Perhaps I may illustrate the problem by reference to the categories of people elected to the Standing Committee of the General Synod in the Anglican Church of Australia. The constitution gives ex officio places to the primate, the five metropolitans, the chairman of committees, the synod secretaries (one clerical, one lay) and the general secretary of the General Synod. There are then four elected from the house of bishops (the diocesan bishops and two indigenous bishops—the house does not include assistant bishops, who are in the house of clergy) and nine each elected from the house of clergy and the house of laity. The category breakdown of the two most recent Standing Committee elections is as follows.

	Church employees	Others actual/ [possible]	Total
Ex-officio members	7	2 (2)	9
Elected members	18	4 (9)	22
Total	25	6 (11)	31

My point, which does not relate to individuals, is that the present operation of the synodical structure makes it hard to regard it as providing representativeness for the generality of the church, and, further, that the categories most under-represented tend to be those at the coal face of mission and engagement with the wider society. Such a pattern is less likely to facilitate a church community marked by interdependent diversity.

Similarly, the fostering of intervening institutional arrangements for ministry and pastoral support which are free to take initiatives is more likely to create the kind of community which is marked by interdependence and diversity. In a tradition committed to the priesthood of all believers, such authority as exists in the organisational arrangements begins with the baptised. The realistic representation of that in church structures would bring decision making into closer contact with the realities with which ordinary Christians are faced. It would make this authority more interactive and more ecclesial in character.

One of the most important challenges facing Australian Anglicanism, particularly in the large metropolitan areas, is the recovery of an episcopate which directly ministers to the church community. We have in our metropolitan cities such large dioceses that the diocesan archbishops find themselves expected to be something more like chief executive officers of large corporations rather than people who have an episcopal ministry to a community of people. If episcopal responsibilities were limited to no more than the equivalent community of thirty-five parishes and were directly related to a network of institutional arrangements including parishes, schools, welfare agencies and others, it would be more likely that genuine episcopacy would be possible for those who inhabit these institutional arrangements. The present institutional arrangements actually frustrate episcopacy and diminish the possibility of interdependent diversity. It is not just the bishop who suffers in the present arrangements, it is also the ecclesial life of the community.

On a global scale the development of regionalism in the Anglican Communion would move in the same direction. In 2001 the Ekklesia Society published some proposals called 'Mending the Net' to deal with what they saw as problems of division around the issues of the ordination of women and sexual ethics. They called for enhanced responsibility for the primates meeting, because this provides 'an authoritative and intimate center'. The problem with the proposals in 'Mending the Net' is that they are a response of corporatism and unreconstructed imperial mentalities. They serve to concentrate apparent authority in the Communion. It is a trend in exactly the opposite direction to one which might have any kind of significant strategic value for the long-term future of Anglicanism.

Engagement as respectful visionaries

In discussing engagement, I argued that providence was a key concept for understanding the presence of God in the creation. I also argued that this theological approach implies that change will be principally by persuasion. We noted that this kind of persuasion was part of the experience of the Reformation in the sixteenth century. It occurred in a variety of social and grassroots circumstances, but it was not the model embedded in the statutory monuments. The model embedded in the statutory monuments was shaped by notions of singular authority and coercive power. The notion of Anglican Christians as respectful visionaries for the society in which they live draws upon this grassroots Reformation persuasive activity and the New Testament model of the Christian community as a discrete voluntary group, a model in some significant contrast with the picture in the Reformation legislation. In this model of engagement, a commonality with the neighbour was seen in terms of the providential activity of God. This understanding implies a conception of life as conversation not only with neighbours and institutions but also with God, who is present in the social order. Such a model of engagement implies imagination as to what the God and Father of our Lord Jesus Christ might be doing in the present and risk in acting upon such a vision. It is in this context that the notion of engagement for Anglicans as respectful visionaries was developed.

Any development of an effective project of Anglicans being respectful visionaries faces major challenges in regard to their inherited tradition. There are major category formation issues to be encountered. The inherited English establishment mentality persisted within Australia until the end of the twentieth century. The assumptions of this inherited mentality no longer are appropriate to the position of Anglicans as they exist today in almost any country in the world.

There is, further, a methodological issue in regard to the way in which we approach this question. Do Anglicans have a model of what the nation state or a society should look like, or is it the case that they have certain kinds of understandings as to what will assist a genuinely human existence and what will facilitate the cultivation of faith? This debate has been long-standing in Christianity and especially in Anglicanism. But a clear point has directly arisen from our consideration of the theological interpretation of the English Reformation and our consideration of the notion of providence as part of the characteristically Anglican perception. That point is that it is most unlikely that Anglicans will have a theory of the state which enables them to lay out an ideal form. Rather, the radical direction in which Hooker pointed and which is drawn from an understanding of providence is that the Anglican tradition brings to the conversation some values and principles with which to engage rather than an ideal form to apply. That is what it means to be a visionary—not in the sense of having some Utopian ideal but in the sense of having some instincts about what is genuinely appropriate for human existence and for faith in God lived in any particular environment.

Theology in this context will need to play a key role in the cultivation of a conversation with the insights of other disciplines. Peter Senge is right. Our best understandings of our human situation today are not to be found in conceptions developed in watertight silos of particular disciplines. They are to be found at the cutting edge of each of these disciplines. Universities around the western world are reshaping the disciplines as they seek to come to terms with the changing situation is which we live out our lives. Christian theologians ought to be engaged in this dialogue directly and vigorously in order not only to contribute but also to understand the nature of their own Christian faith. This model presumes the policy of engaging in order to reflect upon what that engagement might yield for understanding Christian faith and the world in which we are called to live. Anglican theologians, as servants of the Anglican tradition which emphasises social enmeshment, will need to address things like the role of government, human rights, the nature of cities and human demography, the family and the nurture of the human person, power and humility in a plural world, and the nature of institutions. These are questions which do not always figure in the theological curriculum.

This brings us to a profound problem with the practice and character of Anglican theology. The problem differs in its profile and its extent in different parts of the world, but some general points are discernible. Prior to the nineteenth century, in England theology was taught among other broadly conceived disciplines in the universities. These universities (Oxford and Cambridge) were thought of as Christian institutions providing Christian education of a general kind. During the nineteenth century, in line with wider social changes, specific disciplines developed to serve the emerging professions. So theology emerged as a separate discipline, and its professional group was the clergy. They became the custodians of this professional knowledge.[237]

---

237 See Russell, A, *The Clerical Profession*.

This pattern was transplanted to Australia and elsewhere. Because the early universities in Australia were not controlled by the church, they provided a Christian education which excluded the intellectual discipline of the clergy, namely, theology. The consequence was that theology was framed as undergraduate training for ordination, and the content of the theological curriculum has expressed that fact.[238] In the United States of America and Canada a somewhat different pattern has emerged, but similar underlying problems exist in that the theology sustained has been ecclesiastically and ministerially shaped. As a consequence, the character of the intellectual engagement with the host culture has changed. It is not integrated but separated, and the issues of engagement are consequently muted and distorted. Even the theology courses offered to lay people are shaped in this way. The current debate about theology, so advanced in the United States of America, is of crucial importance for Anglicans.[239] If it does not yield a theology which necessarily addresses the contemporary culture but is not captured by that culture, then the capacity of Anglicans to engage with their local host society will be significantly diminished.

An Anglican vision

The present crisis in Anglicanism worldwide calls for vision. Some construe that vision in future-oriented terms so that the vision becomes the goal to which we should all aspire. No doubt in the broad spectrum of human existence such idealist approaches to the vagaries of life have helped in the realisation of the Christian vocation. That is not the kind of vision which has been offered in this book, and it is not the kind of vision which at this stage in our history I believe is of much real value. When Israel perished for lack of vision, it was not such a vision they lacked. The vision portrayed by the prophets was more often a vision of the reality of God's presence and character. When Elisha's servant could not understand his master's confidence in dangerous circumstances, it was because he had no vision of the 'chariots of God' which surrounded them. Paul's vision of the man of Macedonia was an uncovering of the reality that God was preceding him in his missionary activity.

238 Kaye, B, 'Theology for Life in a Plural Society'.
239 See for example Kelsey, D H, *Between Athens and Berlin: The Theological Education Debate.*

The kind of vision offered here is that of a picture of 'the way things are'. It is an attempt to uncover something of the inner dynamic of the Christian truth sustained in the Anglican experience of God. There is much to be said for the idea of a paradigm such as Paul Avis offers, because it gives a shorthand statement of a central way of looking at things. However, I fear it lacks a powerful enough identification of the historicality of the experience of Anglicanism, and the particular paradigm of baptism does not give enough of the differentiating nuances of that historical experience. The image of the failed church–state model elaborated by William Sachs draws attention to a very important truth in the history of Anglicanism. But it does not configure the question sufficiently radically or broadly, so that the particular point of example, the English establishment model, necessarily limits the power of the analysis to reach beyond the departure of the tradition from its English soil. Nor in my view does it sufficiently uncover the theological issues at stake in this matter and, as a consequence, his account has great difficulty in moving into the present post-English colonial phase in which we are now located.

That movement is clearly identified by Ian Douglas, indeed he makes it his central heuristic tool. In this respect he addresses the reality of the present crisis with abundant 'front on' clarity. But English colonialism is not the only colonialism which affects Anglicanism, and I believe the issues need to be handled at a more general and, in a certain sense, more abstract level. It is for that reason that I have made particular use of Hooker's critique of the Royal Supremacy, because it shows that the real problem is the nature of authority and, in this case, the nature and functioning of imperial authority. Stephen Sykes appears to me to have moved in his thinking on these issues and, if I have interpreted him correctly, his focus on the location in the church community of the exercising of authority constitutes a profound and important contribution for the present circumstances.

These contributions are all visions in the sense in which I'm using the term. They are attempts to give an account of what is really going on, an account of what Anglicanism is all about and what the real challenges are which currently face Anglicans worldwide. By vision I do not mean an account of the inner sociological forces which move under the surface to produce the social and cultural conditions of the contemporary crisis for Anglicanism. There is something of that here, but the vision I have sought to present is a theological vision, a vision of the reality of God in relation to this Anglican tradition. It is this kind of theological vision which I have tried to give in this book, and I have tried to do it by providing a picture of Anglicanism as a discrete tradition within the broader tradition of Christianity. That picture has implied that Christianity is itself a tradition necessarily made up of a number of discrete traditions. If Roman Catholicism is seen as a historical attempt to give social and institutional expression to Jesus' words to Peter, '…on this rock I will build my church, and the gates of Hades will not prevail against it' (Matthew 16:18 NRSV), then it seems to me that Anglicanism, taken over the long span of history, might be thought of as a historical attempt to give expression to what Jesus said to James and John, 'You know that among the gentiles those whom they recognise as their rulers lord it over them, and their great ones are tyrants over them. But it is not so among you; but whoever wishes to become great among you must be your servant' (Mark 10:42 NRSV). Neither tradition has escaped the rebuke of Christ, 'Get behind me, Satan' (Matthew 16:23), and neither tradition on its own could ever capture the full dynamic and reality which is the redeeming and creating presence of the Lord of all creation and the crucified Saviour of us all. What I have tried to present is a picture, a vision, of where the Anglican tradition is in relation to the crisis which it now faces.

In putting this picture forward, I have used some of the recent analytical work on traditions in social theory and philosophy, as well as the historical experience of Christians. Because Anglicans today give special place to the literary monuments of the English reformation, I have been at pains to draw attention to the ambiguities that attachment brings in terms of a genuinely critical appropriation of the reformation in England. That has been a strategically important element in this analysis because of the role of imperial notions of authority contained in the language and presentation of these monuments and because of the crucial importance of such notions in the contemporary world in which Anglicans are called to live out their vocation as Christians.

The very nature of this historical tradition makes it important to recognise that there have been significant and dramatic episodes of transition before for Anglicans. We noted some of these moments in detail in the course of the argument in this book, but we should not underestimate the degree to which earlier transitions were perceived by those involved to be of catastrophic proportions. It is worth recalling some of those moments in order to underline the historical resilience of this tradition of faith. They include the Saxon–Celtic interface, marking out a tradition of influence and a monastic presence; the Roman mission (or invasion) of Augustine, marking out a conception of territory and organisation; the Norman conquest, marking out a pattern of control and, for the church, legal separation and some institutional independence; the Tudor revolution, marking out a tradition of nationalism and statutory control; and the imperial colonial phase, marking a tradition taken to foreign parts in the clothes of empire, redolent of the domestic imperial conceptions of Tudor nationalism.

It has been the contention of this book that Anglicanism has survived as one of the discrete traditions within Christianity because it contained within it crucial elements of a theological kind which have made it resilient. Those elements are the following: a conception of God who is participating in the human condition, an incarnational God; connectedness in the church's ecclesial conceptions, a real sense that God is present; an instinct about authority which derives from this and is marked by open-endedness, porous borders, tentativeness and being contingently aware and is an authority experienced and exercised by the whole people of God; engagement in the social and cultural context, so that the church is guided by an awareness of both contingency and providence in regard to both ecclesial and social institutionality.

I began this book with a reference to Abraham going out by faith to a place he did not know. That pilgrim principle has marked the major moments of the journey of Anglicanism from Celtic communities to colonial empire. The present moment for Anglicanism, in terms of its local manifestation in different cultural locations and its global connection in a time of new and changing imperialisms, is fraught with many temptations and opportunities. A better appreciation of its history as a discrete tradition within Christianity will enable a better engagement with the central elements of its present interpretative crisis. That, in turn, will open up for those Christian pilgrims who call themselves Anglicans more opportunities to be effective and faithful.

BIBLIOGRAPHY

This list contains only those items referred to in the notes.

Free to Believe? The Right to Freedom of Religion and Belief in Australia, Human Rights and Equal Opportunity Commission, Sydney, 1997.

Our Nation: Multicultural Australia and the 21st Century, Commonwealth of Australia, Canberra, 1995.

Anderson B, *Imagined Communities,* Verso, London 1991.

Aristotle, *Ethics,* Penguin Books, Harmondsworth 1953.

Atkinson A, *The Europeans in Australia: A History. Volume One, the Beginning,* OUP, Melbourne 1997.

Austin A, *Australian Education 1788–1900: Church, State and Public Education in Colonial Australia,* Pitman, Melbourne 1961.

Avis P, *Anglicanism and the Christian Church,* T & T Clark, Edinburgh 1989.

——, *The Anglican Understanding of the Church: An Introduction,* SPCK, London 2000.

Barrett C K, *A Commentary on the First Epistle to the Corinthians*, A & C Black, London 1971.

Barth K, *The Doctrine of Creation: Church Dogmatics, Volume III, 4*, T & T Clark, Edinburgh 1961.

Bede, *A History of the English Church and People*, Penguin Books, London 1968.

Bellah R, et al, *Habits of the Heart*, University of California Press, Berkeley 1985.

Berkman J and Cartwright M (eds), *The Hauerwas Reader*, Duke University Press, Durham 2001.

Berlin I, *The Roots of Romanticism*, Chatto & Windus, London 1999.

Bettenson H (ed), *Documents of the Christian Church*, Oxford University Press, London 1956.

Bianchi E and Ruether R E (eds), *A Democratic Church: The Reconstruction of Roman Catholicism*, Crossroads, New York 1992.

Biemer G, 'Religious Education — a Task between Divergent Plausibilities', in Jenkins A H (ed), *John Henry Newman and Modernism*, Sigmaringendorf, 1990.

Birrell B, *Federation: The Secret Story*, Duffy and Snellgrove, Sydney 2001.

Black A, *Council and Commune: The Conciliar Movement and the Fifteenth-Century Heritage*, Burns & Oates, London 1979.

——, *Guilds and Civil Society in European Political Thought*, Cornell University Press, 1984.

Blombery T, *The Anglicans in Australia*, Religious Community Profiles, Australian Government Publishing Service, Canberra 1996.

Bollen J D, *Protestantism and Social Reform in New South Wales*, Melbourne University Press, Carlton 1972.

Bollen J D and Leigh College, *Religion in Australian Society: [An Historian's View]*, Leigh College, Sydney 1973.

Bolton G, *Edmund Barton*, Allen & Unwin, St Leonards 2000.

Bonner G, 'Religion in Anglo-Saxon England', in Gilley S and Sheils W (eds), *A History of Religion in Britain*, Blackwell, Oxford, 1994, pp 24–44.

Border R, *Church and State in Australia 1788–1872: A Constitutional Study of the Church of England in Australia*, SPCK, London 1962.

Brett J, *Robert Menzies' Forgotten People*, Pan MacMillan, Sydney 1992.

Broughton W, *Speech of the Lord Bishop of Australia in the Legislative Council upon the Resolution for Establishing a System of General Education*, Sydney 1839.

Broughton W G, *The Counsel and Pleasure of God in the Vicissitudes of States and Communities*, Mansfield, Sydney 1829.

Brown P, *The Rise of Western Christendom: Triumph and Diversity AD 200–1000*, Blackwell, Oxford 1996.

Burgmann E H, *Religion in the Life of the Nation: Four Lectures*, The St John's College Press, Morpeth 1930.

——, *God in Human History*, Morpeth Booklets, No. 4, St. John's College Press, Morpeth, NSW 1931.

Camilleri J and Falk J, *The End of Sovereignty: The Politics of a Shrinking and Fragmenting World*, Edward Elgar, Aldershot 1992.

Campenhausen H v, *Ecclesiastical Authority and Spiritual Power in the Church of the First Three Centuries*, A & C Black, Oxford 1969.

Carter S, *The Culture of Disbelief: How American Law and Politics Trivialize Religious Devotion*, Anchor Books, Doubleday, New York, 1993.

Chandler A D, *The Visible Hand: The Managerial Revolution in American Business*, Belknap Press, Cambridge, Mass. 1977.

Cole C, Brumfitt J and Hall J (eds), *Jean-Jacques Rousseau: The Social Contract and Discourses*, J M Dent, London 1973.

Collinson P, 'The Elizabethan Church and the New Religion', in Haigh C E (ed), *The Reign of Elizabeth*, MacMillan, London, 1984, pp 169–94.

——, *The Birthpangs of Protestant England: Religious and Cultural Change in the Sixteenth and Seventeenth Centuries*, Macmillan, London 1988.

——, 'England', in Scribner B, Porter R and Teich M (eds), *The Reformation in National Context*, CUP, Cambridge, 1994, pp 80–94.

Condren C, *The Status and Appraisal of Classic Texts: An Essay on Political Theory, Its Inheritance, and on the History of Ideas*, Princeton University Press, Princeton, N.J. 1985.

Coombs H, *The Fragile Pattern*, Australian Broadcasting Corporation, Sydney 1970.

Corten D, *When Corporations Rule the World*, Earthscan, London 1995.

Cox E, *A Truly Civil Society*, Boyer Lectures, Australian Broadcasting Corporation, Sydney 1995.

Cross C, *Church and People 1450–1660: The Triumph of the Laity in the English Church*, Collins, Fontana Press, London 1976.

Cunningham D, *These Three Are One: The Practice of Trinitarian Theology*, Blackwells, Oxford 1998.

Day D, *Chifley*, Harper Collins, Sydney 2001.

De Bono E, *Lateral Thinking for Management: A Handbook of Creativity*, American Management Association, [New York] 1971.

De Pree M, *Leading without Power: Finding Hope in Serving Community*, Jossey-Bass, San Francisco 1997.

Douglas I T, *Lambeth 1998 and the 'New Colonialism'*, The Witness, 1998, pp 8–12.

——, 'Whither the National Church? Reconsidering the Mission Structures of the Episcopal Church', in Slocum R (ed), *A New Conversation: Essays on the Future of Theology and the Episcopal Church*, Church Publishing, New York, 1999, pp 60–78.

——, 'Anglican Identity and the *Missio Dei*: Implications for the American Convocation of Churches in Europe', *Anglican Theological Review*, 82, 2000, pp 459–74.

——, 'The Exigency of Times and Occasions: Power and Identity in the Anglican Communion Today', in Douglas I T and Kwok P-L (eds), *Beyond Colonial Anglicanism*, Church Publishing, New York, 2001, pp 25–46.

Douglas I T and Kwok P-L (eds), *Beyond Colonial Anglicanism: The Anglican Communion in the Twenty-First Century*, Church Publishing, New York 2001.

Duck R C, *Gender and the Name of God: The Trinitarian Baptismal Formula*, Pilgrim Press, New York 1991.

Dudley-Smith T, *John Stott, the Making of a Leader: A Biography: The Early Years*, InterVarsity Press, Downers Grove, Ill. 1999.

Dulles A, 'A Half Century of Ecclesiology', *Theological Studies*, 50, 1989, pp 419–42.

Etherington N, 'Missions and Empire', in Winks R (ed), *The Oxford History of the British Empire, Volume V, Historiography*, Oxford University Press, Oxford, 1999, pp 303–14.

Figgis J N, *Studies of Political Thought from Gerson to Grotius, 1414–1625*, Cambridge University Press, Cambridge 1907.

——, *The Fellowship of the Mystery*, Longmans Green and Co., London, New York [etc] 1914.

Fukuyama F, *The End of History and the Last Man*, Penguin Books, London 1992.

Gee H and Hardy J (eds), *Documents Illustrative of English Church History*, MacMillan, London 1921.

Gellner E, *Nations and Nationalism*, Blackwell, Oxford 1983.

——, *Postmodernism, Reason and Religion*, Routledge, London 1992.

Griffiths J (ed), *Certain Sermons or Homilies Appointed to Be Read in Churches in the Time of Queen Elizabeth of Famous Memory*, SPCK, London 1864.

Gunton C, *The Promise of Trinitarian Theology*, T & T Clark, Edinburgh 1991.

——, *The One, the Three and the Many: God, Creation and the Culture of Modernity*, Cambridge University Press, Cambridge 1993.

Guy J, *Tudor England*, Oxford University Press, Oxford 1988.

Haigh C (ed), *The English Reformation Revised*, Cambridge University Press, Cambridge 1987.

——, *English Reformations: Religion, Politics, and Society under the Tudors*, Oxford University Press, Oxford 1993.

Harris M, *The Challenge of Change: The Anglican Communion in the Post-Modern Era*, Church Publishing, New York 1998.

Harris R, *Romanticism and the Social Order 1780–1830*, Blandford Press, London 1969.

Hastings A, 'Christianity and Nationhood: Congruity or Antipathy?', *Journal of Religious History*, 25, 2001, pp 247–60.

——, *The Construction of Nationhood: Ethnicity, Religion and Nationalism*, CUP, Cambridge 1997.

Hatch E, *The Growth of Church Institutions*, Hodder & Stoughton, London 1887.

——, *The Organization of the Early Christian Churches*, Longmans Green, London 1892.

Hauerwas S, *A Community of Character: Toward a Constructive Christian Social Ethic*, University of Notre Dame Press, Notre Dame 1981.

——, *Sanctify Them in the Truth: Holiness Exemplified*, T & T Clark, Edinburgh 1998.

Hempenstall P, *The Meddlesome Priest: A Life of Ernest Burgman*, Allen & Unwin, St Leonards 1993.

Hilliard D, 'The Ties That Used to Bind: A Fresh Look at the History of Australian Anglicanism', *Pacifica*, 11, 1998, pp 272–73.

——, 'The Transformation of South Australian Anglicanism 1880–1930', *JRH*, 14, 1986, pp 38–56.

Hirst J, *The Sentimental Nation: The Making of the Australian Commonwealth*, Oxford University Press, Oxford 2000.

Hobsbawm E J, *Nations and Nationalism since 1780*, CUP, Cambridge 1990.

——, *Industry and Empire: The Making of Modern English Society, 1750 to the Present Day*, Pantheon Books, New York, 1968.

Hogan M, *The Sectarian Strand: Religion in Australian History*, Penguin, Ringwood 1987.

Holt M, *The French Wars of Religion, 1562–1629*, Cambridge University Press, Cambridge 1995.

Hudson W and Bolton G (eds), *Creating Australia: Changing Australian History*, Allen & Unwin, Sydney 1997.

Hughes P, et al, *Believe It or Not: Australian Spirituality and the Churches in the 90s*, Christian Research Association, Kew, Victoria 1995.

Hurd J, *The Origin of 1 Corinthians*, Seabury, New York 1965.

Izbicki T, 'Papalist Reaction to the Council of Constance: Juan De Torquemada to the Present', *Church History*, 55, 1986, pp 7–20.

Jameson F, *Postmodernism, or, the Cultural Logic of Late Capitalism*, Verso, London 1991.

John Paul II, *The Vocation and the Mission of the Lay Faithful in the Church and in the World*, St Paul Publications, Sydney 1989.

Jones C, *The Search for Meaning: Conversations with Caroline Jones*, Australian Broadcasting Corporation, Sydney 1992.

Kaldor P, et al, *Shaping a Future: Characteristics of Vital Congregations*, Openbook, Adelaide 1997.

Kaye B N, 'An Australian Definition of Religion', *University of New South Wales Law Journal*, 14, 1992, pp 332–51.

——, 'Paul and His Opponents in Corinth', in Miller E (ed), *Good News in History: Essays in Honour of Bo Reicke*, Scholars Press, Atlanta, 1993, pp 11–126.

——, *A Church without Walls: Being Anglican in Australia*, Dove, Melbourne 1995.

——, 'Theology for Life in a Plural Society', in Treloar G (ed), *The Furtherance of Religious Beliefs: Essay on the History of Theological Education in Australia*, Centre for the Study of Australian Christianity, Sydney, 1997, pp 203–16.

——, '"Classical Anglicanism" a Necessary and Valuable Point of Reference', *Reformed Theological Review*, 56, 1997, pp 28–39.

——, 'Signposting the Future: Why the Idea of Lay Vocation in Society Has Become a Bad Idea for Australian Anglicans', *St Mark's Review*, 177, 1999, pp 11–17.

——, *The 1850 Bishops Conference and the Strange Birth of Australian Synods*, Trinity College, Melbourne 2000.

——, *Web of Meaning: The Role of Origins in Christian Faith*, Aquila Press, Sydney 2000.

——, 'Unity in the Anglican Communion: A Critique of the "Virginia Report"', *St Mark's Review*, 184, 2001, pp 24–31.

Kelly P, *The End of Certainty: The Story of the 1980s*, Allen & Unwin, St Leonards 1992.

Kelsey D H, *Between Athens and Berlin: The Theological Education Debate*, Eerdmans, Grand Rapids, Mich. 1993.

Kimel A F (ed), *Speaking the Christian God: The Holy Trinity and the Challenge of Feminism*, Eerdmans, Grand Rapids 1992.

Kingdom J, *No Such Thing as Society? Individualism and Community*, Open University Press, Buckingham 1992.

Kinnamon M E (ed), *Signs of the Spirit: Official Report Seventh Assembly. Canberra, Australia*, WCC, Geneva 1991.

Küng H, *Structures of the Church*, Crossroad, New York 1982.

Lansbury R, 'Managing Change in a Challenging Environment', *Asia Pacific Journal of Human Relations*, 30, 1992, pp 16–28.

Lawton W, *The Better Time to Be: Utopian Attitudes to Society among Sydney Anglicans 1885 to 1914*, UNSW Press, Sydney 1990.

——, 'Nathaniel Jones—Preacher of Righteousness', in O'Brien P and Peterson D (eds), *God Who Is Rich in Mercy*, Anzea, Hombush, 1986, pp 361–76.

Limerick D, 'The Shape of the New Organization: Implications for Human Resource Management', *Asia Pacific Journal of Human Relations*, 30, 1992, pp 38–52.

Limerick D, Cunnington B and Crowther F, *Managing the New Organisation: Collaboration and Sustainability in the Postcorporate World*, Business and Professional Publishing, Sydney 1998.

Luhmann N, *Social Systems*, Stanford University Press, Stanford 1995.

Lukacs J, *The End of the Twentieth Century and the End of the Modern Age*, Ticknor and Fields, New York 1993.

Luoma J, *The Primitive Church as a Normative Principle in the Theology of the Sixteenth Century: The Anglican–Puritan Debate over Church Polity as Represented by Richard Hooker and Thomas Cartwright*, PhD, The Hartford Theological Seminary, 1974.

Lyotard J-F, *The Postmodern Condition: A Report on Knowledge*, Manchester University Press, Manchester 1984.

MacCulloch D, *The Later Reformation in England*, MacMillan, London 1990.

——, *Thomas Cranmer: A Life*, Yale University Press, New Haven 1996.

——, *Tudor Church Militant: Edward VI and the Protestant Reformation*, Allen Lane, London 1999.

MacIntyre A, *After Virtue: A Study in Moral Theory*, Duckworth, London 1981.

——, *Whose Justice? Whose Rationality?*, Notre Dame University Press, Notre Dame 1988.

Macintyre S, *The Succeeding Age*, The Oxford History of Australia, 4, 1901–1942, Oxford University Press, Melbourne 1986.

MacKay H, *Reinventing Australia*, Angus and Robertson, Pymble 1993.

Mackay H, *Why Don't People Listen? Solving the Communication Problem*, Pan Macmillan, Sydney 1994.

Mant A, *Intelligent Leadership*, Allen & Unwin, St Leonards 1997.

Marsh I, *Beyond the Two Party System*, Cambridge University Press, Cambridge 1995.

Marshall P, *Enmity in Corinth: Social Conventions in Paul's Relations with the Corinthians*, J C B Mohr, Tübingen 1987.

Mason M (ed), *Religion in Australia: A Bibliography of Social Research*, University Relations Unit, Flinders University, Bedford Park 1982.

McGrath A, *Iustitia Dei: A History of the Christian Doctrine of Justification*, Cambridge University Press, Cambridge 1986.

McLeod A, *The Pattern of Australian Culture*, OUP, Melbourne 1963.

Mead L, *Five Challenges for the Once and Future Church*, The Alban Institute, Washington 1996.

Melleuish G, *Cultural Liberalism in Australia: A Study in Intellectual and Cultural History*, Cambridge University Press, Cambridge 1995.

——, *The Packaging of Australia: Politics and Cultural Wars*, UNSW Press, Sydney 1997.

Moltmann J, *The Trinity and the Kingdom of God: The Doctrine of God*, SCM Press, London 1981.

Nicholls D, *Deity and Domination: Images of God and the State in the Nineteenth and Twentieth Centuries*, Routledge, London 1989.

Nichols A, *The Panther and the Hind: A Theological History of Anglicanism*, T & T Clark, Edinburgh 1993.

Nisbet R, *The Quest for Community: A Study in the Ethics of Order and Freedom*, Institute for Contemporary Studies, San Francisco 1990.

O'Brien P T, *Introductory Thanksgivings in the Letters of Paul*, Supplements to Novum Testamentum; V, 49, E J Brill, Leiden 1977.

O'Donovan O, *The Desire of the Nations*, CUP, Cambridge 1996.

O'Grady J, *They're a Weird Mob: A Novel*, Landsdowne Press, Sydney; London; New York 1974.

Palmer P, 'The Company of Strangers: Christians and the Renewal of Amrerica's Public Life', pp

Pfeffer J, *Power in Organizations*, Pitman, Boston 1981.

Piggin S, *Evangelical Christianity in Australia: Spirit, Word and World*, Oxford University Press, Oxford 1996.

Placher W, *The Domestication of Transcendence*, John Knox Press, Westminster 1996.

Porter A, 'Religion, Missionary Enthusiasm, and Empire', in Porter A (ed), *The Oxford History of the British Empire, Volume III, Historiography*, III, Oxford University Press, Oxford, 1999, pp 222–46.

Powicke M, *The Reformation in England*, OUP, London 1941.

Pusey E (ed), *The Works of That Learned and Judicious Divine, Mr Richard Hooker: With an Account of His Life and Death by Isaac Walton*, Clarendon Press, Oxford 1836.

Raphael D and Macfie A (ed), *Adam Smith: The Theory of Moral Sentiments*, Liberty Press, Indianapolis 1974.

Rorty R, *Contingency, Irony, and Solidarity*, Cambridge University Press, Cambridge 1989.

Russell A, *The Clerical Profession*, SPCK, London 1980.

Sachs W, *The Transformation of Anglicanism: From State Church to Global Communion*, Cambridge University Press, Cambridge 1993.

Schnarch D, *Constructing the Sexual Crucible: An Interrogation of Sexual and Marital Therapy*, Norton, 1991.

Seidman S, *Contested Knowledge: Social Theory in the Postmodern Era*, Blackwell, Oxford 1994.

Senge P, *The Fifth Discipline: The Art and Practice of the Learning Organisation*, Random House Australia, Sydney 1990.

Senge P, et al, *The Dance of Change: The Challenges of Sustaining Momentum in Learning Organizations*, Nicholas Brealey Publishing, London 1999.

Shapin S, *A Social History of Truth: Civility and Science in Seventeenth-Century England*, Science and Its Conceptual Foundations, University of Chicago Press, Chicago 1994.

Sheehan P, *Among the Barbarians: The Dividing of Australia*, Random House Australia, Milsons Point 1998.

Sheil C (ed), *Globalisation: Australian Impacts*, UNSW Press, Sydney 2001.

Shils E, *Tradition*, Faber and Faber, London 1989.

Soskice J M, *Metaphor and Religious Language*, Clarendon Press, Oxford 1985.

Speed Hill W E (ed), *The Folger Library Edition of the Works of Richard Hooker*, I–VII, Harvard University Press and Medieval and Renaissance Studies, Cambridge Mass and Binghamton 1977–1998.

Stump P, *The Reforms of the Council of Constance (1414–1418)*, E J Brill, Leiden 1994.

Sykes S W, *The Integrity of Anglicanism*, Mowbray, London 1978.

——, 'The Genius of Anglicanism', in Rowell G (ed), *The English Religious Tradition and the Genius of Anglicanism*, Ikon, Wantage, 1992, pp 227–41.

——, 'Foundations of an Anglican Ecclesiology', in John J (ed), *Living the Mystery*, Darton Longman and Todd, London, 1994, pp 28–48.

——, *Unashamed Anglicanism*, Darton Longman & Todd, London 1995.

Tacey D, *Reenchantment: The New Australian Spirituality*, Harper Collins, Sydney 2000.

Tanner N (ed), *Decrees of the Ecumenical Councils*, Georgetown University Press, Washington 1990.

Teale R, 'The "Red Book" Case', *JRH*, 12, 1982, pp 74–89.

Tierney B, *Church Law and Constitutional Thought in the Middle Ages*, London 1979.

Tillard J, 'The Church of God Is a Communion: The Ecclesiological Perspective of Vatican II', *One in Christ*, 27, 1981, pp 117–31.

Tonnies F, *Community and Society*, Michigan State University Press, East Lansing 1877.

Turney C, Bygott U and Chippendale P, *Australia's First: A History of the University of Sydney Volume I, 1850–1939*, 1, Hale & Iremonger, Sydney 1991.

Vanhoozer K (ed), *The Trinity in a Pluralistic Age*, Eerdmans, Grand Rapids 1997.

Veliz C, *The New World of the Gothic Fox: Culture and Economy in English and Spanish America*, University of California Press, Berkeley 1994.

Volf M, *After Our Likeness: The Church as the Image of the Trinity*, Eerdmans, Grand Rapids 1998.

Vos D, *Church and Community Conflicts: The Relationships of the Thessalonian, Corinthian, and Philippian Churches with Their Wider Civic Communities*, Society of Biblical Literature, Atlanta 1999.

Ward G (ed), *The Postmodern God: A Theological Reader*, Blackwell, Oxford 1997.

Watson F (ed), *Historical Records of Australia*, Library Committee of the Commonwealth Parliament, Sydney 1914–1925.

Watson W, 'Rethinking the Late Stuart Church: The Extent of Liberal Anglicanism 1688–1715', *Anglican and Episcopal History*, 70, 2001, pp 143–68.

Witherington III B, *Conflict and Community in Corinth: A Socio-Rhetorical Commentary on 1 and 2 Corinthians*, Paternoster Press, Carlisle 1995.

Zizioulas J, *Being as Communion*, St Vkadimir's Seminary Press, Crestwood 1985.